Of the thousands of decompression dives that Gary Gentile has made, 200 of them were on the Grand Dame of the Sea: the *Andrea Doria*. After diving on the German battleship *Ostfriesland* in 1990, at a depth of 380 feet, he became instrumental in merging mixed-gas diving technology with deep wreck-diving by publishing the first book on technical diving: the *Ultimate Wreck Diving Guide*. In 1994, he participated in a mixed-gas diving expedition to the *Lusitania*, which lies at a depth of 300 feet.

Gary has specialized in wreck-diving and shipwreck research, concentrating his efforts on wrecks along the eastern seaboard, from Newfoundland to Key West, and in the Great Lakes. He has compiled an extensive library of books, photographs, drawings, plans, and original source materials on ships and shipwrecks. *The Shipwreck Research Handbook* was based on his lifetime of historical research.

Gary has written scores of magazine articles, and has published thousands of photographs in books, periodicals, newspapers, brochures, advertisements, corporate reports, museum displays, postcards, film, and television. He lectures extensively on wilderness and underwater topics, and conducts seminars on advanced wreck-diving techniques, high-tech diving equipment, and wreck photography. He is the author of nearly five dozen books: primarily science fiction novels and non-fiction works on diving and on nautical and shipwreck history. The Popular Dive Guide Series will eventually cover every major shipwreck along the east coast of the United States.

In 1989, after a five-year battle with the National Oceanic and Atmospheric Administration, Gary won a suit which forced the hostile government agency to issue him a permit to dive the USS *Monitor*, a protected National Marine Sanctuary. Media attention that was focused on Gary's triumphant victory resulted in nationwide coverage of his 1990 photographic expedition to the Civil War ironclad. Gary continues to fight for the right of access to all shipwreck sites.

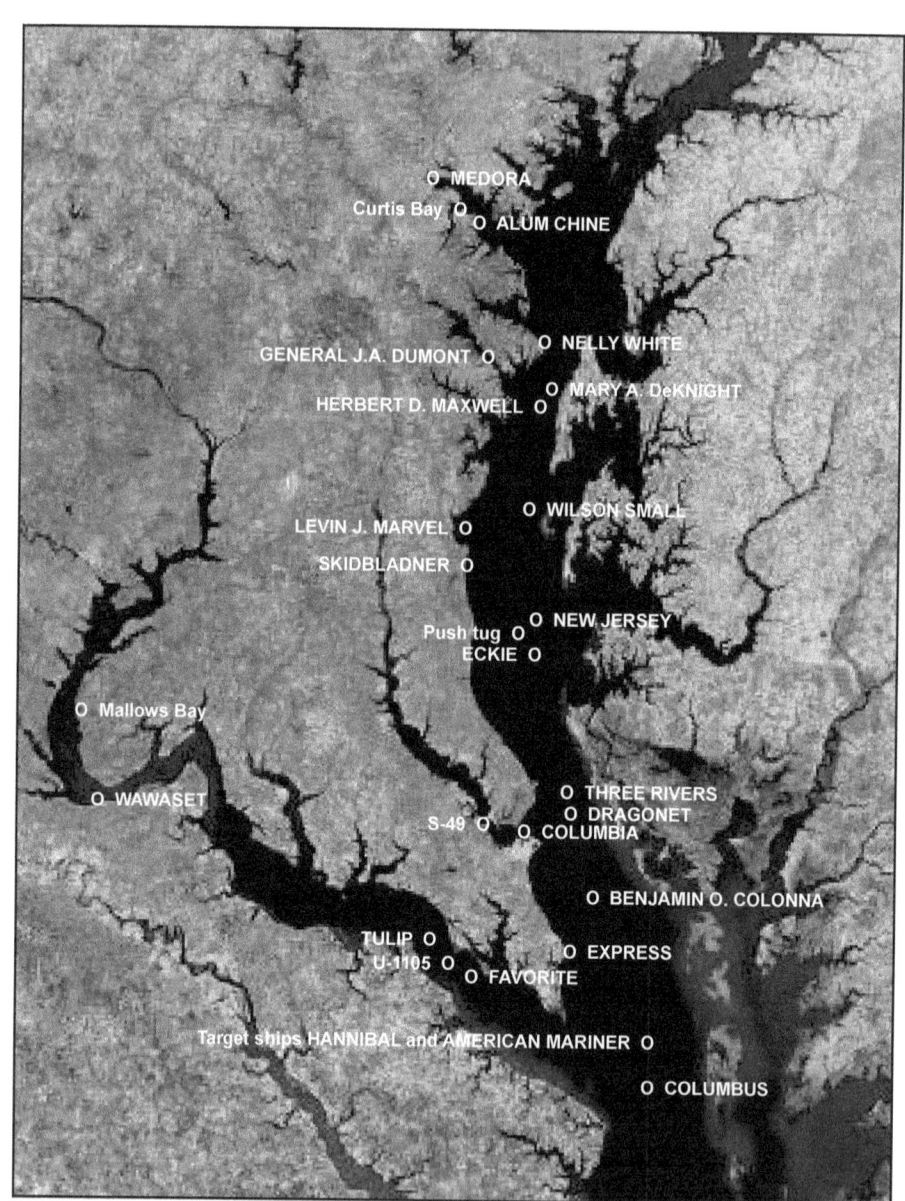

In this Landsat image, the capital O preceding or following the name denotes the approximate location of sites that are mentioned in this volume. See the GPS and Loran section in the back of the book for precise locations.

Shipwrecks of the Chesapeake Bay in Maryland Waters

by Gary Gentile

Gary Gentile Productions

Copyright 2013 by Gary Gentile

All rights reserved. Except for the use of brief quotations embodied in critical articles and reviews, this book may not be reproduced in part or in whole, in any manner (including mechanical, electronic, photographic, and photocopy means), transmitted in any form, or recorded by any data storage and/or retrieval device, without express written permission from the author. Address all queries to:

Gary Gentile Productions
3 Lehigh Gorge Drive
Jim Thorpe, PA 18229

Additional copies of this book may be purchased from the same address by sending a check or money order in the amount of $20 U.S. for each copy (plus $4 postage per order, not per book, in the U.S. Inquire for shipping cost to foreign countries). Alternatively, copies may be ordered from the author's website and paid by credit card:

http://www.ggentile.com

Picture Credits

All uncredited photographs were taken by the author. The front cover photo is the target ship *American Mariner*. The author's photo on page one was taken by Susan Long. Every attempt has been made to contact the photographers or artists whose work appears in this book, if known, and to ascertain their names if unknown; in come cases, copies of pictures have been in public circulation for so long that the name of the photographer or artist has been lost, or the present whereabouts are impossible to trace. Any information in this regard forwarded to the author will be appreciated. Apologies are made to those whose work must under such circumstances go unrecognized.

International Standard Book Numbers (ISBN)
1-883056-46-2
978-1-883056-46-9

First Edition

Printed in U.S.A.

CONTENTS

INTRODUCTION	6
SHIPWRECKS	
Alum Chine	15
American Mariner	28
Benjamin O. Colonna	35
Columbia	38
Columbus	39
Dragonet	46
Express	53
Favorite	58
General J.A. Dumont	60
Hannibal	64
Herbert D. Maxwell	67
Levin J. Marvel	77
Mary A. DeKnight	89
Medora	90
Nelly White	102
New Jersey	106
S-49	113
Three Rivers	135
Tulip	140
U-1105	148
Wawaset	157
Wilson Small	171
MISCELLANEOUS WRECKS	173
AWOIS	186
SUGGESTED READING	196
GPS and LORAN NUMBERS	197
BOOKS BY THE AUTHOR	202

INTRODUCTION

The estuary known as the Chesapeake Bay is gargantuan in all its dimensions. Its surface area covers more than 2,200 square miles – larger than the State of Delaware. It holds some 19 trillion gallons of water (more or less, depending upon the tide and whether the watershed that feeds its tributaries is experiencing flooding conditions or drought). Its coastline is so convoluted that it exceeds 7,000 miles in length: longer than the eastern and western seaboards combined.

It has been estimated that the bay contains more than 2,000 wrecks of ships or boats of various sizes and descriptions. Many were sailing vessels from the early days of colonization. Many are also recently lost sailboats, fishing vessels, motorboats, and the like. In between are Civil War hulks, nineteenth-century passenger vessels, twentieth-century freighters, submarines, tugboats, barges too numerous to mention, and at least one battleship, pilot boat, and lightship. These wrecks exist in varying states of collapse.

Contributing to the present condition of a shipwreck are age and salinity. Older wrecks are generally not as well preserved as newer wrecks, because older wrecks have had more time to deteriorate. Wrecks are preserved better in freshwater than in saltwater because most marine fouling and marine boring organisms cannot survive in freshwater.

The salinity of the bay both differs and fluctuates. The confluence of the Susquehanna River at the north end of the bay – indeed, upstream in all the eastern and western tributaries – is perfect freshwater. The mouth of the bay between Cape Charles and Cape Henry is perfect saltwater. Gradations occur throughout the 200-mile twisting centerline in deference to tide, rainfall, and the outflow of tributaries. Brackish water prevails but with degrees of salinity that defy rhyme and reason.

The Visibility Factor

Nor is sodium chloride the only ingredient in bay water that affects deterioration. The bay is filled with manmade chemical pollutants from municipal storm drains, sewage treatment plants, industrial waste, farm runoff, and the like. One chemical that is often overlooked is oxygen. Water that is depleted of oxygen helps preservation because destructive animals can't live without it.

There is an ongoing cycle in which sediments containing high levels of phosphorus are washed into the bay and nurture the growth of waterborne algae called dinoflagellates. Algae consume oxygen as part of their metabolic process. When most of the free oxygen is consumed, the algae die, settle into the mud, and decompose. Gradually oxygen accumulates in the water until enough is available to create another algal bloom.

As a result of these blooms, visibility is best in November (after the summer plankton has died and before the winter plankton blooms), then again in April (after the winter plankton has died and before the summer plankton blooms).

In addition to these periodic changes are catastrophic vagaries that cause excessive runoff. Hurricane Irene in 2011 is a perfect case in point. Record rainfalls caused massive floods that washed millions of tons of mud, dirt, and debris into the bay, turning the normally dull green water to the color of hot chocolate or coffee with cream: a dirty brown brew that was "too thick to drink and too thin to plow." Visibility was zero for many weeks afterward.

Then again, there are unpredictable changes in visibility that cannot be related to any known cause. For example, on one November morning dive on the *City of Annapolis* I had four feet of visibility; that afternoon I had 10 feet of ambient light visibility on the Tautog Wreck: it was so bright on the bottom that I could not see the beam of my dive light; and the 10-foot vis that I recorded in my log counted only *clear* vis – I could actually see less clearly as far away as 15 to 20 feet, depending upon whether I was on the sunny side of the wreck or the shaded side. Granted that the depth on the latter was 26 feet as opposed to 79 feet on the former, nonetheless I did not have 10 feet of vis while decompressing at 10 feet over the *City of Annapolis*. The two wrecks lie six miles apart.

Two days later, I had zero visibility on the *Dorothy* (half a mile from the *City of Annapolis*). At 123 feet, I humped the shot weight across the bottom in the hope of encountering a high part of the wreck where the visibility was better. After ten minutes I quit looking. I could see the beam of my dive light only when I pointed it directly at my face from a distance of several inches. The water was choked with floating sediment. I could not even read my gauges on the bottom; I had to estimate the depth and the passage of time. Talk about sensory deprivation!

Working entirely by feel, I unclipped a liftbag, secured it to the shot weight, partially filled the bag from the mouthpiece of my regulator so that the weight could be pulled off the bottom with little effort, then ascended to my decompression stop at 10 feet. I began to be able to read my gauges at 50 feet.

That afternoon I had 2 feet of vis at 70 feet on the *C.G. Willis*, two and a half miles from the *Dorothy*. What does this all mean? It means that visibility in the Chesapeake Bay is a crap shoot.

Maryland-Virginia Border

Establishing boundaries for the inclusion of shipwrecks in a particular volume of the Popular Dive Guide Series has always been fairly easy. In most cases I simply extended the coastal boundary between States due east along the parallel, or latitude. This system did not always work because of unusual geographic contours.

For example, the southern boundary of North Carolina occludes the northern boundary of South Carolina. In that case I extended the northwest-southeast diagonal land border between the States. I did the same to separate *Shipwrecks of New York* from *Shipwrecks of New Jersey: North*, by bifurcating the Hudson River and Canyon.

For the borders between Rhode Island and Connecticut to the west and Massachusetts to the east, I extended the borders south along the meridians, or longitudes, of the two adjacent States.

To separate shipwrecks for inclusion in either *Shipwrecks of Delaware and Maryland* or *Shipwrecks of Virginia*, I followed my primary rule by extending due east the border between Maryland and Virginia, where that slightly angled border ended at the coastline on Assateague Island. But the inland boundary between Maryland and Virginia, particularly across the Chesapeake Bay and along the Potomac River, is confusing, so that some explanation is necessary for the reader's understanding.

Generally, when two countries, states, provinces, counties, or other political entities, occupy opposite sides of a river or lake, the border that separates them is drawn along the middle of the watercourse. Occasionally, a border may be drawn along the thalweg. A thalweg is a line on a map that is drawn along the deepest part of a river; this line is not necessarily the midpoint between banks. In cases in which an island exists along the logical border, the border is generally shifted so that the island is not bisected by two political entities.

By way of example, in Lake Superior, the border between Canada and the United States was shifted northward so that all of Isle Royale falls under the dominion of the State of Michigan instead of the Province of Ontario. Likewise, in the St. Lawrence River, the border weaves a circuitous course around and between the so-called Thousand Islands so that some are the territory of the Province of Ontario, while others are the territory of the State of New York.

The border along the inland waterways between Maryland and Virginia is one that defies sane reasoning. The border across the Chesapeake Bay is a jagged line that goes out of its way to cut across several islands, and nips the tip off one island so that the tip is left dangling in political limbo. Whereas the border follows the centerline of the Pocomoke River on the east side of the bay, the border follows the south shore of the Potomac River on the west side of the bay.

This latter State of affairs results in some curious circumstances. If a Virginian steps off his property to cool his heels in the Potomac River, he finds himself standing in a Maryland waterway. Maryland enforces jurisdiction over this water with extreme ferocity, so that the Virginian who is standing in ankle deep water can be accosted by Maryland law enforcement agents, say, for smoking marijuana or for dipping his bobber without a valid Maryland fishing license. It makes me wonder what would happen if the angler stepped back onto Virginia soil, where approaching Maryland game wardens have no legal authority, while his bait is several inches away on Maryland bottomlands. Uncooperative fish licensing agreements between the two States is a twisted ball of string and monofilament that I don't want to attempt to untangle; and anyway, it is irrelevant with regard to shipwrecks.

Adding to the absurdity of this border situation is the manner in which Maryland controls the river and the water that flows in it. Maryland contends that Virginians have no right to siphon water out of the Potomac River for irrigation, municipal drinking supply, or any other purpose. These issues are so complex that they have been in continuous dispute for more than four hundred years: since 1609, when the original British charter established the colony of Virginia.

The history of this waterborne contention would fill a book in itself, and is far beyond the scope of the present volume. Suffice it to say that Potomac River water use and management issues have not yet been put to rest, despite a number of lawsuits that reached the Supreme Court of the United States. At the end of the last round in this ongoing fight over water rights between States, in 2003 the Supreme Court held that Virginia could "build improvements appurtenant to her shore and to withdraw water from the River, subject to the constraints of federal common law and the Award," as long as the improvements did not impede navigation. (The Award refers to a 1785 compact that guaranteed water access and rights, including fishing rights, to Virginians.) In other words, Virginia lawfully retains riparian rights both of the State and of its citizens. Of course, all of this is subject to change in the next round, because unlike boxing matches, battles between States have no limit on the number of rounds that can be fought.

What this boils down to as far as shipwrecks are concerned is that shipwrecks in the Potomac River lie on the Maryland side of the border, the only exceptions being specified Virginia embayments in which a straight line is drawn from one jutting point of land to another. This explains why I have included the *Wawaset*, for example, in the Maryland volume, even though the wreck lies only a couple of hundred yards from the Virginia shore.

Thanks for the Memories

It has always been my policy to give credit to those who have helped me along the way. In this particular book the list is short.

First and foremost I would like to thank my long-time friend Mike Moore for introducing me to Chesapeake Bay wreck-diving in the 1980's. My Chesapeake Bay mentor has since passed away; I miss him sorely. In his heyday, he used to tow one of his boats – either *Come 'N Go* or *Arabia* – to the launch site that was closest to the wreck that we wanted to explore, so that we didn't have to motor very far on the water. We found the sites with loran numbers in those days. Some of the loran numbers in this book I obtained from him.

In addition to being a diver, Mike was also a researcher. He conducted historical research on wrecks that interested him, especially those on which he actually dived. He shared the results of his research with me. I have quoted some of his descriptions as a matter of historical reference. I have also used some of the topside photographs that he collected from various sources throughout the years.

As Mike was wont to say about Chesapeake Bay wrecks, "The wrecks don't *look* like much, but the *feel* great."

I would also like to thank another long-time friend who is still alive and kicking so he can read my gratitude: Ted Green. On his boat *O.C. Diver* we have explored a number of wrecks in the Chesapeake Bay. His favorite saying relates to a couple of instances in which he dropped a downline on a shipwreck, dropped me off to descend and fend for myself, then skedaddled out of the way of approaching superships: "Right of way yields to right of weight."

On those occasions when big ship passed, I held onto the downline, stayed deep, and listened to the Doppler effect as the thrumming engine noise first approached and then receded into the distance. Then I surfaced and looked around for the boat. After Ted returned my wave, I let go of the downline and drifted with the current until he picked me up clear of the wreck.

Rick Younger is another long-time friend and fellow diver who helped me immensely. He has lived on the bay all his life, and has dived in its murky waters since he gained his majority. His insights about bay attributes constitute a depth of expertise that only he possesses. I have melded his hard-earned knowledge with my text.

The Trust that is Not

Susan Langley rules the underwater archaeological division of the Maryland Historical Trust with an iron fist. I knew from previous correspondence that she was uncooperative. In 2000, when I asked her for information about the *New Jersey* (which see), she refused to give me any. Nonetheless, in 2011 I submitted to her a modest request for information that was within her purview, in order to evoke a response. I wrote:

"I would like to obtain a copy of Report Number COMP AN 76 ID Number: 00005283, named 'Underwater archaeological reconnaissance of the *General J.A. Dumont* shipwreck site off Severnside, Severn River, MD." written by Fred W. Hopkins in 1987. Either photocopy or scan will suffice. Please take a second to tap Reply and acknowledge receipt of this request. Many thanks."

I did this more to test her honesty than for any need of the information in the report. I also wanted to determine how far she was willing to go to prevent the report's release. She did not have a second to tap Reply for the likes of me. She did not reply for more than a week, and then it was only to act predictably by denying my request. She not only refused to send me a photocopy or scan, but she also informed me that if I visited the MHT library, she would not permit me to even *see* the report, much less copy it.

Although I expected a dishonorable response, I was disappointed that she failed so simple a test with such flying colors.

It seems that the underwater archaeology division of the Maryland Historical Distrust operates much like a black hole: information goes into it for the benefit of its employees, but does not come out of it for the edification of the public that paid for it with their tax dollars. Information is coveted and kept secret instead of being disseminated to the taxpayers who support the MHT and who pay to have the information gathered, collated, and archived; and who pay the salaries of those who covet the information.

What purpose does the MHT serve if it does not share its public resources with the public? What possible reason can there be for their possessive attitude about a report that is twenty-five years old. This is not a Homeland Security issue; it's nothing more than an out-of-date archaeological assessment that the MHT never followed up on.

By way of comparison, when I was researching *Shipwrecks of North Carolina*, I called the North Carolina Underwater Archaeology Unit, at Fort Fisher, Kure Beach. Head archaeologist Richard Lawrence invited me to visit the facility. He gave me a tour, showed me the location of the filing cabinets that contained the State's shipwreck files, allowed me the use of the photocopier, and left me unattended to copy anything I wanted: charts, photographs, and textual documents. This is how a government-funded agency is supposed to operate: for the people, not against them.

Not so in Maryland. My next step was to test the integrity of the MHT as a whole by submitting a request for the Report pursuant to the Freedom of Information Act. Supposedly this route would go over Susan Langley's head to the top administrators of the Trust. Large federal agencies maintain a FOIA office to handle FOIA requests; the office is staffed by FOIA officers who are supposed to handle requests without the personal bias that exists at lower levels of government. Smaller agencies do not have a special FOIA office or specific officers; requests are passed down through the hierarchy to the lowest rung, to the office that archives the requested information.

You can see the shortcoming in this latter situation. Oftentimes the person who denied your non-FOIA request in the first place is the very person who is assigned to handle your FOIA request. The result is the same, with some trumped up loophole used as an excuse to deny the release of information – and there are *thousands* of loopholes to choose from: more loopholes than are found in the federal tax code.

When I was writing *Shipwrecks of Massachusetts*, I tried to obtain information from NOAA about the wreck of the *Portland*, which was located in the Stellwagen Bank National Marine Sanctuary. So vigorous did NOAA want to keep the information from me – because they knew that I intended to publish it – that they hired a battery of lawyers who spent several months in researching loopholes in the Act, in order to deny the release of the information that I requested. These lawyers were highly creative. Instead of citing only a single loophole, they cited a number of them so that if any one of them was knocked down upon appeal or civil lawsuit, they might still win the case from one of the others.

One of the loopholes they cited was that the wreck might – and I stress the word *might* – be the site of an ancient Indian burial ground. This was patently absurd! The wreck lay twenty miles from shore at a depth of 450 feet. Only a handful of scuba divers in the world today are capable of diving so deep. I do not believe that any Indians could swim that far from shore, and then hold their breath long enough to dive to the bottom and dig a grave. Talk about clutching at straws!

Alternatively, the person who is assigned to handle a FOIA request in a small local agency may be a co-worker of the one who denied your non-FOIA request. This person's desk might be located right next to the desk of the other. The co-worker likely has the same attitude about not releasing information that they want to keep to themselves. So you are back to square one.

My FOIA request read thus: "Under the Freedom of Information Act, 5 U.S.C. Sec. 522 et seq., I hereby request an unredacted copy of Report Number COMPAN 76 ID Number: 00005283, named 'Underwater archaeological reconnaissance of the *General J.A. Dumont* shipwreck site off Severnside, Severn River, MD.' written by Fred W. Hopkins in 1987.

"Either hard photocopy by mail or scan by attachment will suffice."

Whenever you are filing a FOIA request, be sure to specify an unredacted copy, else you may receive a copy that is so blacked out with indelible ink that the very information that you are seeking has been intentionally made unreadable.

The MHT – or the minions who did not wish to let me see the Report – denied my FOIA request by a creative ploy: "There are no records in the possession of the Maryland Historical Trust that are responsive to your request. The report you requested is missing from the MHT library."

I have to give them credit for creativity. What better way to deny a request than to remove the item from the shelf? It could always be put back later.

But a bona fide FOIA officer is bound by the responsibility of his or her appointment to do more than make a cursory glance at a library shelf where the original report is supposed to be filed. They are tasked to look farther than the end of their nose, unless they are in cahoots with the original deniers.

I wasted no time in appealing the Machiavellian scheme of the Maryland Historical Trustless: "The following may be considered an appeal. I think there may have been a misunderstanding about my FOIA request. I did not limit my request to the original report, nor only to the report that might be found on a shelf in the MHT library. If the original report was conveniently missing from the MHT library during the brief search interval pursuant to my FOIA request, I hereby request that a broader search be conducted elsewhere in MHT facilities as well as among the MHT staff, such as but not limited to the personal files and office of Susan Langley, as well as anyone else who might conceivably possess a copy of the report in his or her personal possession.

"I find it difficult to believe that MHT staff members were so incompetent that they lost the original of a valuable archaeological report, or so stupid as not to make numerous copies as backups to be squirreled away in alternative locations for easy access.

"I therefore request that a more thorough search be conducted among MHT personnel who might be harboring either the original report or a copy of it, perhaps stashed away at home where it would not be available for FOIA scrutiny."

I never received a response to my appeal. They simply ignored me and left my appeal in limbo. After three and a half months I wrote to the governor of Maryland, to give him the opportunity to become a modern day trust buster:

> Maryland Governor Martin O'Malley February 20, 2012
> 100 State Circle
> Annapolis, MD 21401-1925
> 410-974-3901
> 800-811-8336
>
> On October 7, 2011, I submitted a request to Susan Langley at the Maryland Historical Trust for an unredacted copy of Report Number COMP AN 76 ID Number: 00005283, named "Underwater archaeological reconnaissance of the *General J.A. Dumont* shipwreck site off Severnside River, MD." written by Fred W. Hopkins in 1987.
>
> Langley not only refused to provide me with a copy of the report, but informed me that if I visited the MHT library in person, she would deny me the right to review the report.
>
> On October 15, 2011, I submitted a FOIA request for the instant report to the MHT.
>
> On November 4, 2011, my request was denied.
>
> On November 8, 2011, I submitted an appeal of the denial. After three and a half months, I have received no response to my appeal.
>
> I cannot imagine why Langley and the MHT conspired to withhold a 25-year-old report from the public. What purpose does the MHT serve if it collects data but refuses to share that data with the public that paid for it?
>
> I do not know how high up the political hierarchy the conspiracy goes, so I am appealing to you to force the release of the report in question – and to see that these kinds of shenanigans are put to an end. The MHT is supposed to be the custodian or trustee of information, not its possessor. The MHT appears to behave like a private club to which the public is denied access. That smacks of discrimination against the taxpayers.

I received a reply three weeks later: not from the governor himself or even from his office, but from the Maryland Department of Planning of which the MHT was a subsidiary. I must presume that rather than deal with the issue at stake and take the side of a taxpayer, the governor was content to let a subordinate office have its way.

Rodney Little, the Director and State Historic Preservation Officer, stated in his reply, "Your email of November 8, 2011, to the Maryland Department of Planning's Office of the Attorney General was not understood to be an appeal." I fail to understand how I could have been misunderstood. When I wrote, "The following may be considered an appeal," I expected that any educated person would understand that I was filing an appeal.

Be that as it may, Little informed me that the file that was missing from the library shelf had still not been located, but "we have requested another copy for our files." This was his tacit admission that other copies existed, and that the original FOIA officer chose to ignore that fact in order to deny my request on the grounds that the library copy was not on the shelf – an easy way to deny the fulfillment of my request.

Little's tactic was little better: "Archaeological reports and site forms (both terrestrial and those on state sovereignty submerged lands) are not copied or disclosed to the general public."

So there you have it. The conspiracy goes all the way up to the gubernatorial office. High-ranking political collusion was evidenced by the fact that Little enclosed copies of Langley's email and the original FOIA denial.

All this begs the question that I reiterate: Why does the MHT exist if not to serve the public? Are the employees enjoying a self-serving sinecure which endows them with the unholy power to keep the information they collect from the public? Is the MHT a private club in which privileged members are placed on the public dole so they can conduct pet projects and play with their hobbies at the taxpayers' expense? What does the government do with the information that it collects at the taxpayers' expense? Only privileged staff members of the MHT are permitted to peruse the information that the MHT collects.

I should also like to draw attention to the fact that the Freedom of Information Act is a federal law. Violating the Congressional Act constitutes a criminal offense. MHT flagrantly violates the law, and the governor is content to let them get away with it.

MHT underwater archaeologists bleat that their goal is to protect the wrecks. Yet they have not done anything to protect shipwrecks except in one single instance: they installed a part-time mooring system on the *U-1105* so that recreational divers could access the site without having to grapple the hull or conning tower. They have not installed mooring systems on any other wrecks, not even those that are favorites among anglers and recreational divers.

They have never marked wrecks with navigational buoys so that watermen could avoid snagging them and dragging them apart with machine-driven oyster dredges.

They have never coated the exposed surfaces of wooden-hulled wrecks with antifouling paint, in order to ward off the devastating effects of clinging and boring organisms such as, but not limited to, barnacles, limpets, chitons, mussels, tube worms, corals, sea anemones, and hydroids. They have never placed cathodic protection on iron- and steel-hulled wrecks in order to combat corrosion. They have never galvanized metal hulls and surfaces. They have never installed systems for electrolytic reduction, which would do much to preserve iron and steel in their original state.

As far as I know, no Maryland State archaeologist has ever discovered a significant shipwreck. Nearly every important wreck in the Chesapeake Bay and off the Maryland coast has been discovered by anglers and commercial oyster operators when they snagged their hooks or gear into it. Nearly every shipwreck has first been explored and described by recreational scuba divers who did not have a degree in archaeology, but who were dedicated enough to pursue the activity by paying their own expenses.

After the U.S. Army Corps of Engineers did an admirable job of recovering the antique engine from the *Columbus* (which see), and donated the engine to the MHT, the MHT let it fall apart through apathetic lack of conservation.

Shipwrecks in Maryland waters are rotting and rusting away, and the Maryland Hysterical Trust has done nothing about the situation except to make prevaricated claims. In fact, the Trust's empty promises and egregious lack of initiative have done more to condemn the wrecks to destruction and devastation than to protect them in any way, shape, or form. What the State of Maryland needs is a staunch Trust buster like Teddy Roosevelt.

Only then can shipwrecks in Maryland waters be protected from accidental ruin, and be enjoyed by multitudinous scuba divers who pay their own way to dive on shipwrecks because of their interest in the exploration of history.

In a way, the decadent posture of the MHT has given me an advantage. The present volume presents more information about shipwrecks in Maryland waters than has been presented to the public by all the people working for the MHT in the entire time of its existence. Go figure.

I took this picture of the Liberty Ship *John W. Brown* in Boston Harbor when she was on a tourist excursion to Massachusetts, in August 2007. She is normally docked at her home port in Baltimore. Note the difference between her superstructure and that of the converted Liberty Ship *American Mariner* (which see).

ALUM CHINE

Built: 1905
Previous names: *Claremont*
Gross tonnage: 1,767
Type of vessel: Steel-hulled freighter
Builder: A. Rodger Company, Point Glasgow, Scotland
Owner: Alum Chine Steamship Company, Cardiff, Wales
Port of registry: Cardiff, Wales
Cause of sinking: Dynamite explosion
Location: Hawkins Point, outside of Baltimore Harbor

Sunk: March 7, 1913
Depth: 35 feet
Dimensions: 269' x 40' x 18'
Power: Coal-fired steam

    March 7, 1913 started like any other day in the Baltimore Harbor area. Slumbering suburbanites yawned with the dawn, and sang praises for the acronym TGIF: Thank God It's Friday. The daily hustle and bustle was about to begin, but at quitting time people could look forward to weekend relaxation. It was no different for stevedores who were working the docks and lighters.
    Down in Panama, construction was progressing nicely on the trans-isthmus canal. After nine years of blasting and digging, it was only a year away from completion. Supplies for the massive engineering job were shipped from port cities on both sides of the continent. On this particular day, the *Alum Chine* was taking on dynamite for transportation to the land of the brimmed straw hat that was so popular among men who were affecting sartorial perfection. Captain F.J. Anstey, master, was attending to business matters in Baltimore.
    The *Alum Chine* was anchored near the main ship channel about half a mile north of Hawkins Landing, outside of Baltimore Harbor. Alongside the freighter was a lightering barge on which four railroad cars were sitting. These cars were piled high with cases of dynamite that had not yet been stowed in the *Alum Chine's* capacious holds: three hundred *tons* of dynamite. Seven carloads had previously been loaded after the freighter's arrival on March 1.
    According to several witnesses, one of the stevedores jammed a pike or bale hook into one of the boxes of dynamite, which caused a small initial explosion when they set the box on the deck. This observation was contested by William Bomhardt, assistant foreman of the stevedores, who testified that a box that he and another stevedore were carrying exploded all by itself when they set it down. "His theory was that the dynamite, which had been frozen, had blistered, and that the friction caused by the blisters on two adjoining sticks produced the explosion."
    Elsewhere on board, and on the lightering barge, neither crewmembers nor stevedores heard any explosion before they saw smoke pouring out of the *Alum Chine's* forward hatch. This was cause for panic.
    Everyone immediately stopped what he was doing. There was no time to try to extinguish the flames. It was every man for himself as they abandoned ship with exceptional celerity. Some leaped blindly into the water; others climbed down to the steam launch *Jerome*; still others jumped from the deck of the *Alum Chine* to the deck of the

tug *Atlantic*. Both boats cut their hawsers and raced away from the conflagration.

Two crewmembers who were left behind clambered out of the hold and shouted for help. The *Atlantic* turned around and returned to the side of the *Alum Chine* to rescue the stranded men. Then she put on steam to get away before the inevitable occurred.

Suddenly there was a titanic explosion. The *Alum Chine* was lifted completely out of the water "as if a torpedo had struck her from below, and then fell to fragments." The blast detonated dynamite on the lightering barge, and a split second later the air was rent with the sound of the secondary explosion – so close in time that it sounded like an echo. The barge was completely annihilated. Railroad cars that survived the blast were sent to the bottom.

"Buildings in Baltimore and scores of surrounding towns were shaken in their foundations by the terrific force of the explosion." The shock wave was felt as far as one hundred miles away. Many people interpreted the ground-shaking concussion as an earthquake. Innumerable windows were shattered, not only in Baltimore but in surrounding towns. Across the bay, "The entire State of Delaware had felt the shock." Buildings shook in Bridgeton, New Jersey. The shock wave was felt in Reading, Pennsylvania.

The Quarantine Hospital was situated twelve miles from ground zero. "Every window in the building was shattered. The patients were hurled from their beds and injured, several having legs and arms broken. Several physicians and nurses also were hurt."

Chunks of iron weighing more than fifty pounds were found three to four miles from the site of the explosion. "In many instances, the concrete foundations of the heavy guns in Forts Hancock, Armistead and Carroll were cracked, while several of the guns themselves were damaged by falling pieces of steel from the wrecked steamer."

Alum Chine engineer J.G. Reese described what he saw from the *Jerome*: "It seemed as though a great column of fire fifty feet high and twenty feet in diameter, topped by another column of black smoke 200 feet higher, came up from the sea, enveloping the ship." A dense pall of smoke shrouded the bay. "It was several minutes before the smoke cleared away and the sea became calm, but when it did there was no sign of either the ship or the barge. Both had disappeared, and not a sign of life was visible."

The *Atlantic* "was caught in the rain of wood and red-hot steel that fell in a shower for a quarter of a mile around, killing some of the crew outright and setting fire to the vessel." The skipper of the tug, Captain William Van Dyke, was one of those who perished; his body was recovered but his arm was severed off at the shoulder. The tug was totally demolished, "her decks strewn with dead and wounded."

The brand new U.S. Navy collier *Jason* lay at a nearby wharf. She had not yet been turned over to the Navy for commissioning. As soon as her skipper, Captain J.R. Thompson, saw smoke, he went below and instructed the engineer to get underway at once. "I was standing near a ventilator when I was tossed six or seven feet into the air. I turned two or three somersaults. I threw out my arms and caught a railing. This kept me from going overboard. In another instant a shower of iron fragments, some pieces as large as my fist and others as large as my head, was falling on our deck. I saw these pieces go straight through our heavy plates. The huge smokestacks of the collier were filled with holes and mashed almost flat.

From *Popular Mechanics*.

"Around me on all sides were men who had been tossed into the air by the concussion. Many were cut and injured by the pieces of iron. Some were killed instantly. The dynamite ship was an iron vessel throughout, and this made the damage to our ship all the greater. The *Chine* was about 500 feet away, but the force of the explosion was so great that our ship was lifted high upon the waves." The *Jason* measured 526 feet in length, and displaced 19,250 tons: a big and heavy ship to be blown completely out of the water.

The tug *Britannia* was proceeding up the Patapsco River at the time of the catastrophe. She plucked wounded men out of the river, then took the burning *Atlantic* in tow, but the latter tug sank before they reached safe harbor.

The death count was initially put at twenty, but by the following day it was learned that more than thirty persons had died in the explosion and its aftermath; others had fatal injuries to which they soon succumbed. More than three score people were hospitalized.

The search for survivors in the water soon turned to recovery of the dead. A flotilla of small vessels combed the river for corpses and body parts: severed arms and legs.

The hulk was a hazard to navigation, and would have to be removed before shipping traffic could proceed safely along the river. Worse, there was a suspicion that one of the railroad cars on the bottom might still contain cases of unexploded dynamite.

In order to avoid having to pay the cost of removing the sunken *Alum Chine* from the waterway, the owners legally abandoned the wreck. This affirmative action of relinquishing ownership was a legitimate mechanism that transferred the cleanup cost to the U.S. Army Corps of Engineers (and to American taxpayers who funded the Corps). The COE wasted no time in getting on the job. "Under the provisions of the law, and by authority of the Secretary of War and direction of the Chief of Engineers of March 8, 1913, the immediate removal of the sunken cars and detached debris by oral agreement, and of the wreck proper by contract, was authorized. The bottom of the river in the vicinity of the wreck was swept by the aid of two tugboats and the United States tender belonging to the district, and use of diver to ascertain the position and condition of the wreckage. The sunken cars and detached parts were removed in open market by Louis E. Broom, a local wrecker, who was engaged on the work from April 11 to 19, inclusive, with a wrecking machine and diver. . . . Contract for entire removal of the wreck proper, including cargo, was made with the Merritt & Chapman Derrick & Wrecking Co., of New York, approved June 20, 1913, commenced June 21 and was in operation at the end of the fiscal year [June 30]. The plant engaged consisted of one steam derrick with a crew of 11, including 2 divers. Portions of the deck, coamings, etc., have been detached by the use of small charges (1 to 4 pounds) of dynamite, and placed aboard scows."

Because the whole forward part of the *Alum Chine* was destroyed, it seems unlikely that all of the hull was recovered. Undoubtedly, many disarticulated parts of the wreck were left on the bottom, where they lay deep enough not to interfere with the draft of vessels of the day. Proof of this came as long as 63 years after the catastrophe that rocked the harbor. In *Baltimore Harbor: a Pictorial History*, author Robert C. Keith published a photograph whose caption read:

"In 1976, workers of the A. Smith and Sons shipyard on Curtis Creek were laying a water main in the harbor when they brought up this severely bent connecting rod and other wreckage believed to be from the *Alum Chine*. Yard owner Jerry Smith has kept the pieces." One large piece of metal measured more than six feet in length and five feet in width.

A disaster of such magnitude as this should have been thoroughly investigated. And it was. Primary investigators were the Army and the Navy. The Army Bureau of Ordnance took testimony not so much to determine the cause of the explosion, but to study the aftereffects of the blast. The results were published under the title "Wave Distribution at the *Alum Chine* Explosion." The second part of the article was technical, but the first part set the stage by describing the circumstances surrounding the explosion. I reproduce the salient features:

The *Alum Chine* "was chartered to transport coal and dynamite to the Canal Zone, Panama, the dynamite to be discharged at Cristobal and the coal at Port Limon. . . . Some 2,000 tons of bituminous coal had been taken aboard when the stowing of the dynamite began.

"The dynamite cargo consisted of 7,000 cases of 45 per cent and 5,000 cases of 60 per cent potassium nitrate dynamite. The dynamite was packed in cartons and these in cases. Each case contained 50 pounds of dynamite. The total weight of dynamite to be shipped was therefore 600,000 pounds, or 300 short tons. The explosives had been brought from the factory by rail some time in advance of stowing on the steamer and as the temperature had been low the dynamite was frozen. It was taken from shore without breaking bulk by placing the cars containing it on a barge and towing this barge alongside the *Alum Chine* when the cases were lifted to a chute, slid down into the hold, and stowed in the forehold on dunnage above the coal so that all of the dynamite was placed near to the water line.

"The loading had been going on during the previous day so that on March 7 at 10.20 a. m., there was stowed on board the *Alum Chine* about 285 tons of dynamite while about 15 tons remained in cars on the barge alongside.

"At about this time the Second Mate of the *Alum Chine*, who was standing between 8 and 9 feet from the forward hatchway, heard a report 'no louder than a pistol shot' and saw 'smoke' issuing from the forward hatchway. Several of the stevedores below this hatchway testified to seeing a foreman grasp a cotton hook and drive it into a box of dynamite that they had had trouble in stowing into place and that immediately there was a report 'like a pistol shot' followed by yellow smoke. This evolution of smoke from the forward hatch was observed by several different persons at different locations in Baltimore Harbor, one of them, familiar with operations at Sparrows Point steel works, likening it in color to the 'blow' from a Bessemer convertor. These observations indicate the smoke to have been colored by nitrogen oxides from burning dynamite. In tests of frozen dynamite by exposure to friction a 'crack' like that from a throwdown torpedo has been observed, followed by the burning of the dynamite. Whatever the source of ignition in this *Alum Chine* disaster it is undoubted that dynamite was set on fire, that some of the dynamite burned, and that the heat from this caused more or less of the remainder to explode.

"The interval between the observing of the incidents above recorded and the final explosion was sufficient to permit the members of the crew and of the party of stevedores aboard, numbering upward of 70 men, to get to a relatively safe distance before the explosion occurred if they acted promptly. Nevertheless the casualties numbered some 32 killed or drowned and 60 injured. Some of these casualties occurred on the U.S. Collier *Jason*, lying to the west of the *Alum Chine* and less than one-fourth mile distant. The major part of the casualties occurred on the tug *Atlantic* due to the fact that when she had gotten some distance from the *Alum Chine* her captain, William E. Van Dyke, in an heroic effort to rescue two men that had been left on the *Alum Chine*, returned to the latter, took the men off, and was able to get but a short distance away when the explosion took place, destroying him and many of the persons on the *Atlantic*.

"The effect of the blast was to shear the *Atlantic* off at the water's edge 'as if cut with a knife' and to keel the *Jason* over more than 10 degrees of arc. The barge with its partly loaded cars was overturned, dumping the cars with their contents into the harbor, but it does not appear that any of this dynamite exploded. While considerable damage was done to the nearby collier *Jason* by the blast and by flying missiles, and while pieces of steel, approximately 150 pounds in weight, were thrown some 7 or 8 miles, yet the destruction wrought was less than might have been expected from so large a mass of explosive. While it is known that unexploded cartridges were thrown from the cargo, as some of these were picked up on the deck of the *Jason*, it is concluded that only a portion of the cargo of dynamite exploded and that it may not have been of the highest order of detonation.

"Nevertheless the earth and air waves created by it were transmitted considerable distances."

At this point the study provided some examples, of which I will reproduce only a few, so that the reader may get an idea of the damage that was caused by the concussion. In Baltimore, at a distance of 4 to 8 miles, "The City Hall vibrated and dust was shaken down throughout the building. The doors of the sanctuary at the Cathedral were shaken open and it was feared the ceiling of the Cathedral was about to fall. At McCoy Hall, Johns Hopkins University, there was a feeling that the windows were pushed in by a slight impact and there was also a slight thud heard. 'The effects of the explosion were felt but to a comparatively slight extent in the northwestern portion of the city while pronounced shocks were felt in the southern, eastern and northeastern sections.' "

At a distance of 12 miles, Towson felt "Only a slight tremble. Few in this direction knew of an explosion until they read of it in the papers."

Houses shook in Aberdeen, Maryland, 28 miles from the blast. "Four windows broken, and one blown into room, cracks in walls enlarged, furnace in cellar moved" in the High School building.

In Havre de Grace, Maryland, "A plate glass window, 9 feet by 14 feet, in Lyon's Pharmacy was demolished. Houses were rocked, windows and dishes shaken from shelves." This was 33 miles from the explosion.

Windows were broken at Delta, Pennsylvania, which was located 37 miles from ground zero. "All the doors and windows went out. The report was loud and distinct. A roar was followed by a roll. The cloud of smoke was seen by several persons."

Wilmington, Delaware (at 67 miles): "Window panes broken and other damage done."

In Delmar, Delaware (74 miles): "In almost every town in Delaware window panes in dwellings were broken."

Philadelphia, Pennsylvania (92 miles): "Caused windows to rattle. Small pieces of furniture shaken and overturned."

According to the report, "The most continuous effects reported were on the N.E. line to Philadelphia and up the valley of the Susquehanna river. The report from Dover, Del., indicates the effect to have been quite severe to the east." Thus the major swath of the blast wave trended east and northeast, with other directions suffering damage only close to ground zero.

"It has been stated that the dynamite on the *Alum Chine* was stowed at about the water line. With a view to ascertaining how the vessel was 'pointing' at the time of the explosion information was sought from official sources. The Chief of the Weather Bureau gives the record for its Baltimore office at 10:30 A. M., March 7, 1913, as: temperature 20° [F], sun visible, wind velocity 10 miles per hour, wind direction (from) northwest, and adds the following extract from the records:

" 'The explosion of a vessel, the *Alum Chine*, loaded with dynamite, in the harbor of Baltimore, Md., made a record on the barograph sheet at 10:45 A. M. A forcible puff of wind was felt at the window by the messenger boy immediately after the explosion. Dust was blown in the fourth story windows of the custom house.' "

The U.S. Coast and Geodetic Survey calculated from the wind and tide that the "*Alum Chine* would have been heading northwesterly."

The chief engineer of the District Engineer of Baltimore stated: "The examination of the wreck made after the explosion showed the steamer lying on an even keel with the front end blown off, the stern still intact, and the wreck headed about west-northwest. . . . It seems probable that the vessel was driven some distance astern by the blast and lay on the bottom with the axis in the same general direction as before the explosion."

Another report on the condition of the wreck stated, "The explosion blew off the front end of the vessel, turning the sides out practically at right angles to the line of the hull, but not destroying the rear of the vessel."

After reviewing all of the above, the Bureau of Ordnance concluded, "When an explosive detonates the products of the reaction are projected into surrounding space at high velocity and a wave motion, analogous to that of sound, is imparted to the surrounding media. . . . With the *Alum Chine*, situated as it was, when the explosion occurred such wave motions would be set up in the circumambient air, in the water in which the vessel was floating, and in the earth beneath it, each with a different rate of propagation as is also true for sound waves with a change of medium.

"From the reports cited above it is fair to conclude that at the moment of explosion the *Alum Chine* was heading to the northwest or west-northwest. An effect of the explosion undoubtedly was to raise the bow of the vessel, depress the stern and, by the recoil, drive the stern of the wreck under water with the result that the blast from the explosion in the bow would issue at an elevated angle and into the eye of the wind. Shot thus into the wind the 'blast' of explosion products and stream of impulses set up in the air by the explosion, would be diverted from its course, a part, in this case, being deflected toward the northeast and other portions being in part reflected to the northwest and in part, perhaps after being in some measure completely overturned in its onward course, borne on to the east, southeast and south. Were these the conditions that obtained the air waves traveling to the northwest would tend to pass over Baltimore and Towson to descend in the valley of the Susquehanna. . . .

"As the cargo of explosive was stored in the forehold near to the water line and (by theory) the bow of the vessel rose as the explosion took place, the effect upon the water, and upon the earth, which was at least 20 feet below the vessel's keel, must have been slight and any water or earth tremors produced must have been quite feeble. . . . It is interesting to note that the region on the line from Aberdeen to Philadelphia has been also thrilled by large blasts fired at the Aberdeen Proving Ground."

While the above discussion was rather technical, it was also informative not only with respect to the explosion and the condition of the wreck, but with respect to the passage of the immense pressure wave.

The Navy report had to do with damage to the *Jason*. At the time of the catastrophe in which so many lives were lost, the collier was in the hands of the contractors: the Maryland Steel Company, at Sparrows Point. According to the Navy report, the *Jason* "had just been docked, filled with a full cargo of coal and provisions, had a full crew on board, and was lying at anchor at a distance estimated by various persons to be from 500 to 800 yards distant from the *Alum Chine*. The *Jason* was to depart the following morning for the Delaware Breakwater to conduct her official preliminary acceptance trials. The *Jason* was lying with her port side toward the *Alum Chine*."

A description of the damage is informative: "The hull was pierced in many places and so badly dented that it was necessary to replace a number of the side plates. The superstructure was badly wrenched and lopped over, the side bulkheads badly bulged, and the woodwork of the interior was a mass of splinters and wreckage. The deck of the superstructure was flattened and the supporting beams badly bent. The A frames of the coaling gear were pierced in many places by flying metal and the rigging of same was cut to shreds. The Ardois (a system of electric light signals) was torn from the mast. The bridge instruments were more or less damaged and the chart house and bridge cabin were wrecked. The watertight covers to the cargo-oil deep tanks was [sic] badly sprung. The smoke pipes and atmospheric exhaust pipes were pierced in many places and so badly wrenched as to require renewal.

"The largest hole in the hull plating was about twelve inches in diameter. One piece of metal about three inches in diameter passed through the steel side of the superstructure, killed a mess attendant, then passed in a straight line through a steel athwartship bulkhead, through a steel fore-and-aft bulkhead, and through a wooden door into a lavatory. Another man was killed in a stateroom by being disemboweled by an airport lens and rim. A few other deaths were caused on the *Jason* by flying metal. The concussion was so great that persons standing on deck were thrown violently from their feet. Subsequent to the explosion the vessel presented the appearance of having been through a bombardment of shrapnel and shells as large as six or eight inches in size. Persons on board the *Jason* at the time stated that the greater part of the flying wreckage seemed to pass entirely over the *Jason*. Great quantities of pieces of metal and torn rivets, and about half a bushel of unburned pieces of dynamite were picked up about the decks of the *Jason*, all in a smoky, grimy condition. The unburned dynamite was promptly thrown overboard in order to prevent further damage, but many pieces of torn metal were carried away by the crew and others as souvenirs of the terrible catastrophe. The cargo of coal was discharged to naval colliers, and the vessel was laid up for a period of approximately three months undergoing repairs.

"The machinery apparently suffered no damage, as it was well below the water line and was therefore well protected.

From *Poplar Mechanics*.

"The vessel was fully insured by the contractors, as required by the Government, and the underwriters were required to meet all costs of repairs."

Imagine the damage that would have been done to buildings had the *Alum Chine* been docked at the time of the explosion. The hull of the *Jason* was built of steel plate, and, according to different witnesses, lay one to four blocks from ground zero. Adjacent wharf buildings would have been totally demolished, and the death toll would have been enormous.

In modern American jurisprudence, there is no such thing as an accident. Although people speak glibly of traffic accidents and highway accidents, they are more correctly called crashes. By definition, an accident is a mishap: an unplanned and unfortunate event that results in damage, injury, or upset of some kind; or the way things happen without any planning, apparent cause, or deliberate intent.

In legal terminology, an incident which unaffected people refer to as an accident, the victims, courts, and lawyers describe as an effect that some individual or corporate entity must have caused. In other words, every undesirable consequence can be traced back to a human agency which must be held financially accountable for damages that resulted from this cause and effect relationship. In legal words, there is no such thing as an accident in which there is no one to blame. Natural causes, acts of God, and other such faultless grounds have been banished from the legal system because they are broke, bankrupt, or otherwise insolvent.

On the other side of the coin, in the case of the explosion onboard the *Alum Chine*, there were widows and children who were left with no viable means of support. There were injured men who required medical treatment, some of whom lost wages during the healing process in homes and hospitals; to say nothing of the pain and possible long-term effects that they suffered. There were owners of buildings who had structural damage to repair, windows to replace, debris to clean up, and so on.

Twenty-five libels were filed against various defendants that were charged with the ultimate responsibility for causing the explosion. According to court documents, "The libelants may be classified as : (1) Stevedores working on or about the ship and engaged in the loading of dynamite thereon, or surviving dependents of such stevedores. (2) the owners of the ship. (3) Persons who had no contractual relation with any of the defendants, but who were lawfully in the vicinity of the ship in the prosecution of their own affairs, and who were injured by the explosion, or who are dependent upon persons in like situation who were killed by it, and owners of property which at the time of the explosion was in the neighborhood and suffered from it.

"In all there are five respondents [defendants], although not all of them have been sued in every case. They are: (1) The General Stevedoring Company. (2) the Joseph R. Foard Company of Baltimore City. (3) the Munson Line. (4) The Maryland Steel Company. (5) The mayor and city council of Baltimore."

I will distill this multifaceted case to its primary elements without incorporating all the distractions and case law citations on which the final opinion was rendered. The facts that were not in dispute correlate substantially with the narrative with which this chapter commenced. The only matters that were in dispute were the origin of the fire, and who should have to pay for the resultant damage.

Stevedore foreman William Bomhardt testified that he was trying to squeeze a box of dynamite in place between two other boxes. "While so doing, the near end of the box farther from him exploded. He was wounded in the face." Bomhardt believed that the dynamite exploded of its own accord, due to the subfreezing temperature; it was 21° F at the time. The reader will note that, after having time to think about the incident, his testimony differs slightly from what he said in interviews with reporters. He did not suggest that two sticks must have rubbed together to create friction that led to ignition.

An explosives expert testified on his behalf that dynamite freezes "as high as 52° Fahrenheit," and that dynamite that has been frozen, thawed, and refrozen, might be less stable that dynamite that has never been frozen.

"On the other hand, 13 persons, who claim to be eyewitnesses, say they saw the box explode when Bomhardt struck it the second time with the hook. These witnesses were examined in open court. . . . The overwhelming weight of the testimony is therefore that the explosion occurred when Bomhardt struck a box of dynamite with a bale hook."

The judge went on to note, "Bomhardt escaped on the *Jerome*. He at first said nothing to anyone. He sat with his face in his hands. It was noticed that he was bleeding. A witness went to him, raised his head, and recognized him. He told the man who bound up his head that a case had burst. This brief colloquy took place before the final explosion. His credibility as a witness is impaired by the fact that it seems to be established that on the morning after the accident he insisted that he never used a bale hook at all," when in fact numerous witnesses testified to the contrary.

Some defendants tried to convince the court that the fire and consequent explosion were caused by spontaneous combustion of coal: either in the cargo holds or in the bunkers. They fantasized that, despite the freezing temperature, the coal generated enough heat to emit methane gas, which accumulated in pockets directly beneath the dynamite that was being stowed. Then, by incredible coincidence, one of these pockets burst into flame at the precise moment when Bomhardt struck the dynamite box with the bale hook. The court didn't buy this scenario.

"Unless the evidence in this case it to be weighed in some unusual way, it must be found as a fact that the small explosion which admittedly took place instantly followed the last blow given by Bomhardt with a bale hook to a box of dynamite.

"The respondents answer that it is impossible that such a stroke could have caused the explosion. They say that it would be extremely difficult for any one to hit a box containing dynamite with a bale hook with sufficient force to explode the contents. It would require a blow harder than any sane man who did not wish to commit suicide would have given." Nice try, but the court didn't buy this scenario either.

When all was said and done, there could be no doubt in any rational person's mind that Bomhardt's act of striking a case of dynamite with a cargo hook was the direct and only cause of ignition that caused the burst of flame which led to the subsequent explosion.

However, it is a well-known verity that in twentieth-century lawsuits, an individual is almost never found liable for loss or damage that said individual has caused; that individuals are seldom held accountable for their own destructive actions. There must always be some higher authority to bear the brunt of responsibility: some authority that possesses the resources to pay big bucks to the plaintiffs. Working-class individuals do not have enough money to pay exorbitant claims which, after all, is the sole purpose for suing in the first place. Blame without adequate compensation is worthless. Defendants are chosen not by dint of their responsibility in a matter, but by the amount of money they have and can be forced to pay. Thus liability is assigned *not* to the party who is actually guilty of commission, but to a wealthy scapegoat.

Americans have long since learned that it is easier to make money by suing for it than by working for it.

Although the court firmly established that Bomhardt was the one who initiated the events that led to the explosion that caused so much death and destruction, the libelants (or plaintiffs) chose to sue companies or the government. In America, it has now become accepted that closure can be obtained only by getting rich in the process. Otherwise, sewers (pardon me: suers) would donate their winnings to charity, and take satisfaction in the fact that innocent stockholders would suffer from a reduction in corporate earnings.

Be that as it may, in the crux of the matter, the court spent more of its time on determining who should be held liable for Bomhardt's action than on determining Bomhardt's guilt.

The court dismissed all claims against the Munson Line (which chartered the *Alum Chine* to deliver the cargo of coal and dynamite to the Isthmus of Panama), the Maryland Steel Company (which built the *Jason*), and the City of Baltimore (which was accused of permitting a dangerous cargo to be loaded near metropolitan environs.

The outfit that actually employed Bomhardt was the duly incorporated General Stevedoring Company. But the authorized capital of the company was only $2,000; the value of its stevedoring gear was $1,450; and its profits from the previous year amounted to $1,517.40.

Therefore, the libelants contrived a strategy to convince the court to find the Joseph R. Foard Company equally liable, because of its close ties with the General Stevedoring Company (and, of course, because that company had more money and assets). An examination of corporate records established that Foard performed its own stevedoring work until 1910. It then split its assets and created a separate corporate entity called Stevedoring. Each company operated independently, and each was incorporated in the City of Baltimore. When Foard needed stevedoring work done, it hired Stevedoring; this arrangement did not prevent Stevedoring from doing other stevedoring work.

The connection between the two companies was such that Foard owned all of Stevedoring's stock, and all of Foard's managing officers also worked as managing officers for Stevedoring. Yet each company was recognized as a separate legal entity: each with its own letterhead, equipment, and employees. Nonetheless, for the purpose of the instant suit, and likely at the insistence of the libelants, the court allowed that Foard should share the liability with Stevedoring.

The court was quick to note, however, that "all its assets will be insufficient to meet the claims."

The court then waxed philosophical: "The conclusions here reached are disastrous to the Foard Company. They will give little satisfaction to the libelants. The findings of fact as to the cause of the accident and the relations between the Foard and the Stevedoring Companies require a decree which will sweep away all the accumulations of years of honest industry. . . . the Foard Company seemed called on to pay a high price for a very trifling error of judgment. On the other hand, if the decree here made shall be affirmed above, all that the Foard and the Stevedoring Companies have will make good to the libelants but a fraction of what they have lost. . . .

"It may be that some day the law will be so moulded that more exact and complete equity may be done. Public opinion has apparently come to the conclusion that workmen should be indemnified against the pecuniary consequences of accidents suffered by them in the course of their employment. Hereafter a step further may be taken. It may then seem just to compensate all persons who without fault of their own suffer from industrial accidents. Such a policy may be wise. . . . Whether indemnification shall be given at all, and if so how, is a complex problem. It is for the Legislature to work out."

I cannot help but end this chapter by noting that the court's ruling took all of thirty-seven pages of typescript to publish. That's a lot of writing in anyone's book. This sheer mass of background information, which was used to support the court's opinion, must have been preceded by hundreds or perhaps thousands of pages of testimonial transcription, affidavits, corporate documents, legal briefs, prayers for motions, and so on. Yet the case was concluded in less than eleven months.

I was once the foreman of a jury that heard a civil trial between two litigants who had suffered a minor auto crash. Each litigant had long since been reimbursed for damages and medical bills by his insurance company. Each was suing for long-term pain and suffering, of which there was *none*. The lawsuit had been ongoing for eight years!

In a case that must have cost the legal system hundreds of thousands or millions of dollars, we found for one litigant in the amount of two thousand five hundred dollars ($2,500). (I voted for zero but was forced to compromise.)

How times have changed since the 1842 explosion of the *Medora* (which see).

Fossil shells embedded in matrix in the Calvert Cliffs.

AMERICAN MARINER

Built: 1942
Previous names: *George Calvert*
Gross tonnage: 7,100
Type of vessel: Modified Liberty Ship
Builder: Bethlehem-Fairfield Shipyard, Baltimore, Maryland
Owner: United States Maritime Commission
Port of registry: United States
Cause of sinking: Scuttled for use as a target
Location: Off the mouth of the Potomac River

Sunk: October 21, 1966
Depth: 20 feet
Dimensions: 441' x 57' x 34'
Power: Oil-fired steam

GPS: 39-02.403 / 76-09.314

With war in Europe in full swing, and with American sentiments siding with the Allies against Germany and the Axis powers, the United States Maritime Commission initiated a shipbuilding program for the mass production of "bottoms" (as cargo vessels are called in the business). Shipyards geared up for a new class of freighter that was designated EC2, which stood for Emergency Cargo vessel with a length between 400 and 450 feet. They came to be known more familiarly as Liberty Ships.

The prototype was based on a British design that was altered to have fewer curves in the hull. The result was a blocky appearance, but the advantage was a faster fabrication time because steel plates did not have to be bent for beauty. In terms of mass production, think of the Liberty Ship as the maritime version of the Model T Ford: a workhorse instead of a sleek yacht or cigarette boat.

The Liberty Ships were uniform in their construction. The hull measured 441 feet in length overall; because of the elliptical cruiser stern they measured 417 feet at the waterline. They had a beam of 57 feet, and a depth of 34 feet. Registered tonnage was 7,176 gross, 4,380 net. This standardized hull design enabled shipyards to prefabricate sections in quantity, then assemble the sections by means of welding (as opposed to riveting). Welding was faster and more reliable than the old-time method of drilling holes in steel plates and then riveting the overlapping plates together. Welding also saved six hundred *tons* of rivets.

The Maritime Commission designated each emergency hull by a consecutive number until a name was assigned to it. For example, while MCE-20 was still on the ways prior to launching, the "bottom" was officially named *George Calvert*.

This official U.S. Coast Guard photo was taken on November 1, 1943

Commander and Mrs. Goddard used this postcard picture as a holiday greeting.

By 1941, there seemed little doubt that the war that had been raging in Europe ever since Germany invaded Poland – on September 1, 1939 – was not nearing an end, and that the U.S. must eventually do more for the war effort than to furnish supplies as part of the Lend-Lease program with England. This meant that the U.S. would sometime have to declare war on Germany. Troops that were sent overseas would need transportation, food, supplies, and materiel. It wasn't enough to just step up the production of Liberty Ships. Crews would be needed to operate those ships. Those crews would have to be trained in the operation and maintenance of those ships.

Of the more than 2,700 Liberty Ships that were built before the global war ended in victory for peace-loving and peacekeeping nations around the world, one of them was chosen for conversion to a training ship. That one was the *George Calvert*. On December 5, 1941, the Maritime Commission started the process of conversion by renaming her *American Mariner*. Two days later, Japan bombed Pearl Harbor, and the United States was dragged into the thick of a two-ocean war against belligerents that were located on opposite sides of the planet: Japan and Germany.

The Maritime Commission authorized the expenditure of $950,000 to have the newly ordained *American Mariner* towed from the Bethlehem-Fairfield Shipyard in Baltimore to Bethlehem's nearby Key Highway plant, where she was to undergo conversion. Launching was scheduled for December 30; the hull was launched on time, and conversion commenced immediately upon its arrival at the Key Highway plant.

In exterior appearance the hull of the *American Mariner* was identical to that of the standard Liberty Ship. The unseen interior, however, was vastly different. Instead of five cargo holds there was only one; that one was hold number 2. Ordinarily there were three holds forward of the midship navigating bridge, and two aft. They were numbered from fore to aft. These capacious holds were divided into three deck levels.

Hold number 1 (closest to the bow) became a recreation room. Cargo could be carried only in the bottom level of hold number 2; above the cargo deck was a berthing deck; and above the berthing deck was the mess hall. Hold number 3 held stores and a galley. Hold number 4 became a machine shop and sick bay. Hold number 5 became a carpenter shop. Above this room and the two shops were berthing spaces for as many as 500 instructors and trainees, plus showers, laundry, medical and dental facilities, and various shops: barber, tailor, and cobbler. The top deck was divided into compartments for heads (both forward and aft), mess hall, galley, stores, workshop, and classrooms. In essence, the *American Mariner* became a home away from home, or a miniature city with all the essentials and necessities. The top deck was pierced for more portholes than the standard Liberty Ship possessed.

The superstructure was more than a small midship navigating bridge. It consisted of three deck levels, the lowest of which measured more than 150 feet in length; this contained a stage, a movie projection room, and an auditorium that seated more than 300 people. The deck above was shorter and was reserved for officers; it contained staterooms, heads, library, pantry, and scullery. The topmost deck was the navigation deck; it contained the wheelhouse, chart room, radio room, and fire control room (for the armament). In outward appearance, the *American Mariner* now looked more like a passenger liner than a Liberty Ship. In actuality, due to the number of instructors and trainees onboard, she *was* more of a passenger vessel than a cargo carrier.

Due to interior alterations and the expanded superstructure, the gross tonnage was calculated at 7,100, while the net tonnage (cargo carrying capacity) was reduced to 1,562.

The *American Mariner* bristled with guns. Her battery consisted of three 3-inch deck guns, eight .50 caliber machine guns, and two 20-millimeter antiaircraft guns. All this armament required a slew of gunners who had to be housed and fed. The vessel's large population required extra lifeboats, life vests, and life preservers: enough to accommodate every individual onboard.

The *American Mariner* could attain a speed of 11 knots, but her most efficient cruising speed was 10 knots; this enabled her to steam for 16,000 nautical miles without refueling.

Because the *American Mariner* was intended for training purposes instead of for delivering cargoes, she may have invented the concept of the "voyage to nowhere." She would depart with a convoy that was destined to cross the Atlantic Ocean, but she generally turned back or steamed along the coast long enough to give her trainees a "feel" for the sea, and to learn what it was like to be a real merchant mariner.

While this portion of the *American Mariner's* career may seem boring by comparison with her later duties, her importance with regard to winning the war cannot be stressed strongly enough. Building thousands of bottoms to replace those that were torpedoed by German U-boats was only one part of the equation; there was a need for educated mariners to operate those vessels. Only so much can be learned from a book. Experience at sea was a crucial part of the learning process.

After passing written examinations, deck officers and able bodied seamen had to acquire the practical applications of their craft: everything from navigation to engine maintenance. During the war, the U.S. Merchant Marine Academy graduated nearly 200,000 men (and some women). That was three times the number of American mariners who were employed at the start of the war. Many of those graduates saw service on the appropriately named *American Mariner*.

After the war, the *American Mariner* was assigned to the Massachusetts Maritime Academy at Buzzards Bay, on the bank of the Cape Cod Canal. Under this new aegis she visited Maine, stopped at Cuba and Bermuda and Jamaica, toured the West Coast, and steamed up the Mississippi River.

In 1950, she was laid up at Kings Point, New York. In 1953, she was towed up the Hudson River to join the reserve fleet in deactivated status (better known as "mothballed"). This remained her home for the next five years.

She was given a new lease on life in 1958. After reactivation, she underwent a massive conversion to a U.S. Army vessel for service as a missile range instrumentation ship. The 1950's was the era that popularized such concepts as the Iron Curtain, the Cold War, the ICBM (intercontinental ballistic missile), the DEW line (Distant Early Warning system), and the less-well-known Downrange Antimissile Measurement Program (DAMP).

There was very real concern that the Soviet Union might launch a nuclear missile attack against the mainland of the United States. There was no way to prevent such an attack, but there could be ways to detect the approach of ballistic missiles. The DEW line consisted of a series of Air Force bases in the Canadian arctic and waterborne platforms along the eastern seaboard: the most probable directions from which a Russian attack would come. These facilities were equipped with huge radar dishes that could detect incoming missiles, and hopefully provide sufficient warning time to enable a full-scale counter attack while strike zones were being evacuated.

A ballistic missile was one which followed a predetermined trajectory that could not be altered after the missile was launched. This type of missile differed from the guided missile, which contained a remote-controlled guidance system that enabled re-targeting by means of inflight maneuvering. Due to the distance from Russian-held territory to the U.S., an enemy intercontinental ballistic missile would have fly out of the atmosphere into the vacuum of space in order to strike an American city.

Upon re-entry, such a missile would create disturbances in the atmosphere such as bright incandescent light, infrared and ultraviolet radiation, ionization, polarization, scintillation, and perhaps as-yet unknown phenomena. The purpose of DAMP was to study these atmospheric disturbances and develop electronic means to detect them.

The *American Mariner* was equipped with an array of antennas, the largest of which was a parabolic reflector that measured sixteen feet in diameter. Communication subsystems included transmitters and receivers in ranges of high, very high, and ultra-

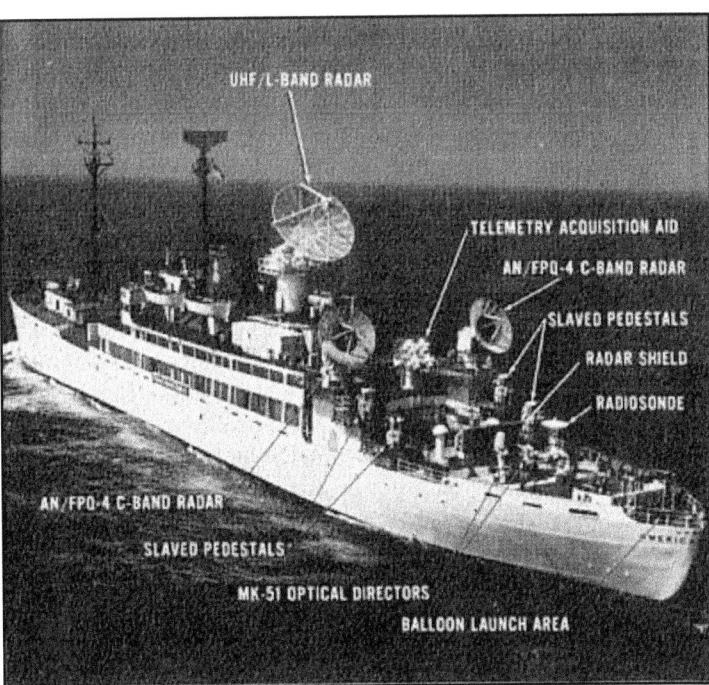

This official U.S. Army photo indicates and names the primary functional features, instruments, and radar dishes.

This stern view shows the radar dishes. (Official U.S. Army photo.)

high frequencies. Detection apparatus occupied large spaces below deck. All this electronic gear functioned on vacuum tube technology. The interior of the vessel was air-conditioned – not for the comfort of the crew but because vacuum tubes generated vast quantities of heat, and would cease to work if they became overheated (or perhaps vacuum tubes had a stronger union than merchant mariners).

The vessel was managed by civilian personnel who were furnished by the Mathiasen Tankers Industries. The electronic equipment was operated by civilian scientists and technicians, who were employed by the Radio Corporation of America (RCA) and the Barnes Engineering Company. The total complement consisted of about one hundred fifty persons.

Actual operations commenced in January 1959. The *American Mariner* proceeded to an impact area with electronics experts monitoring detection and communication consoles. A friendly (and unarmed) missile was then launched into the area. The missile was detected and tracked by optical scanners, radar, and telemetry equipment. Still cameras captured visual effects, and motion-picture cameras filmed the missile during its progression to the strike zone. A complete photographic processing lab was maintained onboard. Re-entry data were collected for later study.

In essence, the *American Mariner* was a floating laboratory. She carried no armament of any kind; her guns and gun tubs had long since been removed. In this most fascinating phase of her career, her missions took her throughout the North and South Atlantic Oceans. Naturally, this work was highly classified at the time, and only in retrospect has the vessel's clandestine occupation become known to the general public.

In 1962, the *American Mariner* passed through the Panama Canal and proceeded to her new area of operation in the Pacific Ocean: Johnston Atoll, about 750 nautical miles west of Hawaii. Here she participated in nuclear bomb tests by tracking missiles that were launched from the island in order to detonate their payloads high in the atmosphere.

One critical feature of these tests was the study of the electromagnetic pulse (EMP) that was generated by an atomic blast in the upper atmosphere. EMP is a surge of free electrons that are stripped off atoms by shock waves and are focused away from the detonation point at the initiation of the blast. This surge, or pulse, lasts for only nanoseconds, but is intense enough to disrupt the Earth's magnetic field and damage unshielded circuitry. The EMP from one of these blasts – on July 9, 1962 – knocked out street lights and other electric and electronic apparatus in Hawaii. Hawaiians also observed the flash of light in the western sky, as well as the auroral effects that resulted from ionic interactions and the change of energy states in affected atoms.

Because vacuum tubes are less vulnerable to EMP than solid state electronics, the *American Mariner* did not suffer significant damage from the pulse: a strange case of older being better. More sophisticated electronic equipment was badly damaged by the pulse. The avionics of two observation aircraft were badly impaired, although both planes managed to land safely.

The 1963 nuclear test ban put an end to atmospheric detonations of atomic bombs, which came to be called "nuclear devices." A rose by any other name would smell as sweet, and an atomic bomb with a different designation would kill just as many people. Underground testing continued, however, until 1971.

The *American Mariner* returned to the Atlantic Ocean. She was phased out of Army service and transferred to the U.S. Air Force. Her outdated instrumentation was upgraded. Again she was used to track missiles that the Air Force was testing. She operated in this capacity until December 1965, at which time she was deactivated. Her essential electronic equipment was removed for other uses.

When the Liberty Ships were built they were considered to be expendable. It was hoped that these assembly-line vessels would survive until the end of the war. Many did not. Those that did survive were sold by the U.S. Maritime Commission to private industry both at home and abroad. Their distinctive profile was seen around the world in dwindling numbers for the next couple of decades.

By the time the *American Mariner* was laid up for the last time, only a handful of Liberty Ships remained on the high seas. By 1971 they were all gone: bombed, torpedoed, sunk by marine casualty, or scrapped – all except for three.

On August 11, 1994, I was diving off the Diamond Shoals of North Carolina when we spotted a freighter in the distance. Because we were diving on a wreck that had been torpedoed during World War Two (the *Empire Gem*), we joked about how the distant vessel would have looked through the eyepiece of a German periscope. Artie Kirchner said casually if somewhat facetiously, "It looks like a Liberty Ship."

I took a second glance. Suddenly I felt a creepy sensation in the back of my mind, much like déjà vu. I grabbed a pair of binoculars and stared at the vessel on the horizon. I could hardly believe my eyes. "It *is* a Liberty Ship!" I shouted. I would recognize that profile anywhere, anytime. But I also knew that what I saw was impossible. It was as if the dive boat had gone through a time warp back to those perilous days of 1942.

It turned out that it *was* a Liberty Ship. It was the *Jeremiah O'Brien*. She and the *John W. Brown* were the only two Liberty Ships that were still afloat and operational. Each had been saved from the wreckers, and through private subscription and the heroic efforts of a large body of volunteers, had been reconditioned as tourist attractions. The *Jeremiah O'Brien* is currently docked in San Francisco; the *John W. Brown* in Baltimore (see page 14 for a comparative photo).

On the day we spotted her, the *Jeremiah O'Brien* was returning from the semi-centennial D-Day celebration. She made the voyage from San Francisco to France and back again entirely under her own steam. On the return passage, she sighted the eastern seaboard precisely where we happened to be diving; she then turned south and proceeded to the Panama Canal.

The third Liberty Ship whose profile can still be seen on the water is the *American Mariner*. After a long and distinguished career, the hulk was transferred to the U.S. Navy and towed into the Chesapeake Bay for use as a target ship. It seems that after the Navy bombed the *Hannibal* (which see) to smithereens, they needed another target ship for their aviators to devastate. The *American Mariner* was not commissioned into the Navy like the *Hannibal*, but was transferred simply as a piece of property, much like a discarded radio or a crumbling building or a broken-down jeep.

She was positioned adjacent to the remains of the *Hannibal* in 20 feet of water. The Underwater Demolition Team set scuttling charges on the hull. After a test charge was detonated on October 19, 1966, the final charges delivered the coup de grace two days later. The *American Mariner* settled slightly to the bottom so that the hull was exposed above the normal waterline, and she (a ship) became it (a shipwreck).

The location is marked on nautical charts with a visible wreck symbol. A warning notice that reads "Bombing Area" is appended. Pilots are supposed to do a flyby before dropping bombs and making strafing runs. Fishing is good around the hull, but anglers are cautioned to leave the area quickly if a jet screams past overhead, in case the pilot fails to notice a boat close to or possibly hidden by the wreck. Watch out for helicopters that might fire guns and rockets at the hulk.

Because of the enlarged superstructure, the *American Mariner* does not display the silhouette of the standard Liberty Ship. Only the contours of the hull (which now resembles a slab of Swiss cheese) conform to the original design. Nonetheless, perhaps it is fitting that after nearly fifty years of target practice, the shot-up hull has maintained its general shape – if not its structural integrity – and serves as a stark reminder of the turbulent times in which the vessel and her sisters were constructed and went to war in search of peace – and found it at last in the Chesapeake Bay.

BENJAMIN O. COLONNA

Built: 1903
Previous names: None
Gross tonnage: 145
Type of vessel: Menhaden fishing trawler
Builder: Pocomoke City, Maryland
Owner: Joseph C. Jett, Inc., Reedville, Virginia
Port of registry: Reedville, Virginia
Cause of sinking: Collision with SS *Tullahoma*
Location: off the Hooper Islands, between the Patuxent and Potomac Rivers

Sunk: October 26, 1948
Depth: Unknown
Dimensions: 121' x 20' x 8'
Power: Diesel engine

Very few vessels live to the ripe old age of 45 years. By that age most vessels have long since been retired, scrapped, or simply left to rot on some out-of-the-way river bank. The *Benjamin O. Colonna* was one of the exceptions. She enjoyed a long and fruitful career in the fishing industry, between 1903 and 1948.

In the old days, the loss of a fishing vessel was seldom followed by in-depth news reports. Even an accident that involved loss of life seldom rated more than a couple of column inches. In this case, the *Benjamin O. Colonna* was *not* one of the exceptions – even in local papers.

During the pre-dawn hours of October 26, 1948, the Chesapeake Bay was shrouded in pea-soup fog. Small craft advisories were posted as the fishing vessel plowed through whitecaps in seas that were described as "very rough." The twenty-one men onboard were eager to return home after a season of hard work in purse-seining for menhaden: an inedible fish that was caught mostly for its oil and for use as a fertilizer. The *Benjamin O. Colonna* transited the Chesapeake & Delaware Canal, then turned south.

Meanwhile, the 10,296-ton tanker *Tullahoma* was upbound from Baytown, Texas to Baltimore, Maryland with a cargo of crude. As the two vessels approached each other, the fishing vessel suddenly veered off course directly across the path of the behemoth. The tanker did not even shiver as her steel stem sliced through the wooden hull of the *Benjamin O. Colonna*, severing the fishing vessel in twain. The after section sank shortly thereafter; the forward section capsized and continued to float because the air that was trapped in the interior compartments buoyed the weight of the hull above the surface. The time was 4:42 in the morning.

The *Tullahoma* hove-to at once, notified the Coast Guard by radio, and put lifeboats in the water to search for survivors. They scoured the vicinity of the floating forward section, and picked up sixteen soaked survivors. Five men were lost in the collision. "Victims, all of Reedville, were listed as Bennie Browns, Harding Jones, Nathan Rich, Harry Smith and a fifth as yet unidentified."

The Coast Guard dispatched a search plane from Elizabeth City, North Carolina; the cutter *Chinook* from Baltimore; and the cutter *Jonquil* from Portsmouth, Virginia. The aircraft and surface vessels converged on the still-floating forward section, but were unable to locate any more survivors. Coastguardsmen of the *Jonquil* searched the forward section for bodies, but found none. Later she took the broken section in tow.

According to one newspaper account, "Capt. William Miller, master of the undamaged tanker, said a broken steering chain caused the trawler to cut across the tanker's bow." If this was true, Miller must have obtained the information from one of the survivors.

Ordinarily that would be the end of the story. But due to serendipity and an unusual set of circumstances, I was lucky to have additional facts brought to my attention by Rebekah Satterwhite Haynie, the granddaughter of chief engineer Howard Pratt Haynie, Sr. In 2006, after reading my book *Shipwrecks of Virginia*, she wrote to me about the World War Two loss of the *Menominee*: "The boat has special meaning for my husband, as it was his grandfather [Lester] Haynie who was captain of the tug *Menominee*. My husband also had an uncle, Willard T. Haynie, son of Captain Les, who lost his life when the tug was torpedoed. His body was never found."

Ironically, after fifteen years of searching, I had finally located the wreck of the *Menominee* only the year before she wrote to me.

After her lead-in, she proceeded to tell me "of another shipwreck, this one involving *my* grandfather." In her handwritten letter she provided me with a summary of events about the *Benjamin O. Colonna*. In my reply, I informed her about my discovery of the *Menominee*, and asked her for details about the *Benjamin O. Colonna*. At that time I was still compiling a list of vessels to cover in the book that you hold in your hands, and was not very familiar with the loss of the fishing vessel.

Rebekah sent a newspaper article from her grandmother's scrapbook. Her grandmother was Elizabeth Haynie, wife of Howard Pratt Haynie. She also sent a typed account that she put together "from interviews I had with members of my family who were aboard, and my mother and uncle."

According to Rebekah, the skipper was R. Bernice Shelton, the pilot was Rosser Carey, the mate was John Shelton (brother of Bernice), the chief engineer was her grandfather, and the second engineer was Loren Perciful (her great uncle).

"The boat was headed back to Reedville to dock for the season. They were coming from the Hayes Factory in Lewes, Delaware. My grandfather said the seas were so rough there that they washed over the breakwater. The cook was serving breakfast early in order to clean up the galley before they docked. Some of the men were stirring, some were still below deck.

"One of the crew, Bennie Bowen (the dryboatsman, or striker), was serving as trick man for the pilot Rosser Carey. That is, Rosser was on watch but Bennie was at the helm steering. Mr. Carey had left the deck to go to breakfast.

"The fish boat saw the tanker coming. The helm signaled 'four bells and a jingle' to the engine room, which meant Full Astern (they were going Full Ahead.)

"Around four A.M., the tanker struck the fish boat on the starboard side and cut through the fish hold. (The hold was empty since it was the end of the season. But there was a dog in the hold that belonged to John Shelton that went down with the boat.)

"In the engine room, the impact threw Loren into the bulkhead and broke his watch. The fish boat went over. Pratt was hanging on to the rail in the stern and thought to himself, Well, this is the end. (He told me later that he could not swim.) He and the rail both went under, then the stern righted itself. The boat was cut in two; the stern floated long enough for some of the men to get off in one of the purse boats. The second purse boat was lost. The bow of the fish boat was kept afloat because of the wooden

The upside-down forward section of the *Benjamin O. Colonna*. (Courtesy of Rebekah Satterwhite Haynie.)

mast. The pilot house got knocked off of the boat.

"Both Pratt and Loren said that the lights kept burning and the whistle got stuck and blew until the boat sank.

"The tanker came back to pick up survivors. All but five of the crew were saved. John and Bernice hung onto the pilot house until picked up. Pratt and Loren got off in the purse boat with the others. The caging around the wheel of the purse boat got bent, and the men on it were afraid they would get run over by the tanker, as they could not maneuver and also it was still dark. They didn't have a light and scrambled to find something to signal the tanker. They finally set the cook's apron on fire so they could be spotted.

"The survivors were initially picked up by the *Tullahoma*. Only Rosser Carey was taken to the hospital with injuries. As stated in the magazine article, the rest of the men were brought home to Reedville on the *Elsie I*, John Lowry captain. The Coast Guard had arrived on the scene, but Mr. Lowry radioed them that he had the survivors on board. He brought them back to Reedville.

"On a personal note: my uncle Pratt Haynie, Jr. was six years old when the boat was wrecked. The image of the incident that sticks in his mind is seeing my grandfather get off the fish boat in Reedville holding one shoe in his hand. My mother remembers my grandfather sitting by the stove in the kitchen crying."

Rebekah also stated that an inquiry was held. "I cannot find out anything about who held the inquiry into the collision. I know there was one because my grandfather had to go testify. He also had to help identify the lost. A friend of mine, who is retired from the Coast Guard, researched the incident and tried to find information in the records of the Coast Guard ships named in the newspaper article, but he could find nothing."

It is likely that the inquiry report has been lost or was never archived.

In her handwritten letter, Rebekah wrote, "My grandparents had a party line phone system then. My grandmother picked up the phone that morning, listened, and the people on the line were talking about the collision. My mother said she screamed 'My husband's on that boat!' Can you imagine?" (If you don't know what a party line is, or was, ask someone from an earlier generation.)

My thanks go to Rebekah Satterwhite Haynie for saving this fascinating bit of history, and for making it available to me and my readers.

COLUMBIA

Built: 1911
Previous names: None
Gross tonnage: 359
Type of vessel: Wooden-hulled barge
Owner: Arundel Corporation, Baltimore, Maryland
Cause of sinking: Collision with *Lillian Ann*
Location: Off Drum Point, Patuxent River delta

Sunk: December 17, 1942
Depth: 50 feet
Dimensions: 168' x 23' x 10'
Power: None

GPS: 38-18-45.35 / 76-24-59.42

Many wrecks in the Chesapeake Bay have little or no historical interest. While the barge *Columbia* may be one of these, the site draws the attention of recreational divers because it is fun to explore.

Barges tend to receive short shrift when it comes to accounts of their sinking, and the *Columbia* is no exception to this unfortunate rule of thumb. The following newspaper account is the best description that I have been able to find:

"Coast Guard officials have reported that the barge *Columbia* was struck and sunk by an outbound tugboat yesterday off Solomon's. There was no loss of life.

"The Barge [sic], owned by the Arundel Corporation, was loaded with gravel and was being towed to an anchorage off the island."

"The tug *Lillian Ann*, operated for the Navy, struck the barge, which was third in a four-boat tow.

"Two men, Capt. J.H. Posey and Seaman G.L. Loessler, who were onboard the barge, were rescued by crewmen from other craft in the tow."

Some secondary sources give the date of sinking as March 15, 1943. This cannot be correct because the article quoted above was published on December 18, 1942, in which case "yesterday" would be December 17, 1942. Obviously the article could not have been published three months before the collision occurred.

Contemporary steamboat *Daniel Webster* is similar in appearance to the *Columbus*. Note how the deck is even with the outside of the paddle box, and how angled beams from the hull support the deck extension. (From *Early American Steamers*, by Erik Heyl.)

COLUMBUS

Built: 1829
Previous names: None
Gross tonnage: 416
Type of vessel: Wooden-hulled side-wheel steamer
Builder: George Gardner, Baltimore, Maryland
Owner: Maryland & Virginia Steamboat Company
Port of registry: Baltimore, Maryland
Cause of sinking: Fire
Location: Off the mouth of the Potomac River

Sunk: November 27, 1850
Depth: 60 feet
Dimensions: 133' to 138', then 174' x 30' to 53' x 11'
Power: Wood-fired steam

GPS: 37-57-49.56 / 76-11-54.61

Steamboating was big news in the 1800's. Ever since the inception of steamboats on the Chesapeake Bay, in 1813, newspapers fell over themselves to report the construction, launching, maiden voyages, and appurtenance descriptions of every new paddle-wheeler and screw steamer, whether designed for the conveyance of passengers, freight, or, in most cases, both. Modern historians can thank the old rags for such in-depth coverage, even if it was not always accurate.

If you look at the sidebar, you will notice that I gave the length of the *Columbus* as a range between 133 feet and 138 feet. That is because the published sources differed in this regard. Then you will notice the length given as 174 feet. You will also notice the vast ranges of the beam: from 30 feet to 53 feet. These difference require some explanation.

The published sources agreed that the beam of the hull was 30 feet. Those same sources gave the extreme width of the deck as a range between 51 feet and 53 feet. In side-wheel construction, the paddle boxes were located outboard of the hull. Thus the extreme width was measured from the outboard side of one paddle box to the outboard box of the other paddle box. By simple subtraction, each paddle box extended between 10-1/2 feet to 11-1/2 feet beyond the top of the hull.

In some side-wheelers, mostly those in ocean-going service, the width of the deck conformed to the beam of the hull. In other side-wheelers, mostly those in bay and river service, the deck was extended beyond the beam of the hull to the outboard side of the paddle box, then was gradually curved fore and aft to the hull at the bow and stern. Wooden beams extended from the hull above the waterline on an angle to the bottom of the platform, to support the parts of the deck that extended beyond the top of the hull. This latter system provided more deck space, but was liable to structural damage from rough seas that were encountered on transoceanic voyages. The normally placid inland waterways permitted deck extensions with little opportunity for harm.

In 1848, the steamer was lengthened to 174 feet by cutting the hull in two and inserting a newly built section.

Here is the first description of the *Columbus*, published on May 25, 1809: "The new steamboat *Columbus*, belonging to the Maryland & Virginia Steamboat Company, made an excursion yesterday for the purpose of a trial of her machinery. She proceeded [from Baltimore] down the Patapsco to its mouth, and up the Chesapeake Bay beyond

Pool's Island. On her return, she performed the distance from Pool's to Fort McHenry in a few minutes over two hours, and from North Point in about an hour. Her rate of speed, at the closest calculation, was at *least* twelve miles per hour, and this was attained under the various disadvantages, attendant on a first experience. The trial was perfectly satisfactory to the President and Directors of the Company, and to the other persons on board, and no doubt is entertained of her accomplishing an increased degree of speed as soon as she is in proper trim.

"The *Columbus* is propelled by an engine of 100 horse power, made by that excellent machinist, Mr. Charles Reeder. The machinery is of the best and handsomest workmanship, and in its operation elicited the unqualified approbation of all who witnessed it. The length of the *Columbus* on deck is 137 feet; breadth of beam 30 feet; depth of hold 11 feet; and extreme width of main and upper decks 53 feet. She was built by Mr. George Gardner, in the most faithful and substantial manner, and combines great strength of frame with beauty of model.

"The principal object of this boat is to transport merchandise between Baltimore and Norfolk, and an idea of her capacity may be formed, when we state that she is able to carry two thousand barrels under deck. A large space on the main deck may also be appropriated for the transportation of cotton when required. The accommodations for passengers consequently are not so extensive as usual, but the arrangements in this respect are nevertheless excellent, and will afford every comfort to travellers. The after cabin contains ten state-rooms, in each of which are two berths, a writing desk and other conveniences. An upper deck extends the extreme length and breadth of the boat, and affords a most spacious and delightful promenade in fine weather. The *Columbus* is altogether a first rate boat, and we have no doubt, from the facilities which she will offer to commercial operations between Baltimore, Norfolk and Richmond, she will make a profitable return to the enterprising Company to which she belongs. On the subject of our trade to Norfolk by this line, we propose to speak at a more leisure moment."

A slightly different description of the *Columbus* was provided by a competing newspaper on May 28: "The new large and elegant steam boat *Columbus*, belonging to the Maryland and Virginia Steam Boat Company, arrived here [Norfolk] yesterday at 11 o'clock, A.M. in 19-1/2 hours from Baltimore. She is commanded by Capt. J[ohn]. D. Turner, and is intended for the conveyance of freight and passengers between Baltimore, Norfolk, City Point and Richmond; her engine is of 100 horse power, her burthen 416 tons, length 133 feet, extreme width of deck 51 feet 1 inch, breadth of beam 30 feet 10 inches, depth of hold 10 feet 9 inches. The forward or gentleman's cabin contains 18 berths, and the after or ladies' cabin the same number. In the latter, (which is fitted up in very handsome style, ornamented with rich carved and gilt work, the doors and panel work of mahogany and curled maple, and richly carpeted,) there are eight state rooms, each having two berths, a wash stand, &c.; the curtains are of white dimity, neatly and tastefully arranged.

"So far as a trial of her speed has been obtained . . . it is thought [she] will make the run from Baltimore to Norfolk in 16 hours."

In case you didn't notice, this second description has a mathematical error with regard to the number of ladies' berths: either the same as the gentleman's cabin (18 berths), or two berths in each of eight staterooms which, when multiplied, equal 16 berths.

Elsewhere it was noted that the *Columbus* "had the conventional 'square' or 'crosshead' steeple engine with a single 50-inch cylinder and a six-and-a-half-foot stroke that gave her a speed of ten miles an hour."

Yet another description was provided by Irish comedian Tyrone Power, the great-grandfather of the American actor of the same name. The elder Power wrote a book about his 1834 visit to the States, the title of the book being *Impressions of America* (1836). He was onboard the steamboat *George Washington* when he witnessed this event which, we are to presume, was common practice at the time:

"Whilst steering through the waters of the Chesapeake, perceived a large steamer standing right for us, with a signal flying. Learned that this was the *Columbus*, bound for Norfolk, Virginia, for which place we had several passengers, who were now to be transshipped to the approaching vessel.

"We were out in the open bay, with half a gale of wind blowing, and some sea on; it therefore became a matter of interest to observe how two large ships of this class would approach each other.

"The way they managed this ticklish affair was really admirable; before we neared, I observed the Norfolk ship was laid head to wind, and just enough way kept on to steer her; our ship held her course, gradually lessening her speed, until, as she approached the *Columbus*, it barely sufficed to lay and keep her alongside, when they fell together, gangway to gangway: warps were immediately passed, and made secure at both head and stern; and in a minute the huge vessels became as one.

"Here was no want of help; the luggage and the passengers were ready at the proper station, so that in a handful of minutes the transfer was completed without bustle or alarm. Meantime the interest of this novel scene was greatly increased by the coming up of the inward-bound Norfolk-man, which fitted close by us amidst the roar occasioned by the escaping steam of the vessels lying-to, a noise that might have drowned the voice of Niagara. . . .

"As we thus lay together, I noticed that the upper or promenade deck of the *Columbus* was completely taken up by a double row of flashy-looking covered carts, or tilt-waggons [sic], as they are called here. Upon inquiry, I found that these contained the goods, and were, indeed the movable stores, or shops, of that much enduring class, the Yankee pedlars [sic], just setting forth for their annual winter cruise amongst the plantations of the South: where, however, their keen dealing may be held in awe, they are looked for with lively anxiety, and their arrival greeted as an advent of no little moment.

"Arranged in a half circle about the bow on the main-deck, I observed the horses of these royal pedlars [sic]: they stretched their necks out to examine us with a keenness of look worthy of their knowing masters' reputation and their own education. . . .

"Our business being completed, the hissing sound of the waste-steam pipe ceased, this force being once more applied to its right use; the paddles began to move, the lashings were cast off, and away the boats darted from each other with startling rapidity: the *Columbus*, with the gale aft, rushing down the great bay of the Chesapeake, and the *Washington* breasting its force right for Baltimore."

Another account puts nineteenth-century steamboat travel time into perspective with modern forms of transportation. On May 10, 1833, boldfaced headlines proclaimed

"FROM NORFOLK TO NEW YORK IN 33 HOURS!!" According to the accompanying article, "The new arrangement of the Baltimore steam boats *Columbus* and *Pocahontas*, which we publish today, and which goes into operation on Sunday next, proposes to give a degree of dispatch unexampled, to the conveyance between Richmond, Norfolk and New York, transporting the passengers from Richmond to New York in 41 hours, and from Norfolk to the great commercial emporium, in 33 hours. This is really next to flying, and we are bound to believe that it is the ultimate point of expedition to which the ordinary means of transportation can arrive."

Considering the time it takes to check luggage and pass through airport security, and stand in endless lines prior to actual boarding, it might have been faster to travel from the Big Apple to Norfolk by steamboat than it is to fly today. Not only that, but steamboat passengers did not have to suffer the indignities of identity confirmation, frisking, groping, wanding, metal detecting, and x-raying that modern air travelers must endure.

When I am stuck in bumper-to-bumper commuter traffic around Philadelphia, Baltimore, Washington DC, and Richmond, I think about how much less frustration steamboat passengers must have felt as they relaxed in their cabins or passed time in the lounges while someone else did the driving. It once took me seven hours to drive the 100-mile stretch on Interstate 95 between the District of Columbia and Richmond. By comparison, travel in the "good old days" doesn't seem all that bad.

On the other hand, steamboating was not without unanticipated events such as stranding and collision. Shoals were not charted, and those whose positions were known sometimes shifted location; navigational aids were largely nonexistent.

Records indicate that the *Columbus* ran aground on the James River in 1829 (her first year of operation). In 1848 she went ashore near the Magothy River (between Baltimore and what is now the Bay Bridge off Annapolis); the *Planter* and *Thomas Jefferson* helped to pull her off the bar.

In 1831, the *Columbus* was involved in a minor collision with the *Rappahannock*. No explanation was given for the cause of the accident, although it is likely that darkness was the primary contributing factor, perhaps because the navigating lights were either not shown or were misinterpreted. The crash occurred on March 14 at 2 o'clock in the morning, when the wind was blowing "very fresh."

The *Columbus* was southbound. Near Smith's Point light, the northbound *Rappahannock* was spotted dead ahead from a distance of four miles. According to Captain Turner's succinct account, the *Columbus* steered southwest "in order to bring the *Rappahannock* well on the larboard [port] bow, about a point or a point and a half; she still nearing the *C*. and showing no side lights, kept up S.S.W., ordered the helm put hard aport, ran forward, rang the bell and stopped the boat, when nearly at the same instant the *Rappahannock* struck us a little forward of the wheel house on our larboard bow, our head being W. by N. when she came in contact, and hers about N.W."

The passengers provided a bit more detail: "The damage was principally confined to the wheel house, and is comparatively of a trifling nature, occasioning only the delay of a few hours. From the nature of the accident and the situation of the boats, it is very apparent that no blame can possibly be attached to the commander of this steam boat, and the passengers have voluntarily assembled for the purpose of exonerating Capt. Turner and his officers from any imputation of neglect, and to return him their thanks for his polite attention and seamanlike conduct, during the accident and the remaining part of the passage."

Although newspapers were overwhelming in their praise of transportation by steamboat, and published departure and arrival times, they were often less demonstrative when it came to reporting crashes and losses, perhaps because it went against the grain of promotion, in an attempt to prove to a gullible public that steamboating was perfectly safe. In short, steamboat collisions and catastrophes were often downplayed unless accompanied by tremendous loss of life, in which case they could not go unnoticed.

Consider this report, which was published twelve days after the event. Under the small heading "Burning of the Steamer *Columbus*," and the smaller subheading "*Deplorable Loss of Life*," the correspondent wrote, "The steamer *Columbus* took fire in the Chesapeake Bay, at the mouth of the Potomac, about 3 o'clock on Thursday morning week, and in a few minutes the vessel was in a sheet of flame. There were but 16 persons on board at the time. Of these, 9 perished, either by flames, or were drowned! Their names were Capt. John Hollingshead, L. S. Godwin (mate,) and his son, John Sherman, Henry Bowie, Henry Estep, Hynson Brown, Saul Lane, and L. Saligman. The survivors escaped in a boat."

The value of the loss was given as $150,000.

Given the depth at which the *Columbus* sank – 60 feet – the smoke stack and the steeple engine would not have stood high enough to be a hazard to navigation. The hull collapsed over the years and its identity was lost. The location, however, was known to anglers and divers in the twentieth century; they commonly fished and dived on the site.

In 1987, NOAA vessels *Rude* and *Heck* brought official attention to the site when they found it resting on the muddy bottom during a routine hydrographic survey. NOAA divers described the wreck as "a jumbled mass of large diameter pipe, possibly ship's mast. Wooden hull, copper clad." For navigational purposes, the least depth was given as 42.3 feet, as taken by a diver's pneumatic depth gauge. The wreck was then charted on NOAA's nautical chart of the Chesapeake Bay, and put into the AWOIS database (which see at the back of this book).

In 1991, the Army Corps of Engineers conducted another survey in preparation for dredging and widening the shipping channel. By this time in the evolution of federal intervention with regard to digging on land sites and dredging under water, a host of agencies was involved in giving approval to such projects. Full compliance was necessary before the dredging operation could proceed. Permission was not limited to the Environmental Protection Agency and similar agencies, but to historical and archaeological groups. The COE contracted with R. Christopher Goodwin & Associates to conduct an archaeological assessment of the wreck.

Through historical research, Goodwin & Associates determined the identity of the wreck, and ascertained that the *Columbus* had been propelled by a crosshead steeple engine, the broken and rusted remains of which still existed on the site. The COE decided to recover the engine, claiming that it was the only one of its kind that was known to exist. This was either an exaggeration or a belief that was based on ignorance.

The *Express* was propelled by a crosshead engine, and her remains lay only some ten miles away. Likewise the *Pocahontas*, which stranded on the Outer Banks of North

Carolina in 1862. And these are only two that come to mind without doing any research. Undoubtedly there are crosshead engines on shipwrecks in the Great Lakes, where they exist in a better state of preservation.

Be that as it may, recovering the engine was a massive undertaking because of the weight of its components, which was estimated at some eighteen tons.

Recovery operations commenced in 1992. A huge derrick barge was moored over the site; the crane had a lifting capacity of one hundred tons. The barge contained living quarters, galley, "and complete facilities to take care of the 19-person crew and equipment." The barge "required the help of the 100-foot tugboat *Sgt. William Seay*. A 65-foot tugboat towed the barge that would house the archaeological treasures recovered from the bay."

A bevy of tugs and other barges were employed for support. Army divers secured lifting straps to disarticulated engine parts. Much of their work had to be done by feel because the bottom sediment was frequently stirred to thick soup by contrary winds, tide, and current. Visibility was often less than two feet; sometimes it was zero.

"The divers, working in two man teams, spent up to three hours at 60 feet before surfacing. To keep from getting the 'bends,' The teams spent 30 minutes in a recompression chamber after every dive. The chamber was carried on board an LCU [Landing Craft Utility] which also housed the divers' living quarters, air pumps and diving equipment."

Divers fastened cables to part of the engine. The crane lifted the part a couple of feet. "When crane operator Sgt. Michael Brandt began the first lift, the rigging straps came together and bent the frame designed to lift the engine. While members of the 949th [Transportation Company at Fort Eustis, Virginia] worked on a new, stronger engine frame, the divers returned underwater to attach cables to the 7,000 pound paddle-wheel shaft.

The thickly encrusted paddle-wheel shaft first saw the light of day on August 26. The shaft measured twenty feet in length and included one of the hubs. This harbinger of things to come soon turned into a solo recovery. Hurricane Andrew swept through the area and arrested diving operations. One delay led to another until finally the entire operation was postponed until the following spring.

The good news for 1993 was the recovery of most of the major engine components: "The four-foot cylinder; and the piston, rod, steam chest and other assorted parts." In addition, divers recovered "the ship's anchor and part of the rudder, along with bottles, ointment jars, and a complete women's sewing kit." All this for the expenditure of $364,000!

The bad news was the cost and ultimate failure of conservation. Many of the components had "degraded from iron into fragile graphite."

The *Columbus* engine components were taken to the Army depot at Curtis Bay. Each part – some weighing several tons – was meticulously wrapped in burlap. The parts were sprayed continuously with fresh water to prevent them from drying out and crumbling. A special transportation bed was built for each component. The dismantled engine was trucked more than a thousand miles to the International Artifact Conservation and Research Laboratory in New Orleans, Louisiana. The parts were then placed in oversized tanks and immersed in preserving solutions. The process was expected to take three years.

Sodium hydroxide was used as the electrolyte for electrolytic reduction: an electrochemical process in which direct current is applied from one electrode (the anode, or the object to be cleaned) through a conductive medium (the liquid electrolyte) to a sacrificial cathode. The flow of electricity loosens organic surface encrustation, removes corrosive chloride compounds from the interior, and adds electrons to the depleted iron. The ferrous corrosion (or oxidized iron) is returned to his original metallic state.

By way of comparison, conservation of the engine that was recovered from the Civil War ironclad *Monitor* was expected to take fifteen years, and cost upwards of $27 million.

Press releases claimed, "The restored engine, 65 feet across and 40 feet high, will eventually be a centerpiece in the atrium of the Columbus Center for Marine Research and Exploration, now under construction on Piers 5 and 6 in the Inner Harbor" of Baltimore. The Center was named for Christopher, not for the steamship.

In 1998, the New Orleans research lab packed up the partially conserved engine parts and shipped them back to Maryland without first conferring with the recipient. This created great consternation in Baltimore because the Maryland Archaeological Conservation Laboratory had no building in which to store them, and no way in which to continue treatment. Construction of the building had not yet been completed. Said Betty Seifert, the lab's chief conservator, "We could not wait for the formal dedication, set for May, so on January 27, 1998 the building was turned over to us so we could receive the *Columbus* engine."

A tractor-trailer loaded with twenty crates and the paddle-wheel delivered the parts. The lab had to rent a 30-ton crane to unload the crates. A palette jack and a forklift carried the crates individually through the lab's 12-foot-high receiving door.

Then came near catastrophe: "The wooden cradle holding the massive iron paddle wheel and shaft breaks [sic]. The paddle wheel and shaft, covered in plastic sheets, waited in the driveway from February to June while Jerry's Welding in Prince Frederick constructed a new steel cradle." The shaft eventually joined the other engine components in a temperature- and humidity-controlled storage room.

The rest of the engine saga is unfortunate. According to a 2006 report that was published by the National Park Service, "As of this writing, the engine is still in the laboratory and has suffered irreparable damage." It seems that the valve chest assembly "and other portions of the engine" collapsed "under their own weight" while no one did anything to alleviate the problem as it was occurring. They simply let it collapse.

It was estimated "that the engine will require several more years of conservation and reassembly at a minimum before it could potentially be incorporated into an interpretive display."

Sadly, twenty years after the paddle-wheel shaft was raised, and nineteen years after the engine parts were salvaged, none of these components is on display to the public. Through neglect, everything continues to collapse and rust away out of sight, out of mind. This is a typical example of careless and uncaring Maryland underwater archaeology.

DRAGONET

Built: 1944
Previous names: None
Displacement tonnage: 1,526 (surface), 2,424 (submerged)
Type of vessel: Twin screw submarine
Power: Four Fairbanks-Morse diesel engines, four Elliot electric motors
Builder: Cramp Shipbuilding Company, Philadelphia, Pennsylvania
Owner: U.S. Navy
Armament: Ten 21-inch torpedo tubes (six forward, four aft), one 5-inch deck gun, one 40-millimeter gun, two 50-caliber machine guns
Cause of sinking: Scuttled in explosives test
Location: Off the mouth of the Patuxent River

Sunk: September 17, 1961
Depth: 150 feet
Dimensions: 311' x 27' x 15'
Official designation: SS-293

GPS: 38-20.521 / 76-18.213

At the time the *Dragonet* was constructed – during World War Two – she and her sisters were the most modern submarines in the American naval fleet. The U.S. Navy designated her as a *Gato*-class submarine; many secondary sources designated her as a *Balao*-class sub. The differences between these two classes are so minor as to appear befuddling.

The *Gato* and *Balao* were identical with respect to length and beam; their depths were 19' 3" and 16' 10" respectively. Each had the same surface tonnage, but their submerged tonnages varied by ten tons: 2,424 for the *Gato*, 2,414 for the *Balao*. The speeds of each were identical: 20.25 knots surfaced, 8.75 knots submerged. The *Gato* had a complement of 60, the *Balao* 66. Each had ten torpedo tubes. The *Gato* was armed with one 3-inch deck gun and 4 machine guns; the *Balao* was armed with one 4-inch deck gun and one 40-millimeter gun.

The *Gato* was commissioned on December 31, 1941; the *Balao* on February 4, 1943; the *Dragonet* on March 6, 1944.

The *Dragonet* had the same length and beam as both the *Gato* and the *Balao*. Her depth was 15' 3": less than either the *Gato* and the *Balao*. Her speeds were the same as the *Gato* and the *Balao*. Her complement was 66: the same as the *Balao*. Her armament consisted of one 5-inch deck gun, one 40-millimeter gun, and two machine guns: unlike either the *Gato* or *Balao*.

All these specifications are published in the *Dictionary of American Naval Fighting Ships*, which was published by the Naval Historical Center. The DANF is known for its inaccuracies and poor attention to detail. On the other hand, I do not put extra weight on the fact that more than one secondary source designated the *Dragonet* as a *Balao*-class sub, because many secondary sources copied their information from previous secondary sources. So there you have it. Take your pick and shovel.

The *Dragonet* had a short but interesting career in which she sank twice: once by accident and once by intent, both times at the hands of the U.S. Navy. She departed Pearl Harbor for her first war patrol on November 1, 1944. Her destination was the Kurile Islands and the Sea of Okohotsk. It took eighteen days to reach her assigned patrol area. Then came four weeks of adverse weather, rough seas, and "no enemy ship contacts worthy of torpedo fire."

The early morning hours of December 15 found her off the island of Matsuwa To. "Although the sea was flat calm there were pronounced tide rips which rendered depth control difficult." She submerged at dawn, first to periscope depth at 63 feet, then down to 70 feet "when a slight jar forward was felt." Her speed at this time was 3 knots into a 2 knot current, with an actual speed of 1 knot over ground. The time was 7:18.

A fascinating blow-by-blow account of this casualty was published by the U.S. Hydrographic Office as "War Damage Report No. 58," from which I will quote extensively.

The bow bumped upward, the hull assumed at "three degree up angle and started to rise." The bump and rise were interpreted as the detonation of either a nearby aerial bomb or a distant depth charge. "Following this reasoning, it was decided to seek safety in depth as quickly as possible, and by the time the boat had risen to 58 feet, the negative tank was flooded. These actions enabled the boat to gain depth rapidly but when 90 feet was reached, only 10 or 15 seconds after receiving the first slight jar forward, a series of heavy jolts accompanied by loud noises shook the entire boat and caused it to lurch violently. *Dragonet's* speed at this time is estimated to have been about 6 or 7 knots by shaft turns, or about 4 or 5 knots relative to the bottom. This second and violent jolting was also at first interpreted as another depth charge or bombing attack and orders were issued to proceed to 150 feet and rig the ship for depth charge. Almost immediately afterwards, however, it was noticed that the boat was hanging at a depth of 92 feet with a dive angle of 20 degrees, the log recorded zero speed, and further jars oc-

Port bow view of the conning tower. The white enclosures highlight alterations that were made at the Mare Island Navy Yard shortly prior to March 25, 1945. (Courtesy of the Naval Photographic Center.)

curred forward accompanied by loud grinding sounds. It was then realized that the boat had gone aground on a submerged reef or pinnacle and both shafts were stopped at once. The ship had no appreciable list at this time."

The situation worsened immediately when it was learned that the forward torpedo room was flooding rapidly. "The collision alarm was sounded and the forward torpedo room was ordered abandoned. Only four members of the crew were present in that space and they promptly retired to the forward battery compartment. A watertight boundary was immediately established at the after bulkhead of the forward torpedo room by closing the bulkhead door and the bulkhead supply and exhaust ventilation flapper valves. Salvage air (225-pound) was then bled into the torpedo room through the bulkhead connection in an effort to halt the flooding, but was secured when the pressure within the compartment had reached about 55 pounds per square inch. Shortly afterwards, word was received in the control room that the torpedo room was 'completely flooded.' Complete flooding could not have occurred, however, since the rupture in the compartment was just above the watertight deck flat, allowing air to be entrapped in the overhead, and it is presumed that this report was made after the water passed over the top of the sight glass in the bulkhead watertight door. Later inspection disclosed that the water level in the compartment reached a height of about 1 foot above the upper bunks, or about 1-1/2 feet below the overhead of the torpedo room. Since a clock located just below the maximum flood line in the torpedo room stopped at 0720, it appears reasonable to assume that flooding of that space took place in approximately two minutes or less.

"As *Dragonet* was pounding violently and lurching with the surge of the current at this time, it was feared that further serious damage would be sustained and that the hull might possibly break up unless the ship were quickly taken off the rocks. Word was passed to all hands to obtain objects that would float in case the boat might have to be abandoned. At about 0721, 3 minutes after the grounding occurred, the first attempt was made to get off the bottom. All main ballast tanks were blown plus bow buoyancy, negative and safety tanks. Nos. 3, 4 and 5 fuel ballast tanks were empty of oil but due to unfavorable sea conditions had not yet been converted to main ballast tanks by removing the riser blanks, and therefore were not blown since subsequent rapid venting, if the boat were required to again submerge, could have been impossible.

"The increase in buoyancy resulting from the blowing of the main ballast tanks caused the stern of the boat to rise to the surface, but the bow remained either on or near the bottom, due to the flooded compartment forward. When the stern rose, it acquired sufficient momentum to considerably overshoot its point of static buoyancy and surged out of the water far enough to project the extended No. 2 periscope above the surface for a second or two. The Commanding Officer had time only to make a partial sweep to port, but this brief observation disclosed that all was clear in the direction of Matsuwa To. The stern then settled back in the water until it reached its equilibrium point for the static buoyancy condition, the boat assuming a down angle of about 30 degrees. Since both periscopes went under the surface, no further observations could be taken.

"As the stern was protruding out of water and therefore might be sighted by the enemy, and the bow could still not be raised due to the loss of buoyancy forward, all tanks were again flooded to submerge the ship. This action was taken at about 0730. *Dragonet* once more settled to the bottom, in a depth of about 92 feet and with a 16 degree down angle. The ship's heading had now swung from 090°(T[rue]) to 110°(T[rue]) and the action of the current once again caused *Dragonet* to pound heavily on the reef. It was thought at this time that perhaps the bow had been prevented from rising by being wedged in the rocks, so a brief attempt was made to back clear of the reef using emergency power. This proved unsuccessful, however, and the plan was abandoned.

"At 0732 a report was received that the 55-pound per square inch air pressure which had originally been built up in the forward torpedo room had now diminished to 40 pounds and that the water in that compartment was below the eyeport in the bulkhead door and continuing to recede. A few minutes later, air could be heard blowing outside the torpedo room hull, indicating that the water level in the compartment had been lowered to the point of rupture and the down angle on the boat began to decrease slowly. The order was then given to blow the forward main ballast tank group, bow buoyancy, safety and negative tanks. As this caused the ship to trim by the stern, the after group of main ballast tanks was then blown. The ship rose slowly and surfaced at 0738, in clear sight of the shore establishments on Matsuwa To. When 26 feet was reached, the upper conning tower hatch was opened and the tanks were then blown with the low pressure (10-pound) air system as in any normal surfacing.

"All four main engines were started immediately and the area was cleared as rapidly as possible by proceeding south at emergency speed. All automatic weapons were manned and ammunition was broken out. Fortunately, no enemy interference was experienced as *Dragonet* retired. Course was then set for Midway, the nearest Allied base.

"The boat was only slightly down by the head on surfacing but was reported to have assumed about 15 degrees port list, for ruptures in the outer plating of port MBT Nos. 6B and 6D prevented those tanks from being blown below a few feet from the tank tops. Steps were taken immediately to increase freeboard, to reduce trim by the head and to correct the excessive list. Flood valves on Nos. 3, 4 and 5 fuel ballast tanks, both port and starboard, were opened and these tanks were blown in order to increase freeboard. MBT No. 6A and FBT No. 3A on the starboard side were then made free-flooding to compensate for the 15 degree port list. All variable tanks were pumped dry with the exception of No 3 auxiliary, which was flooded as an additional list correction, and after trim tank, which was left about 3/4 full in order to add weight aft. No. 6 normal fuel oil tank was put on service to add weight aft by displacing fuel oil with heavier sea water. Air pressure was maintained on the forward torpedo room through the salvage air system and this kept the water within the damaged compartment at a low level. The after bulkhead of the torpedo room held tight with the exception of a few minor electrical cable stuffing gland leaks.

"Heavy seas and high winds built up on 16 December. The bow planes were still rigged out and pounded so heavily that the entire ship vibrated and it was feared that further serious hull damage forward might result. A slight air leak developed around the top of the bulkhead door to the forward torpedo room but did not become serious. One of the bulkhead cable packing gland leaks increased somewhat, allowing water to enter the pantry. The gland nut was located in such a position that it was inaccessible and could not be tightened. When the grounding occurred and the forward torpedo room flooded, the Mk. 18 electric torpedoes in tubes Nos. 1 and 4 were in a partially withdrawn position for charging. Consequently, the inner doors of these tubes were open and the outer doors were closed but not locked. As the water level in the torpedo room was noted to be rising during this period of heavy weather, and salvage air had to be used in increasing quantities to maintain the air bubble in the torpedo room, it was believed that air must be leaking through one or both of the torpedo tube outer doors. Both high pressure air compressors had to be run continuously to provide sufficient salvage air. The three air banks on service were never allowed to drop below 2500 pounds pressure while the two emergency banks were kept at full pressure.

"By 1800, the storm had increased in intensity. In order to decrease the draft forward and, therefore, the water level in the torpedo room, the contents of NFO tank No. 1 were blown aft into FBT Nos. 5A and 5B. During this transfer, *Dragonet* developed a 20 degree port list, indicating that most of the water and oil in NFO No. 1 had ended up in FBT No. 5B, the port tank. The list shortly decreased to about 10 degrees but the ship commenced to roll heavily, reaching a maximum of 40 degrees to port. Compensation was accomplished by opening the floods of FBT No. 5B and blowing its contents to sea but this apparently over-corrected the list, for No. 3 auxiliary tank was then pumped dry.

"By morning of 17 December the seas had abated somewhat, the bow was riding higher and the water in the forward torpedo room was down to about 12 inches above the floor plates and appeared to be maintaining this level. However, the bow planes were still pounding heavily. It was therefore decided to attempt to enter the forward torpedo room to rig in the planes, tighten up the torpedo tube outer doors and to determine the extent of damage.

"A party of three officers and two men entered and secured the forward battery compartment. Rescue breathing equipment and 'lungs' were carried in case chlorine gas might be generated should sea water inadvertently enter the battery cells from the forward torpedo room. Air pressure was built up in the battery compartment by the salvage air system and the control room bulkhead was then inspected and found tight. The small line to the salvage air gauge for the torpedo room was then disconnected in order to equalize the pressure between the two forward compartments. Bulkhead flapper valves in the hull ventilation system were not opened to accomplish this for fear they could not be securely closed again. When the pressure between the compartments had equalized, the bulkhead door was opened and the party entered the forward torpedo room. As the water level in that compartment was well below the bulkhead door, no water entered the battery compartment and the rescue breathers and 'lungs' were discarded. By working in relays, the bow planes were rigged in by hand and the torpedo tubes were secured. The air in the torpedo room was foul with oil fumes, so oxygen was bled into the compartment to improve working conditions. When the bow rose in the seaway, daylight could be seen through a ruptured area in the pressure hull plating, centered at frame 23, port side, just above the top of the forward trim tank. This was the first positive information that any of ship's company had as to the nature of the damage causing the flooding. Upon completion of the work, the torpedo room was again abandoned and sealed, and the air in the forward battery compartment was bled into the control room. The success of this well-executed and potentially hazardous operation for the safety of the ship removed many of *Dragonet's* difficulties. The bow

Port stern view of the conning tower. The white enclosures highlight alterations that were made at the Mare Island Navy Yard shortly prior to March 25, 1945. (Courtesy of the Naval Photographic Center.)

planes were subsequently further secured by running chains through the rigging gear quadrants in the superstructure.

"Heavy seas and winds of gale force were again encountered late in the evening of 17 December and continued until the afternoon of the next day. At 0245 on 18 December, with the seas approaching from the starboard quarter, *Dragonet* took a very large roll to port and 'hung' at an extreme angle for an appreciable period of time. This roll was measured on the clinometer in the control room as 63 degrees. Men were thrown from bunks and mercury spilled from the flotation chamber of the master gyrocompass, completely disabling it. Seas filled the port side of the bridge, but fortunately did not reach the upper conning tower hatch. The rudder was put at full left and the ship's heading was swung through 105 degrees before the ship slowly came back to about 20 degrees port list. When MBT No. 6A and FBT No. 3A were vented, the ship came upright again, indicating that the flood openings of these tanks may have become exposed by the coincidence of a deep wave trough at the extreme roll, allowing the water within to escape and causing air pockets to form. Both MBT No. 6A and FTB No. 3A had been previously flooded to compensate for the port list which *Dragonet* had assumed on surfacing.

"*Dragonet* arrived at Midway on 20 December 1944 and was docked the same day in ARD-8 for inspection and emergency repairs. Temporary patches were installed over the holes in the forward torpedo room pressure hull and the outer plating of MBT Nos. 2B, 6B and 6D. The ship departed Midway on 23 December for Navy Yard, Mare Island, and arrived on 4 January 1945. Complete repairs together with many outstanding alterations were accomplished there and *Dragonet* was returned to service on 26 March 1945."

Thus ended a somewhat ignominious maiden war patrol. Nonetheless, Vice Admiral Charles Lockwood, Commander Submarines Pacific Fleet, had nothing but admiration for the men of the *Dragonet*. He wrote, "The courageous action of the commanding officer, officers and crew of the *Dragonet* throughout the harrowing period of clearing the almost fatally damaged ship from the grounding and while en route to base in typhoon weather are deserving of the Navy's highest praise."

The *Dragonet* was assigned to lifeguard duty for her next two patrols. She recovered four downed pilots on her second patrol, and one on her third patrol. She never had the opportunity to launch a torpedo or fire her guns in anger.

The submarine was decommissioned at the Mare Island Navy Yard, near San Francisco, California on April 16, 1946. She was never recommissioned. She remained in mothballs for the next fifteen years. In 1961, the U.S. Navy fleet ocean tug *Takelma* towed the *Dragonet* more than 5,000 miles from Mare Island through the Panama Canal to the Norfolk Navy Yard, in Virginia. This was one of the longest hauls in the "modern history of Navy deep-water towing."

The *Dragonet* was destined to be employed as the victim of an underwater explosives test. However, prior to that ultimate duty, it was reported: "Experts on underwater explosions already have subjected the sub to repeated submergings and surfacings and shiftings from side to side. The latter shaking-up is achieved by remote control of ballast.

"Purpose of the tests is to find means of improving shock resistance for the Navy's underseas fleet. The remote control of the *Dragonet*, which the Underwater Explosions Research Division says involves 'some pretty delicate balancing,' is achieved by adjusting the amount of water in the sub's ballast tanks through air lines."

The end came on September 17, 1961, when an underwater explosion sent the *Dragonet* to the bottom of the Chesapeake Bay in 150 feet of water, off the mouth of the Patuxent River, on a heading of 240° true. Six pipe flagstaffs were erected on the hull "for whipping study." These pipes rose to a depth of 95 feet.

In 1968, the Naval Research and Development Center toyed with the idea of raising the *Dragonet* in order to gain "experience in salvaging by use of urethane foams." They then intended to scrap the hull "to help pay for expenses," but only after making "a damage survey of the hull structure." Some correspondence was bandied about among various Navy commands, in particular the Judge Advocate General. JAG confirmed that the Navy "has no further use for this submarine and has no objection as to future disposal of the ship," but nothing ever came of it, and the *Dragonet* was left on the bottom of the bay, where she still rests and rusts today.

Rick Younger noted that the hull rises 15 feet off the bottom. He also noted that visibility on the site is poor to bad. He has heard rumors that in the 1980's, the salvage tug *Lulu* tested explosives on the site; these rumors were somewhat verified by large numbers of dead fish that floated to the surface at the time the tests were conducted.

EXPRESS

Built: 1841
Previous names: None
Gross tonnage: 275 or 602
Type of vessel: Wooden-hulled side-wheel steamer
Builder: Lawrence & Sneeden, New York City
Owner: Potomac Transportation Company
Port of registry: ?
Cause of sinking: Foundered
Location: Between Barren Island and Pt. No Point

Sunk: October 23, 1878
Depth: 20 feet
Dimensions: 201' x 23' x 8'
Power: Coal-fired steam

The steamboat *Express* led an interesting if somewhat catastrophic career that lasted thirty-seven years under a host of successive owners. Additionally, the side-wheel steamer grew in length on three separate occasions. The hull was launched in 1841 at a length that measured 151 feet; it was propelled by a crosshead engine. She operated along the Hudson River between Albany and New York City. In 1845 she was involved in a minor collision with the *Empire of Troy*.

In 1847, she was transferred from river duty to the protected ocean, running between the Massachusetts ports of Boston and Plymouth. Her route took her from Boston Bay to Cape Cod Bay, which was inside the "hook" of Cape Cod.

In 1848, the *Express* steamed to Philadelphia, Pennsylvania, where Simpson &

From the collection of Mike Moore.

Neal lengthened her hull to 172 feet. The way the wooden hull of a paddle wheeler was lengthened was by sawing across the beam either forward or aft of the propulsion machinery, pulling the two sections apart, then building a new section between the separated sections, and connecting the new section to the two adjacent original sections.

The hull was lengthened again in 1854, by eight feet, and her superstructure and accommodations were rebuilt.

The year 1860 found the *Express* operating on the Patuxent River. In 1861 she caught fire, and was subsequently rebuilt in Baltimore by William Skinner. The hull was then lengthened to 201 feet.

After the start of the Civil War, the *Express* was chartered by the U.S. Quartermaster Corps. She remained in that capacity for the next three and a half years.

On January 6, 1865, she was sold to the Potomac Transportation Line. She had hardly returned to civilian commerce when, on January 21, she was "so badly chafed by ice that she sank off Indian Head, after the passengers and a large number of Government horses had been rescued from their danger." Indian Head is on the Maryland side of the Potomac River about 25 miles downstream from Washington, DC. She was later raised, repaired in Baltimore, and returned to service along the Potomac River and in the Chesapeake Bay.

The demise of the *Express* occurred in the "gale of '78."

Hurricane warnings were initiated in 1870. That was the year in which the War Department designated the U.S. Signal Corps as the agency responsible for tracking and reporting the advance of tropical storms. The gale of '78 was tropical storm number 9 in the 1878 hurricane season. The storm was first detected on October 20. It passed west of Jamaica, crossed the middle of Cuba, marched northward off the coast of Florida, and made landfall in North Carolina between Wilmington and Cape Lookout. The eye of the storm then proceeded north-northwest through Virginia and Pennsylvania, passing westward of the Chesapeake Bay. It spent the worst of its fury on the bay during the night of October 22-23.

Of the seventy-one persons who perished as a result of the storm, approximately one quarter of them were lost on the steamer *Express*. Wind speed of 84 miles per hour was recorded at Virginia Beach. The wind diminished slightly as the storm proceeded northward, but nonetheless remained at hurricane force; it uprooted trees and pulled the roofs off of buildings in Washington, DC. Massive flooding occurred from record rainfall. Tornadoes touched down causing injuries and fatalities. A bridge on the Schuylkill River was swept away by flood waters that inundated riverfront buildings in Philadelphia.

The schooner *John Russell* was blown ashore north of the mouth of the Potomac River; receding water left her high and dry in a corn field. All along the eastern seaboard – from North Carolina to Massachusetts – scores of other vessels suffered a similar fate. It was into this tempest that the *Express* steamed southward, on a passage that was scheduled to take her from Baltimore down the Patapsco River, south along the Chesapeake Bay, then up the Potomac River to Washington, DC. Some of her crew and passengers, and all of her freight, failed to reach the vessel's destination.

According to the most detailed contemporary account of her loss, the *Express* "was wrecked in the Chesapeake Bay on the morning of October 23d. Of the crew of twenty-two men, and of the nine passengers, sixteen were lost. The vessel was struck by the

Woodcut from *Frank Leslie's Illustrated Newspaper*.

force of the gale about ten o'clock in the morning; about half-past four a fearful sea broke over her on the port bow, staving in her upper works. The entire mass of water rushed through the saloon, carrying away the furniture and lifeboats. Again and again waves swept over her, and the captain abandoned all hope. While procuring life-preservers, he found two of the lady passengers, upon each of whom he adjusted a life-preserver. He then carried the two ladies on deck, placed them in the stern of the vessel, and warned them that the boat was going to pieces. He promised, if possible, to aid the ladies. The captain then lashed his young son to the saloon and again turned his attention to his vessel. The wind was blowing at a rate that would not allow any one to stand up to it, while the only thing that could be seen in the pitch darkness was the white foam of the raging waters.

"The second mate, Joseph Haney, was knocked down by a fearful sea, which boarded the steamer as he endeavored to cross her deck, and was swept into the smoke-hole. Before he could be rescued the boat rose on a wave mountain-high and pitched headlong into the trough of the sea, the whole of the succeeding wave rushing over her and sweeping her decks clear. Captain Barker heard the despairing shrieks of the passengers above the roar of the waves as they were swept away. In the darkness that followed it was impossible to discover or help any one.

"About ten of those on board clung to the saloon when it was carried away, and found thus a temporary refuge from death. This frail support was, however, swept again and again by the waters, every time carrying away one or more of those clinging to it. The captain clung to the saloon until it went to pieces, and then getting astride a part of the wreck, held on until daylight.

"As the gray dawn broke he found that John Douglass, one of the quartermasters, was clinging to the same piece of wreck with himself. As their frail support mounted on the tops of the enormous waves a glimpse of their surrounds was obtained. About half a mile off was the steamboat, turned bottom up, and just visible above the water. Nearer to them was a part of the saloon, to which were clinging several persons. The storm was yet raging in unabated fury, and there appeared little hope of their being able to withstand the buffetings of the waves. They could see the numbers clinging to the wreck gradually diminish, as, one by one, their strength failed them and they were swept away.

"After clinging for eight hours to the wreck, the captain and his companions sighted a small pungy near them, by the sailors of which they were rescued. They were nearly unconscious from the effects of their long exposure.

"The other part of the wreck drifted ashore on Barren Island, the men clinging to it being rescued by a boat from the steamboat *Shirley*, of the York River line, which was also ashore on the island. The *Express* and cargo were valued at $30,000."

A substantially different but complimentary account was given elsewhere. "Captain Barker gave the following account of the disaster: The *Express* left Baltimore at 4 o'clock Tuesday afternoon [October 22] with freight and passengers for Washington and other points on the Potomac River. About midnight the wind freshened, and continued to increase in violence until 2 o'clock, when it blew a heavy gale, veering from east to southeast. The steamer labored heavily, and the waves broke clear over her upper deck. About 4:30 o'clock her joiner-work began to give way, and efforts were made to head her for the shore. The storm was now so furious that it was impossible to stand against it, and the rolling of the boat prevented the engine from working fast enough to keep steerage way on her. It was evident that the upper deck was fast giving way, and it was deemed advisable to let go the anchors to bring her head to the wind in the hope of her riding out the gale, or at least until it should subside. This effort was futile, as the cabins parted as soon as she broached to, and the steamer went adrift, being no longer manageable. every possible means was employed to bring her under control, but all to no purpose. The *Express* was now off Hooper's Straits. A driving rain helped to beat down the sea, which was now running at a great height, every wave washing the boat from stem to stern. Shortly after 5 o'clock there came a terrific crash, and the joiner-work had started from the stanchions. The passengers and crew had hardly time to realize what had occurred before a wave tore the saloon deck like so much paperwork, and the following billow swept it off to sea, and with it all on board. Everybody had secured life-preservers at the beginning of the gale. Some of the officers tried to secure the boats, but they were washed away and broken up. A moment after the upper deck had been carried away the hull rolled over and sunk bottom upwards. Those of the passengers and crew that could reach portions of the wreck clung to them, but the heavy sea washed them off again, and in the breaking down only about eight persons could be seen. These, as well as could be made out, were Captain Barker, James A. Douglass, quartermaster, and a colored passenger, whose name could not be learned. They were clinging to a part of the saloon deck. Some distance off, on another portion of the wreck, were F.J. Stone, purser; John Douglass, quartermaster; Wm. Gant, colored cook; George Green, baggage-master, and Hiram A. Dekhar. These latter drifted towards Barren Island and were picked up by a boat from the steamer *Shirley*, which is ashore high and dry. The captain and his companions were picked up at 2 o'clock in the afternoon by an oyster pungy, Captain Parker, and taken to Crisfield. James Douglass, the wheelman, who was rescued, was badly hurt by being struck by timbers from the wreck."

Sources differ as to the number of persons lost. The number may have been as high as twenty. "The tug *Dupont* has arrived [at Baltimore], bringing William Holt and Charles L. Cassell, colored, deck hands of the *Express*, who were picked up Wednesday morning from a floating raft by a schooner and thence transferred to the tugboat, making a total of 15 saved and 16 missing, some of whom may have been rescued."

William Barker, the son of the captain, was listed by one source as lost.

Another source wrote: "When last seen the wreck was keel upward. Her boilers and engines are supposed to have dropped out and gone to the bottom. The other portion of the wreck will probably be broken up by the action of the waves, and may drift ashore at Barren Island or other points along the bay. The bay is twelve miles wide where the disaster occurred, and the water from twenty to thirty fathoms deep. The agent is of the opinion that the number of passengers did not exceed seven. These, with the officers and crew, would make twenty-eight souls on board. The *Express* was one of the best known boats in the harbor, having been built in 1841 in New York. In 1873 she was rebuilt at a cost of $20,000. She was 200 feet long, 25 feet beam and 602 tons. She had a horizontal engine with an upright beam and piston. Last winter she was thoroughly overhauled and repaired, and went into the Washington and Potomac river trade. She was owned by the Potomac Transportation company. The value of the vessel and cargo is estimated at $30,000. There was no insurance on the vessel."

Initially the tonnage of the *Express* was given as 275. The tonnage that is given in the paragraph above may have been the result of recalculation after the hull was lengthened and the passenger accommodations were enlarged.

Some sources claimed that the *Express* sank off the mouth of the Potomac River.

Fossil shells embedded in matrix in the Calvert Cliffs.

FAVORITE

Built: ?
Previous names: ?
Gross tonnage: ?
Type of vessel: Wooden-hulled schooner
Owner: Confederate States of America
Cause of sinking: Foundered
Location: Mile and a half southeast of Piney Point, Potomac River
GPS: 38-06.927 / 76-30.625

Sunk: July 18, 1861
Depth: 47 feet
Dimensions: 98' x 17' x 7'
Power: Sail

The *Favorite* was one of a number of insignificant sailing vessels that the Confederates used to transport cargoes along the South's inland waterways. To state that her career was lackluster is to ignore her value to her owners; it is equivalent to stating that the career of a modern eighteen-wheeler was dull and dreary because it delivered its freight on time and without being involved in any newsworthy road hazards.

At the time of her demise, the *Favorite* was in the business of transporting coal. Whereas today the Potomac River is the diving line between Maryland and Virginia, during the Civil War it was the dividing line between the North and the South. Similarly, whereas today Maryland owns the Potomac River all the way to the Virginia shore, the Union controlled the river through vessel superiority. Confederate vessels lacked such impunity; they hid in Virginia creeks and backwaters, and slunk along the Potomac under the cloak of darkness.

The *Favorite* was one such "slinker."

Union navy vessels made frequent forays into Confederate-held territory, dodging sniper bullets that shot from the untamed forest like angry bees. In 1861, Commander T.T. Craven was in command of the Potomac Flotilla. That summer found him leading offensive operations on the Potomac and Rappahannock Rivers onboard the USS *Yankee*.

On July 19, 1861, Craven wrote the following report: "On Monday, with the *Resolute* and three boats from the *Pawnee* in company, I made a thorough reconnaissance of the Yeocomico and its branches. We found several small schooners there, but all except one had their sails unbent and had apparently been laid up for some time. The one with her sails bent, the *Favorite*, was evidently preparing for a trip outside. We took her in tow and anchored her off Piney Point, when, on my return yesterday, I found she had sunk, either by being carelessly run into by another vessel or from the neglect on my part to leave men on board to watch and keep her pumped out."

The *Favorite* and her cargo of coal lay in 47 feet of water, seemingly lost forever.

Although her end was somewhat ignominious, today the site of her loss represents one of the more interesting wrecks to explore. The hull is contiguous so that a diver could possibly circumnavigate the perimeter and return to his point of origin – but I wouldn't necessarily recommend attempting it without deploying a guideline. One section of wooden hull looks pretty much like any other. If the grapnel hooks on the outside of the wreck, and the visibility is decent, you might go completely around the hull and be fairly certain of relocating the grapnel. If the grapnel falls inside the wreck, you might be trusting to luck to relocate it by zigzagging back and forth before your air runs out. In this case you could move the grapnel to the outside perimeter.

I repeat: the use of a line reel is strongly recommended.

The relief averages two to three feet, with occasional upright timbers rising five feet above the muddy bottom. Much of the wood is badly decayed: it has the appearance of joists that have been desecrated by termites. In this case the "termites" are called shipworms; they are not actually worms but wood-boring mollusks. The effect is the same: wood whose surface is pockmarked and fibrous like rotting logs in a forest.

The small rocks that aggregate in the bottom of the hull are chunks of coal.

Divers are warned that there are lines or ropes stretched across sections of the wreck: probably the remnants of lost fishing nets. Be careful of entanglement.

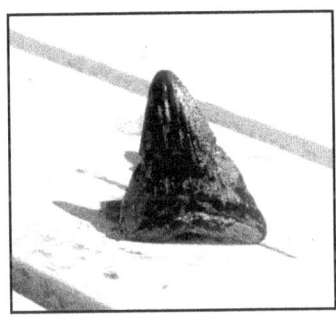

Above is a fossil shark tooth that I found in the water along the Calvert Cliffs. It measures three inches in length. Teeth can also be found on the beach at the base of the cliffs, as they erode out of the Miocene formations or are washed up out of the water during storms. These famous cliffs stretch for more than twenty-five miles along the western shore of the bay, extending north from the Patuxent River. In places the cliffs rise more than one hundred feet above the water.

GENERAL J. A. DUMONT

Built: 1862
Previous names: *James F. Freeborn, Nansemond, W.H. Crawford*
Gross tonnage: 340 reduced to 309
Type of vessel: Wooden-hulled side-wheel steamer
Builder: Fletcher, Harrison & Company, Williamsburg, New York
Owner: Eastern Short Development Company, Annapolis, Maryland
Port of registry: Baltimore, Maryland
Cause of sinking: Fire
Location: North shore of the Severn River
Sunk: December 22, 1914
Depth: 9 feet
Dimensions: 146' x 26' x 9'
Power: Coal-fired steam
Lat/lon: 39-00.20 N / 76-29.30 W

The *General J. A. Dumont* led an illustrious career that spanned more than five decades. This is an extraordinarily long time for a vessel to survive, especially for one that was constructed of wood.

Her hull was laid down the year after the commencement of the Civil War. At that time she was named *James F. Freeborn*. She was a side-wheel steamer that grossed 340 tons. Her paddle wheels were turned by a vertical beam engine with a 40-inch diameter and a 9-foot stroke. In her original configuration she was equipped with auxiliary sails. She could reach a maximum speed of 15 knots, but her normal cruising speed was 10 knots.

She was home-ported in New York City for barely a year when owner Richard Squires sold her out of commercial service.

Both belligerents were sorely in need of fighting vessels. On August 18, 1863, the Union navy purchased the vessel for $65,000. The following day she was commissioned and renamed *Nansemond*. She was immediately armed with a 30-pounder Parrott rifle and two 24-pounders.

In May 1863, Secretary of the Navy Gideon Welles cited Lieutenant Roswell Lamson for his "energy and gallantry and executive ability" in preventing the advance of the Confederates against Norfolk. As a result, Lamson was given command of the *Nansemond* as soon as her purchase was consummated. Only five days after her commissioning, the *Nansemond* joined the North Atlantic Blockading Squadron off Wilmington, North Carolina. Both Lamson and the *Nansemond* then saw a great deal of action as a blockader.

That same year the *Nansemond* destroyed the blockade runners *Douro* and *Venus*. She captured the *Margaret and Bessie*. On December 14, the "little *Nansemond* was caught off the coast in a terrific gale and nearly foundered. Lamson was compelled to throw his guns overboard, and by so doing he saved his vessel and brought her safe to port, and he was commended by the admiral for his efficient conduct and skill on that occasion."

After the government purchased the *Margaret and Bessie*, she was converted to a blockader and renamed *Gettysburg*. Lamson then shifted his command from the *Nansemond* to the newly commissioned *Gettysburg*.

In 1864, the *Nansemond* was serving in the squadron that was attacked by the CSS *Raleigh* off the Cape Fear River. She participated in attacks on Fort Fisher in December of that year and in January 1865.

During her wartime service, the navy spent $31,474.82 on maintenance and repairs. She was placed out of commission on August 8, 1865. Barely a fortnight later – on August 22 – the Navy sold the *Nansemond* to the Treasury Department for $20,000. Her new owner kept her Navy appellation for the first eight years of her new career.

According to quasi-sources, the *Nansemond* "was stationed at Savannah, GA [Georgia], until 1869 and then transferred to Key West, FL [Florida]. In 1873 she was under repair at New York and was eventually sent to Wilmington, NC [North Carolina]. She became the *W.H. Crawford* 20 November 1873 [for service as a revenue cutter]. Afterward, she was at Savannah, Key West, Wilmington, and Pensacola, FL. She was advertised for sale in 1884, but bidding was not high enough; she then underwent repairs. She subsequently served at Key West and Charleston, SC [South Carolina]. In 1890 she was stationed on the Chesapeake Bay and was sold 24 April 1897."

With her return to merchant service – after almost 34 years – her new owner, Edward Booz, changed her name to *General J.A. Dumont*. By this time her tonnage was registered as 309 tons instead of her original 340. This reduction in tonnage must have been due to modifications in the superstructure or interior spaces that resulted in recalculation of her usable enclosed-space capacity.

Booz chartered the vessel to whichever shipping line needed her, for however long she was needed. By way of example, in 1901 he entered into an agreement with the Philadelphia and Lewes Transportation Company to charter the vessel for $1,500 per month, plus the costs of maintenance and repair. The charterer (Philadelphia and Lewes Transportation Company) was also responsible for keeping insurance on the vessel in the amount of $30,000, for damage or loss, despite Booz's claim that the actual value of the *General J.A. Dumont* was $35,000. As collateral to ensure payment, Booz had a lien against the wharf in Lewes, Delaware, which wharf was owned by the chartering company.

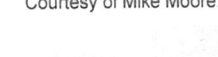

Courtesy of Mike Moore.

In the event, the charterer defaulted in living up to its end of the bargain. Not only did it renege on four of its monthly payments, but it failed to pay the wages of the crew, and it "failed and neglected to deliver the said steamboat in substantially the same condition as when delivered." After Booz paid off the crew, his lien against the charterer amounted to $8,181.83. He moved to take possession of the wharf as per the agreement.

The Philadelphia and Lewes Transportation Company objected to losing this valuable piece of property, and defended Booz's lawsuit in the Circuit Court of Delaware in order to retain possession. The attorney for the defendant company (the "demurrer" or "demurrant" in the words of the court) attempted to muddle the issue by citing "a large number of cases." However, the court noted that "a careful examination of them fails to disclose that they have any material bearing upon the case in hand."

The judge wrote, "The demurrer must be overruled, with costs to the plaintiff in this cause hitherto accrued."

In 1912, the Eastern Shore Development Company assumed ownership of the aging *General J.A. Dumont*. The paddle-wheeler now ran ferry service across the Chesapeake Bay, between Annapolis and Claiborne, a distance of about twenty miles. (This was 40 years before the Chesapeake Bay Bridge was built.) She continued in this service for two years.

In 1914, a fierce wind blew the *General J.A. Dumont* onto the north shore of the Severn River. There were no fatalities. No attempt was made to pull the vessel off the lonely strand. Several months later – on December 22 – she caught fire for reasons unknown and burned to the waterline. And there she remained.

My long-time friend Mike Moore used to dive on the wreck in the early 1980's. He wrote directions to the wreck site and composed a cumulative report of his dives: "The closest launching ramp is the excellent state ramp at Sandy Point. Go under the Bay Bridge, give Greenbury Point a wide berth and turn into the Severn River. Pass under the Old Severn River (Rte. 450) Bridge and steer in the direction of Manresa, the large white building with the cross in front on the north shore of the river. As you pull close into Manresa you will notice a small cove to the right. To the right of the cove entrance is a small, weatherbeaten [sic] fisherman's shack. The wreck is immediately in front of the shack in about 8-9 feet of water.

"The *Nansemond* is not a very exciting dive, but its location in the river away from most boat traffic, clear of waves and out of the current, makes it a good dive for new divers or bad weather. Some of the frames (ribs) and some machinery protrude out. It appears that the main part of her machinery must have been salvaged as no large parts of her engine or boilers has been found. Some interesting bottles and some ornate pieces of Victorian gingerbread woodwork show up occasionally."

Things have changed since Mike's early diving days, but not much. The Manresa mansion was constructed piecemeal starting in 1926. Throughout the following decades, Manresa on the Severn – as the Jesuit retreat was called – spread along the spacious riverfront grounds as new wings were added to the initial structure and chapel. In 1995, the property was purchased by Ewing Health Services and was converted to an assisted living home for the elderly; the building has been restored with those accommodations in mind. The present name of the mansion is Atria Manresa; the address is 85 Manresa Road, Annapolis.

The shack that Mike referred to no longer exists. Modern houses now stand prominently along the cliff above the bank, and piers extend into the river from shore. The Maryland Historical Trust claims to know the precise location of the wreck, but refused to give it to me (see the Introduction for an explanation of this refusal). I interpolated the GPS coordinates from Mike's directions. Because of the hull's relief, it should show up on a fish finder or depth recorder.

Another way to locate the wreck is to start from the rock jetty on the east side of the cove entrance, move outward from the inlet to where the water is 8 to 9 feet deep, and drag a grapnel along the depth contour. You are certain to snag the wreck in just a few minutes. Sweep back and forth if you miss it on the first try.

I took this picture from the bulkhead on Atria Manresa property. The wreck is located approximately in the upper middle of the picture, between the short row of piles in the foreground and the long pier in the background. Drag a grapnel back and forth in 8 to 9 feet of water to find the remains of the hull.

HANNIBAL

Built: 1898
Previous names: *Joseph Holland*
Gross tonnage: 1,785
Type of vessel: Collier
Builder: J. Blumer & Company, Sunderland, England
Owner: U.S. Navy
Armament: One 4-inch gun, two 3-inch guns, eight .50 caliber machine guns
Cause of sinking: Scuttled for use as a target
Location: Off the mouth of the Potomac River

Sunk: March 1, 1945
Depth: 20 feet
Dimensions: 264' x 39' x 17'
Power: Coal-fired steam
Official designation: Miscellaneous auxiliary
GPS: 38-02.438 / 76-09.209

For a vessel that lasted as long as the *Hannibal*, she certainly had a lackluster career. That is not necessarily a bad thing, for she performed valuable if not noteworthy service in several capacities as a naval auxiliary for forty-seven years – and then some.

The U.S. Navy purchased the *Joseph Holland* in preparation for the Spanish-American War. She was converted to a collier, and was officially commissioned as the USS *Hannibal* on June 7, 1898. Her usual complement was 244 officers and men. Her armament was light, consisting of one 4-inch gun, two 3-inch guns, and eight .50-caliber machine guns. She saw no action in the war that lasted for only four months. Yet her duties kept her busy for thirteen years in the transportation of coal along the U.S. eastern seaboard.

The *Hannibal* was decommissioned for two months in 1911. After recommissioning, she "was assigned to the U.S. Survey Squadron to make depth soundings and surveys in preparation for the opening of the Panama Canal. Hydrographic surveys continued in the Caribbean until 1917, including operations in Panama, Nicaragua, Honduras, and Cuba."

When the Great War loomed on the horizon, the *Hannibal* was overhauled and modified to serve as a tender to submarine chasers, a duty that she held until August 1919, when her services were no longer needed and she was decommissioned again.

Two years later, she "sailed for Cuba to resume survey operations which lasted until 1930. During the next decade *Hannibal* surveyed waters near Trinidad, Venezuela, Costa Rica, and the Canal Zone. During World War II she operated out of Norfolk, Virginia in the Chesapeake Bay degaussing range. *Hannibal* decommissioned 20 August 1944 and was sunk as a bombing target" on March 1, 1945.

This thumbnail sketch shows a workaday vessel that was never called upon to do anything grand. Yet as a collier, tender, and survey vessel, she always performed her duties to her utmost ability – and to the utmost abilities of the men who commanded her.

How many Navy flyboys made passes over the *Hannibal* during the next couple of decades cannot be determined with any degree of accuracy. Speaking of accuracy – or inaccuracy, as the case may be – an interesting sidelight to the *Hannibal's* last assignment at her final duty station occurred in 1957.

The hull of the *Hannibal* lies about twenty-five miles south-southeast of the Patux-

The picture above was taken in 1907. Compare it with the one at the bottom of the page, which was taken in 1943. (Both courtesy of the Naval Photographic Center.) Below is a commemorative cachet that was postmarked onboard on July 20, 1934. U.S. Navy vessels served as government post offices. Mail that was posted onboard was "sent" whenever a vessel docked or entered harbor. Mail that was addressed to a shipboard sailer was forwarded to that sailor's vessel at the next port of call.

ent Naval Air Station, from which the bombing and strafing runs were conducted. In the 1950's, a lighthouse stood on the Holland Island Bar, off of South Marsh Island, at about the same distance from the air station. The Holland Lighthouse marked the entrance to Kedges Strait, and warned mariners off the dangerous shoal. The lighthouse was located about four miles from the *Hannibal*.

On February 19, 1957, a flight of Navy planes took off from the air station and flew toward the target ship for a nighttime practice session. Unfortunately, the pilots' bombing skill was better than their navigational skill. Their flight pattern was a few degrees off course. They struck the target a devastating blow – but they struck the wrong target!

Commander William Pack, of the all-weather attack squadron, explained what happened: "Three of our attack bombers were on a routine night rocket flight, with the *Hannibal* their target, a sunken ship in Chesapeake Bay, as their objective. One of the planes dropped a flare and the others, mistaking Holland light, about four miles from the sunken vessel, for their target, fired four rockets at the lighthouse structure."

It can happen to anyone.

Damage was described as moderate to severe, depending upon whether the deponent was a naval defense attorney or the two members of the lighthouse crew who were injured by flying debris. "The rockets tore away one of the main support structures, ripped an 18-inch hole in the lighthouse, and pierced a storage tank."

The *Hannibal* has long since been shot to pieces by pilots who were better trained in nighttime navigation and target recognition; it is no longer visible above the surface of the water. The wreckage consists of little more than the lower hull which is surrounded by a debris field. The sunken metal hull rests about a hundred yards from the *American Mariner* (which see), which as of this writing is standing tall.

The Holland Lighthouse doesn't look like a ship to me, but then I'm not a Navy flyboy bombing a target at night. (From the author's collection.)

HERBERT D. MAXWELL

Built: 1905
Previous names: None
Gross tonnage: 772
Type of vessel: Wooden-hulled four-masted schooner
Builder: New England Company, Bath, Maine
Owner: William Quillen
Port of registry: Seaford, Delaware
Cause of sinking: Collision with *Gloucester*
Location: Off Kent Island, 4 miles south of Chesapeake Bay Bridge

Sunk: March 16, 1912
Depth: 70 feet
Dimensions: 185' x 38' x 14'
Power: Sail

GPS: 38-55.593 / 76-23.610

The *Herbert D. Maxwell* was built at a time when wooden-hulled sailing vessels were gradually yielding to steel-hulled steamships as the major carriers of freight. Sailing vessels were subject to the vagaries of heaven's breath, whereas steamers could proceed anytime in any direction without having to tack against contrary winds. Yet domestic-built schooners had some advantages: they were inexpensive to build and operate, and if speed of delivery time was not a factor, they could transport non-degradable freight cheaper than it cost to transport the same by steamer.

The *Herbert D. Maxwell* was a coastal schooner. She plied the inland waters and hugged the shore during voyages that carried her to sea. On May 11, 1909 – at the age of four years – she was transporting rails from Baltimore to Savannah, Georgia when she went aground off Sparrows Point in the Patapsco River barely five miles from her port of departure. She soon backed off without assistance and proceeded on her way none the worse for wear.

She was not so fortunate three years later. At 7 o'clock on the evening of March 15, 1912, the *Herbert D. Maxwell* departed her berth on the Magothy River (15 miles southeast of Baltimore). Her holds were loaded with 1,150 tons of fertilizer that was bound for Wilmington, North Carolina. The cargo was owned by the Virginia-Carolina Chemical Company. Onboard the graceful four-masted schooner were Captain William Quillen, master and owner, and a crew of eight. The windjammer turned to starboard where the Magothy River entered the Chesapeake Bay, then proceeded south.

She was only an hour from the dock when the wind died. Without nature's motive power, a sailing vessel is controlled by current and tide. Captain Quillen dropped anchor near the east side of the bay south of Sandy Point (the current location of the Chesapeake Bay Bridge). The wind picked up around 3 a.m. First Mate J.C. Cott called all hands to get the schooner under way. Captain Quillen took the helm at first, then turned it over to a crewmember. The captain and the mate stood watch on the poop deck as the schooner proceeded southward.

At that time the steamship *Gloucester* was on a northern heading. The 295-foot-long steamer was a monster compared to the 185-foot-long schooner. She grossed 3,200 tons against 772 tons of the schooner. She was built of hardened steel instead of crunchable wood. She was on her regular passage from Boston, Massachusetts to Baltimore. She was owned by the Merchants & Miners Transportation Company.

Although the Chesapeake and Delaware Canal had opened for business as long ago as 1829, it was not until 1938 that it was broadened and deepened enough to permit the passage of vessels the size of the *Gloucester*. The deep-draft steamer was forced to round Cape Charles in order to enter the Chesapeake Bay, then proceed some 160 miles north to reach Baltimore.

On the morning in question, darkness cloaked the bay but the sky was clear and the stars shone brightly. Both the schooner and the steamer were showing navigation lights to warn oncoming vessels of their presence. Due to a crook in the bay off Tolly Point, the shipping channel made a small change in direction, requiring downbound vessels to veer slightly to port, and upbound vessels to veer slightly to starboard. At this point the navigable waters measured two miles in width; there was more than ample space for approaching vessels to avoid each other.

There are two versions of events that ensued. According to witnesses aboard the *Herbert D. Maxwell*, the schooner was proceeding at 4 to 5 knots when lookouts spotted the lights of a steamer dead ahead a little over a mile away; they saw both of the side lights as well as the range lights on the mastheads. When less than half a mile separated the two vessels, lookouts (including the captain and mate) claimed that the red light disappeared so that only the green or starboard light showed, indicating that the oncoming vessel had turned to port (westward) in the same direction in which the schooner was heading.

This gave Captain Quillen cause for concern. The jibboom sometimes blocked his line of sight. He walked from one side of the quarter deck to the other, in order to keep the steamer's lights in view. Now it looked as if the steamer would clear the schooner by passing her on her starboard side in a starboard to starboard passage. The skipper had barely relaxed his vigil when he saw the steamer change course. The masthead range lights aligned themselves on the schooner, and the red or port light came back into view. This meant that the steamer was now turning to starboard, and that there would not be enough space between the vessels to complete the turn for a port to port passage.

Captain Quillen yelled for the helmsman to "put the helm hard up. The wheel jammed, and before the order could take effect the collision happened.... In brief, the schooner's story is that the steamer crossed the schooner's bow from port to starboard. After it had gotten safely over, it suddenly turned from starboard to port, and ran directly into the schooner, and cut the latter down."

The story differs from the viewpoint of the *Gloucester*. She was steaming between 13 and 14 knots when her lookouts first spotted the lights of the schooner from a distance of about a mile. At that time the schooner showed only her red or port light; schooners did not show masthead lights, this difference being the mariner's way of distinguishing between a steamship and a sailing vessel. The first officer was on watch. He told the helmsman to port his helm "some."

The reader must understand that at that time, porting the helm turned the vessel to starboard, and vice versa. "Porting the helm" mean pushing the uppermost spoke to the left, or turning the helm counterclockwise. This action was due to the arrangement of the linkage between the helm and the rudder. This arrangement was a holdover from the days when vessels did not have helms, but were steered by means of a tiller. The tiller was linked directly to the rudder, so that pushing the tiller to port (or left) pushed the rudder to starboard (or right), and consequently turned the vessel to starboard. This convention was gradually changed in the 1930's, so that today the helm works the same as the steering wheel of an automobile. When you turn your steering wheel counter-clockwise, your car turns to the left; when you turn the steering wheel clockwise, your car turns to the right. There is no such thing as turning a steering wheel left or right; the correct terminology is counterclockwise and clockwise; the same holds true for turning screws, nuts, bolts, and control knobs.

The *Gloucester* continued on her port helm until about one-third of a mile separated the two vessels. All this time the schooner was showing her red or port light, indicating that the schooner was continuing her course for the traditional port to port passage. As the distance closed, the mate thought to increase the space between them, and ordered the help put hard aport (which turned the vessel hard to the right).

"While the steamer's stem was swinging under the influence of a hard aport helm farther to starboard – that is, to the eastward – those on its deck saw the schooner also swing over in the same direction, and change her red light to green [starboard]." The mate then considered that his condition was in extremis. Collision was imminent. There was no time to check the steamer's speed by ordering reverse on the telegraph. Instead he ordered the helm put hard astarboard in the hope of passing the schooner starboard to starboard.

The vessels collided less than half a minute later. The steel stem of the *Gloucester* knifed into the port side of the *Herbert D. Maxwell* abaft number three hatch (the aftermost hatch), neatly slicing off a section of the after hull. Bay water rushed into the ruptured hull with such abandon that there was no time to launch the lifeboat before the schooner sank and left the crewmembers to fend for themselves in the dark open water.

A postcard picture that was taken prior to launching.

Damage to the *Gloucester* was slight by comparison. Her mainmast fell by the wayside, her rails were crushed in the area of contact, and her wireless apparatus was demolished. She stopped and lowered lifeboats to search for survivors. They managed to rescue Captain Quillen and four crewmembers, but First Mate Cott, Gertrude Cardozo, Miguel Silva, and Joaquino Suares were not found and were presumed to have drowned.

In the resulting lawsuit, the judge noted appropriately that the *Gloucester* was the burdened vessel: "It must explain why it did not keep out of the schooner's way." This notion may seem arrogant and unfair to a landsman, but there is reason behind the legal premise. As mentioned above, a sailing vessel is limited in its ability to maneuver. It cannot always proceed in a perfectly straight line, but might have to tack from side to side in order to move forward against a contrary wind. Nor can it turn or come to a standstill with ease. Therefore, in accordance with the International Rules of the Road, a sailing vessel has the right of way over a steamship, which is burdened to yield.

By the same Rules, when a sailing vessel and a steamship approach each other, the sailing vessel *must not* alter course, but *must* proceed in the same direction until the vessels have passed each other. This Rule is imposed upon a sailing vessel so that the steamer can be assured of the sailing vessel's course, in order for the steamer to maneuver out of its way without interference.

Furthermore, according to U.S. Coast Guard Rules of the Road for inland and river traffic, a vessel moving downstream with a following current has the right of way over a vessel moving upstream into the current. This is because a vessel that is being pushed by current cannot stop and therefore its maneuverability is restricted.

The Chesapeake Bay is tidal, and brine is found as far north as Baltimore, but the tidal flow at the point of collision is minimal, with southbound current predominating. This put additional burden on the *Gloucester* to yield right of way.

Nonetheless, the judge was not convinced that the *Herbert D. Maxwell* did not contribute to the collision, by changing course at the last minute and steering into the way of the *Gloucester*. "Upon these findings of fact, it follows that both were at fault – the schooner for its change of course, a change which would probably not have taken place had the steamer seen the schooner as soon as it should have done. The steamer is to blame because it continued, after seeing the danger, with unchecked speed. It must have had time after it saw the schooner to materially reduce its speed. Such reduction would almost certainly have avoided the collision."

In the meantime, efforts were being made to both salvage the wreck and to remove it has a hazard to navigation. The U.S. Army Corps of Engineers took control of the situation.

The after portion, which had been nipped off in the collision, "floated down the bay, grounding on the shoal off Poplar Island in 11 feet of water. It subsequently floated across the bay to near Governors Run Wharf [about 30 miles downstream] in 10 feet of water. The character and position of the wreckage rendered it probable that it would again get adrift, when it would become a dangerous obstruction to navigation at night. Accordingly, under the emergency and the provisions of law, and by authority of the Secretary of War and direction of the Chief of Engineers, on March 25, 1912, the destruction and removal of this wreckage was undertaken, the work being done by hired labor and use of Government plant [vessel]. Three hundred and fifty pounds of 60 per cent dynamite were used, which shattered the wreckage. The large debris was put ashore entirely out of the way of navigation. Operations were commenced and completed April 4, 1912, the original depth (10 feet) was restored at the site. The total cost of removal was $100, which included all expenses of first examination, subsequent inspection, and other superintendence in the field and office." You can hardly get your lawn mowed for that amount today.

The schooner was valued at $45,000. The main hull lay at a depth of 70 feet, with the masts protruding above the surface of the water in the way of shipping traffic. Quillen arranged with the Lighthouse Service to place a lighted buoy on the wreck as a warning to passing mariners. He then tried to interest a commercial salvage company in raising the hull intact, but negotiations in this regard proved unproductive. He then abandoned the vessel to the insurance underwriters.

Once again the Corps of Engineers was called upon clear the shipping lane of obstruction. "After repeated unsuccessful efforts on the part of the owners (A. D. Cummins & Company, of Philadelphia, Pa. [which apparently purchased salvage rights from the underwriters]) to raise the wreck, which was deemed by them to be of considerable value, the removal of such portions of it as rose to within 50 feet of mean low water was authorized, under the provisions of law and by authority of the Secretary of War, dated October 10, 1912, and direction of the Chief of Engineers, dated October 11, 1912. The work was done by the owners, under circular poster advertisement and written proposal and acceptance. The low bid ($50) was made, it is understood, to enable the owners to secure the award and salve the wreck, after the obstructive portions had been removed. Actual operations under this award commenced January 2, 1913, and were completed February 24, 1913, being prosecuted in an intermittent and desultory way. The masts were pulled out and broken off, and the bowsprit and jib boom sawed or blown off, so that the least distance of any part of the wreck was 52 feet below mean low water. It is no longer an obstruction to navigation. The total cost was $341.41, including all expenses of first examination, subsequent inspections, services of the steam tender belonging to the district and a diver, and other superintendence in the field and office."

The *Herbert D. Maxwell* was then forgotten and its location was lost. The discovery of the wreck in the twentieth century was both accidental and coincidental. The fascinating saga began in 1939, with the loss of the *Floating Pile Driver No. 7*, which was owned by the McLean Contractors Company, in Baltimore.

The pile driver's steel hull measured 65 feet in length and 26 feet in width. The derrick stood 75 feet high. Within the hull were two boilers to provide steam for a 3-drum hoisting engine. The platform was not motorized; it had to be towed.

On November 20, 1939, a lighted bell buoy was placed on the wreck to warn passing mariners of a possible menace to safe navigation. The Army Corps of Engineers investigated the site on January 20, 1940. They found that when the pile driver foundered in 65 feet of water, it landed on its side; five feet of the hull settled into the mud. The least depth over the wreck was 45 feet. This was not considered a hazard to navigation. The lighted bell buoy was discontinued, but the location was marked on the nautical chart. Although the examiners didn't know it at the time, the site of the pile driver lay only one mile from the wreck of the *Herbert D. Maxwell*.

Two decades later – on October 23, 1959 – the U.S. minesweeper *Ability* was testing her minesweeping gear in the vicinity of Kent Island when her gear hung on an obstruction. She ascertained her position by means of distance to and bearing on a navigational buoy, and by means of sextant and chronometer. She shortened her gear, and cleared the obstruction at a depth of 30 feet. This hazard to navigation was reported to the Coast and Geodetic Survey (NOAA's predecessor), which shared responsibility with the Corps of Engineers for keeping the inland shipping lanes clear of hazardous obstructions.

Instead of searching only for the singular hang site, the Coast and Geodetic Survey decided to sweep a large swath across the shipping lane off Kent Island, a project area that measured some eight miles in length (north to south) and a mile and a half in width (east to west).

The Coast Guard cutters *Wainwright* and *Hilgard* were employed to wire-drag the area. The hydrographic survey was conducted from April 21 through April 27, 1960. Three shipwrecks were found during the course of the investigation. The locations of these wrecks were triangulated from eight stations (although not all eight stations were employed for each triangulation). In the report, the wrecks were numbered from one to three. Viewed from today, it is interesting to note that, due to the parameters of the survey area, the easternmost wire-drag strip barely missed snagging the *Mary A. DeKnight* (which see), which had to wait until a 1996 survey to be discovered.

Wreck number one was determined to be the pile driver (later to become AWOIS Record 4456), which now cleared to a least depth of 50 feet.

Wreck number two was unidentified; it cleared with a least depth of 49 feet.

Wreck number three was determined to be the wreck that the *Ability* hung. It was not identified. It cleared to a least depth of 22 feet. This later became AWOIS Record 9738. A side-scan search in 1996 found a rise of ".5 meters off the steeply sloping bottom in 12 meters of water. Evaluator recommends deleting from chart since it does not represent a danger to navigation." The designation of the item was changed from wreck to obstruction.

In reality, the hydrographers misdetermined wrecks one and two. Number two was the pile driver, and number one was an unidentified target. This survey put the *Herbert D. Maxwell* on the chart, but failed to identify it as such.

A full generation passed before the next hydrographic survey was conducted in the vicinity of Kent Island. In August 1987, the NOAA survey vessels *Rude* and *Heck* conducted a survey of the area. They were unable to locate the pile driver. No explanation was given, but it is likely that the hull had collapsed and the derrick had settled into the mud.

They had better success with the other site. Not only did they locate the wreck, but they put divers down on it. After three descents, the divers described the wreck as that of a steel derrick barge. The divers ascertained the least depth as 50.4 feet by means of pneumatic depth gauge. Interoffice evaluators concluded that the derrick barge was in fact the pile driver, and that the proximity of the two locations led to on-site confusion.

A dozen years passed. On November 5, 1996, the NOAA survey vessel *Bay Hydrographer* conducted a side-scan sonar survey of the so-called derrick barge. The image that appeared was most definitely not that of a derrick barge (nor that of a pile driver). According to the written report, "Sonargrams depict the wreck of a large sailing

This marvelous side-scan sonar image resembles a detailed pen-and-ink drawing. Clearly shown is the bowsprit, which was supposed to have been removed by salvors, who cleared the wreck to a safe depth for the purpose of surface navigation. Note the three hatch openings and the truncated after end. (Courtesy of EdgeTech.)

vessel as evidenced by images of prominent bowsprit and mast stubs. Also clearly shown were three large square cargo hatches. All these attributes plus the size of the wreck (185.9 feet) and local history (below) indicate that this is the wreck of the *Maxwell*. Due to poor vis. no dive ops undertaken. Echo-sounder LD [least depth] of 52 feet obtained on tip of bowsprit."

This last point is interesting in that the Corps of Engineers claimed that the bowsprit had been "sawed or blown off." (See report above.)

A new group of evaluators concluded that the three survey divers from twelve years earlier had dropped into a steel deck house during a time of extremely poor visibility, and thought they were inside a derrick barge. This scenario could make sense were it not for the fact that the *Herbert D. Maxwell* never had a steel deck house. The hull and superstructure were made entirely of wood. However, I can testify to the fact that in extremely poor visibility, it is often difficult if not impossible to obtain a clear mental image of a shipwreck that a diver is seeing – or feeling, as the case may be – by piecing together scores or hundreds of fleeting images after the dive. I am reminded of the three blind men who felt different parts of an elephant – the trunk, a foot, and the abdomen – and who gave totally different descriptions of the animal at their fingertips. The survey divers are to be forgiven for the error of their ways.

The interesting part of this report was the mention of "local history." The local historians to whom they referred turned out to be local historians to *which* they referred:

the National Ocean Survey in Rockville, Maryland, and the Marine Physics Branch of the U.S. Naval Research Laboratory in Washington, DC. Both these agencies demonstrated unique knowledge about the *Herbert D. Maxwell*, and stated that they used the wreck "for demonstrations of various sonars and other instruments."

How did these putative "historians" come to know so much about the *Herbert D. Maxwell*? The answer was simple: from recreational divers who had dived on the wreck, who had done their homework, and who did not mind sharing the results of their research (unlike the Maryland Historical Trust; see Introduction for details of its disinclination to share information).

I first dived on the *Herbert D. Maxwell* on July 26, 1987 – the month before the *Rude* and *Heck* "discovered" the site's actual location, and when NOAA divers described the wreck as a steel derrick barge – and I was by no means the first recreational diver to explore the aged hull. Mike Moore took me there on his boat *Arabia*. He had loran numbers for the wreck because he had dived on it before and knew its true identity. How many other such divers had visited the site in prior years is anyone's guess.

I was more fortunate than the three NOAA divers who dropped blindly into a "steel derrick barge" several weeks later. I had one foot of clear visibility, and I could see unclearly another two to three feet; I could vaguely discern structure some five feet away: enough to avoid swimming into a fouled fishing net. Of course, this was with a powerful dive light. Ambient light visibility was zero, like a night dive. I also had one other advantage over the NOAA divers: I was a wreck-diver with years of experience in recognizing features on shipwrecks to which divers who were unfamiliar with wreck sites might be oblivious.

According to Mike, "Loran doesn't do any particular good on the *Maxwell* as the Navy transmitter at Greenbury Point is too close and too powerful. To find the *Maxwell* you need a good depth finder, a scale expansion (zoom) capability helps, and a good hand bearing compass. A VHF radio is mandatory, otherwise you and your boat will wind up a scratch in some freighter's bottom paint."

I should mention at this point that Mike Moore was the most brilliant person I have ever met. He had a mind like a computer. He had perfect recall, and could instantly relate the minutest details of everything he knew or read with absolute accuracy. I knew that he was an engineer, but because the projects he worked on were so highly classified, I never learned exactly what *kind* of engineer he was, or who he worked for: whether he worked directly for an agency of the federal government, or was employed by a private company that did secret contract work for the government. Only once during all the years I knew him did he remark about his current work: on homing torpedoes for nuclear submarines. He also had a subtle sense of humor, as the previous paragraph demonstrates.

Here are his directions for finding the *Herbert D. Maxwell* in the days before the advent of the global positioning system (keeping in mind that this was in the mid-1980's): "The *Maxwell* is about a four mile run from the excellent State of Maryland ramp at Sandy Point. Head south of the Bay Bridge favoring the east (red buoyed) side of the shipping channel. About a mile south of red buoy '78' there will be a white and orange buoy 'N' marking the north end of a measured mile course. Head away from the buoy on a magnetic heading of 262 and watch your depth sounder. The bottom will fall away to a little over a hundred feet and then start to rise up again. When you hit a depth of 72 feet drop a marker buoy. Check the buoy's position by taking a bearing on the water tower on Kent Island to the northeast. It should bear 064 magnetic. This is your initial position to start the search. The wreck lies on that 72 foot contour in a sort of notch on the side of the channel. The best way to find the wreck is to start a couple of hundred yards south of your initial point and follow the contour to the north. You'll find that the east tower of the Bay Bridge makes a good visual reference. [The 1960 surveyors used this same landmark as a triangulation station.] When you come upon the wreck the bottom will fall away sharply to about 80 feet and then shoot up to the deck of the wreck at about 60 or 65 feet. . . .

"Most of the time the current is ebb (flowing toward the south) so it's easiest to hook the wreck by dragging the anchor from north to south hooking the port side. Once you've confirmed this you can keep yourself oriented to the port side and work either toward the bow or toward the stern from the anchor."

Mike followed these directions and told me precisely when to drop the grapnel. It caught on the first drop. He stayed on board to watch the boat while I went down alone. He warned me that he might have to leave on a moment's notice in order to avoid being run down by a large tanker or freighter. Even though the Rules of the Road specified that an anchored vessel with restricted maneuverability had the right of way, big ships generally ignored that particular Rule when small boats were concerned. As Ted Green has been wont to note, right of way often yields to might of weigh.

If Mike had to leave, he would slip the anchor line from the cleat and secure it to a buoy which he would then toss overboard. He would idle the boat nearby until the vessel passed and I surfaced. If the buoy did not get run down, I could ascend the anchor line and decompress on it. Otherwise, I was on my own, and would have to send up a liftbag on a line and do a drift decompression after I heard the Dopplering engine noise receding. He would not take a chance on running me over to pick up his buoy.

These emergency procedures are standard protocol for diving in the Chesapeake Bay, especially in or near the shipping lanes.

In addition to these instructions, Mike described the highlights of the layout of the wreck. He wrote it this way: "She lies with her bow facing east. The bow is a graceful clipper design with most of the bowsprit intact. Swimming down the port side you'll get a feel for the slender lines of the ship. Down the centerline you'll find that, of the four masts, two are missing, presumed salvaged, and the other two are broken off. . . . About 40 feet of the stern is broken off. . . . A small deckhouse in the bow contains the Hyde windlass machinery and the galley. . . . Starting about 30 feet aft of the bow the starboard side is gone."

I descended silently and weightlessly through pitch black water that was reminiscent of a sensory deprivation tank. My only hold on reality was the anchor line. After I bumped into the wreck, I switched on my light and checked my gauges. Then I swept the beam across the deck. The wood was as clean as that on wrecks that I had seen in the Great Lakes. I could clearly see the grain. I had a job to do before I could afford to go sightseeing. I dropped over the side and went down to the bottom to check the security of the hook. I reached a depth of 70 feet. The temperature was 78°.

Back on the deck I was lucky enough to be able to orient myself immediately. No bulwarks, posts, or rails were in evidence, but the anchor line was draped over the inward curve of the port side so that the bowsprit was in view. I swam to the end of the bowsprit, noting deadeyes and bull's-eyes: remnants of the standing rigging. Then I turned and worked my way aft along the port gunwale.

Most of the decking in this area was intact, as were the hatch combings. About midship I saw that some of the planks were missing. I peered down into the capacious hold. I saw nothing but blackness beyond the beam of my light. I did not dare to venture inside. I used the plank to lead me to the starboard side of the hull. There I saw that some of the outer planks were missing. I wouldn't go as far as to say that the starboard side was gone, but the vertical hull did not appear to be fully intact.

I followed the starboard gunwale to the break. At this point the after planks existed in complete disarray, much like Brobdingnagian splinters, or perhaps a colossal game of Pick-Up Sticks. The break cut diagonally toward the port side, but I made no attempt to follow the trail of debris. I turned back toward the bow, then crisscrossed the deck several times now that I felt comfortable within the perimeter of the hull, and felt confident that I would not get lost.

Although I was unaware of the description that NOAA's divers would make in the not-too-distant future, as I now look back in memory I can honestly state that I saw nothing that reminded me of a steel derrick barge. I had the advantage of greater visibility than that which the NOAA divers were soon to behold.

I heard no deep-throated throbbing of large vessel engines. After an hour of bottom time, I returned to the anchor line and ascended to ten feet, for ten minutes of decompression in 84° water.

I cannot end this chapter without relating a couple of cautionary anecdotes about diving on the *Herbert D. Maxwell*. Mike Moore's best friend, Coast Guard officer Mike Monteith, told the first story: "At one point I made a penetration deep into the fo'c'sle where the crew slept. While I was in there, the glass in my dive mask fell out.

"Whereupon I attempted to exit through a hole in the wreck, becoming hopelessly entangled in netting. Ten minutes later, Stu Marder, who was my buddy, found me and cut me free and led me by the hand. I had no vision as it was pitch black; mostly I moved by feel. He led me back to the anchor rope, then up to our first decompression stop, then up to the top.

"Whenever I see him, I thank him. We had agreed on a time I would go into the wreck. If I was not out in five or six minutes, he was to come looking for me."

Mike Moore related the other story. "A diver got away from us one time in 1985. He was unable to find the anchor line within his air supply so he did a straight ascent. Then he had trouble venting air from his dry suit so he had to stop his ascent.... Soon he drifted further aft, then came to the surface abeam of the dive boat, but off to the side.

"By the time he swam over, he just missed our 200 feet of trail line. We did our Chinese fire drill, brought in our divers, slipped our anchor line, got under way, took a bearing on him and ran down the bearing two miles down the bay.

"He knew we would come to get him. Meanwhile, he was almost hit by an oyster boat. Farther on he drifted by a naval frigate anchored off the Naval Academy.

"The crew saw someone swimming toward them, figured he was a terrorist and called out their Marine detachment. So he drifted past them, looking up at M-16 barrels manned by scared Marines. All he could do was wave and smile.

"We had trouble getting him back on the wreck." Enough said!

LEVIN J. MARVEL

Built: 1891
Previous names: None
Gross tonnage: 184
Type of vessel: Wooden-hulled ram schooner
Builder: J.M.C. Moore, Seaford, Delaware
Owner: Chesapeake Windjammer Vacation, Annapolis, Maryland
Port of registry: Baltimore, Maryland
Cause of sinking: Foundered
Location: Herring Bay, east of Fairhaven

Sunk: August 12, 1955
Depth: 22 feet
Dimensions: 125' x 23' x 7'
Power: Sail

GPS: 38-45-23.30 / 76-31-26.27

    The *Levin J. Marvel* belonged to a class of sailing vessel that was known as a ram, or a ram schooner. Ram is a local name for "a three-masted, bald-headed schooner used inside the Chesapeake and on the Delaware Canal."

    The dictionary definition of bald-headed is, "A term used in connection with various rigs and usually denoting that some of the regular spars and sails are temporarily or permanently absent. When used in connection with a square-rigged ship it denotes that no sails are set above the top-gallants; in a schooner that no topmasts are rigged. Also called bald."

    The ram schooner design was only two years old when the *Levin J. Marvel* slid down the ways, in 1891. Robert H. Burgess described the ram schooner "as homely a vessel as ever cleaved the waters of the Bay. Her cumbersome hull resembled a canal barge. The characteristics of these craft were wall sides, bluff bows, flat bottoms, little sheer, and no topmasts." I disagree with Burgess. Although the hull may be somewhat tublike, the bowsprit and counter stern add a touch of class when the vessel is proceeding under billowing sails. Despite either opinion, the ram schooner design was popular enough on the Chesapeake Bay that twenty-nine of them were built, the last one in 1911.

    One important feature of the design was a beam that was narrow enough to permit the vessel to pass through the Chesapeake and Delaware Canal. This canal connects the Chesapeake Bay with the Delaware Bay. In 1891, the canal was not as wide as it is today. In addition, because of the Albemarle and Chesapeake Canal – which connects the North Landing River in Virginia with the Elizabeth River in North Carolina – small vessels could trade as far north as Trenton, New Jersey (beyond Philadelphia) and as far south as Wilmington, North Carolina, without having to leave inland waters. (These canals eventually became part of the Intracoastal Waterway.)

    Another important design characteristic was the shallow draft. This feature enabled the vessel to navigate farther up Chesapeake Bay tributaries than deep-draft vessels could go. Sleek lines and aesthetic appeal were unnecessary for the kind of labor for which the vessels were intended. They were workhorses, not thoroughbreds.

    Furthermore, because the ram was equipped with a donkey engine for handling the anchor and sails, the vessel could be operated by only three sailors. The low outlay for wages made the vessel economical to operate.

Like the others in her class, the *Levin J. Marvel* was employed in the cargo trade: primarily transporting lumber, coal, and sometimes fertilizer. She sailed along the bay immodestly for the next sixty-four years under a variety of owners and skippers but always with the same name.

No vessel could go for so many years without leaving her mark in the historical record. Here is a sampling of incidents in which the ram schooner was involved.

On December 7, 1904, the *Levin J. Marvel* was being towed from Elizabeth City to Norfolk through the Albemarle and Chesapeake Canal when the tugboat *Nettie* attempted to pass in the Dismal Swamp. The *Nettie* was towing two scows and a barge. One of the scows sheered across the canal and collided with the ram. Neither vessel sank. J.B. Wright, master and part owner, libeled the tug for $529.95 in damages.

In 1906, the skipper of the ram was Irving Houston. April 27 found Houston at the Protestant Hospital in Norfolk with a bullet wound in his right breast. According to his mate, "Houston shot himself while despondent."

There are several references to the *Levin J. Marvel* carrying lumber in the early part of the twentieth century, but by the 1940's she was taking on a completely different kind of cargo: biped livestock on the hoof. In a trade that was referred to disparagingly as the "dude cruise," she engaged in the business of sailing along the Chesapeake Bay with a boatload of tourists who wanted to see the local sights while experiencing a few hours of life before the mast.

From the collection of Mike Moore.

Her longest charter in this regard took place after the close of the Second World War, in the autumn of 1945: 1,271 miles from Baltimore to Miami along the Intracoastal Waterway. The ram was under the command of Captain Marshall Pritchard; he was ably assisted by a mate, a cook, and a steward. Twelve eager passengers were wined and dined in splendor (except for one toddler who, because he was under the legal age for imbibing alcohol, had to suffice with soft drinks. Ironically, one of the passengers was soft-drink executive John Hughes.)

Eagerness soon yielded to anxiety as the vessel encountered one problem after another. A report of the trip described the *Levin J. Marvel* as "the biggest and certainly the clumsiest vessel ever to sail the Inland Waterway's narrow canals and locks. She has no engine and seemed as out of place as a duckbilled platypus in the 20th century. Much of the time was spent getting disentangled from bridges or hauled off mud banks. . . . In a good breeze, with sails close-hauled, the best the *Marvel* could do was about four knots. She went sideways almost as fast. But with a good stiff following wind she would hustle along at eight knots or better. . . . At New River, N.C. the *Marvel* spent most of Thanksgiving Day aground. She managed to get herself off once, but [the] second time she had to be pulled off into deeper water by a Marine crash boat. . . . Altogether she ran aground fifteen times."

This was not an enviable record. The constant delays caused some passengers to "jump ship" because they ran out of vacation time before reaching their destination. The intended two-week passage turned into a thirty-three-day ordeal – and that was only one way! Those who endured the entire trip to Miami "gained five to ten pounds" because the food was so delicious. They needed extra helpings to generate heat against an unseasonable drop in temperature that often went below the freezing mark. Florida greeted them with a snowstorm!

Short Chesapeake Bay cruises were undoubtedly more profitable. June of 1954 found the *Levin J. Marvel* once again under new ownership. H.E. Knust sold his interest in the aging lumber schooner to John Meckling for $18,000. John Thomas Evans retained his portion of ownership. The new company name was called the Chesapeake Windjammer Vacation. The vessel now advertised accommodations for forty passengers.

A month and a half later, Meckling and a crew of eight commenced a summer cruise schedule in which they planned to depart from Annapolis every Monday and make stops at "four or more ports according to the wind and tide." Nine weekly excursions were planned, but on the way to Annapolis to embark passengers for the first cruise of the season, the ram sank on a Wicomico River mud bank. She was eight and a half miles downstream from her port of departure in Salisbury, Maryland.

"The Salisbury fireboat, the *Fred A. Grier*, with a six-man crew headed by Capt. Richard Dana, went to the rescue about 10:30 a.m. yesterday [July 16] after the boat's pumps failed to make any headway against water coming in through seams around the stern.

" 'We pumped for four hours,' Capt. Dana said. But the boat filled again on high tide and the Coast Guard from Crisfield was called in to help. It was about 5:30 p.m. when the Coast Guard cutter arrived with nine men aboard.

"The *Levin J. Marvel* floated on high tide and was towed into White Haven by a work boat, captained by Corrie Wilkerson of Salisbury. He had left here [Salisbury] towing the boat yesterday.

"It is believed the seams in the stern, where the boat began leaking, later swelled, stopping her leaks. The water at times was 12-1/2 feet deep in the cabins.

"Captain William Tawes of Salisbury was in command of the schooner. He was captain of a sister ship, the *Edwin and Maud*, last summer for Chesapeake Bay Cruises. That schooner is operating similar cruises along the northern Maine Coast this summer.

"Captain Tawes said he noticed the boat settling just after he passed the Harcum farm and the only thing he could do was to run her aground in shallow water on the east bank."

Three pumps were put onboard as the ram idled at Brown's Marine Railway in White Haven. These pumps had a combined capacity to eject 1,200 gallons of water per minute. Prospective passengers who were scheduled for the first cruise were notified that their windjammer cruise had been cancelled. On July 24, a 25-foot yawl put her bow to the stern of the ram and began the long push down the Wicomico River and up the bay to Baltimore. The push took three days. Not until the night of July 27 did the ancient ram schooner reach the Booz Marine Railway, where she was hauled out of the water to have her seams caulked and her hull painted.

The *Levin J. Marvel* was back in operation by August 10. On that date she departed Annapolis for a week-long cruise with ten passengers. The remainder of the cruising season went without further hitches.

The 1955 cruising season commenced without the travails of the previous year. Everything was going well for Meckling until August 8. As the *Levin J. Marvel* departed Annapolis with four crewmembers and twenty-three passengers for a six-day cruise, the Coast Guard hoisted flags that signaled small craft advisories along the Chesapeake Bay. A big storm was brewing – not just any storm, but one with a name. This tropical storm was called Hurricane Connie.

The *Levin J. Marvel* was accompanied by a motorboat that could tow the vessel up the confines of rivers where sailing maneuverability was restricted, or on the bay whenever the wind died. The schooner weathered out the worst of the hurricane by remaining dockside in Cambridge, Maryland. Connie's eye did not make landfall, but as the hurricane tracked northward it dropped as much as ten inches of rain on both sides of the Chesapeake Bay; gale-force winds created huge waves in the bay where the fetch was long. Small craft advisories remained in effect after the storm passed northward.

The schooner had a schedule to keep, so after the passing of Connie's eye, the *Levin J. Marvel* slid down the Choptank River, poked her bowsprit into the bay, and proceeded northward for her final port of call. The weather at the time was favorable. By the morning of August 12, however, wind speeds increased to 40 miles per hour out of the northeast, "with gusts of higher velocity." This was the remnant of the hurricane.

The tail of the tempest struck with a fury that the eye didn't possess. The wind was so strong that the schooner couldn't buck it. She was forced to turn around and run before the wind toward Herring Bay, "anchoring at 0930 one and one-half miles to the eastward of Fairhaven. Due to the inability to close defective shipside airports and probable leakage because of the deteriorated state of the hull, the vessel began making water which, as the morning progressed and the weather worsened, got beyond the control of the pumps on board. By 1200 one power bilge pump had failed and the other was ineffective. The radio transmitter on board was inoperative and although efforts were made, signals of distress could not be put on the air and the plight of the *Levin J. Marvel* was unknown to anyone except those on board. By 1400 the wind was north-northeast, force 7 to 8, squally, overcast, with very rough sea. The uncontrolled ingress of water caused the bow of the vessel to lose buoyancy and become awash, and the persons on board gathered aft in preparation to abandon ship. At 1430 the vessel rolled heavily, lay over on her beam, and foundered. There being no lifesaving equipment on board and the accompanying motorboat having been previously lost, the passengers and crew were forced to enter the water with jacket-type life preservers and the floating wreckage as their only means of survival. Fourteen passengers perished and nine passengers and all four crew members survived."

This official Coast Guard summary was all too succinct: strictly factual without any attempt to portray the human drama. This was where newspaper accounts took up the slack. The miracle of the situation was that *anyone* survived after jumping overboard into tempestuous seas.

John Meckling, the skipper, was one of the lucky survivors: "The water started coming in over the deck . . . quicker than we could pump it out. A big wave came along and laid the boat on its side."

Passenger Nancy Madden praised Meckling for saving her life: "I was just preparing to leave the ship. We were evacuating the ship. But I couldn't make any headway at all. The captain got me and shoved me over near the ship so I could hold on. There was a lot of confusion. I never heard even one person call out for help. The captain collected a bunch of us together. I would never even see them, but he would get them. The captain just prayed out loud. We were in a circle holding hands. I'm sure the fact that we were together helped us."

Separated from the rest and left on her own, passenger Margaret Deborah Killip was the first survivor to make it to shore. She alerted a local resident who called Barrack H of the Maryland State Police. This was the first notice of the casualty that anyone ashore received.

People who assisted in subsequent rescue operations were police, National Guardsmen, firefighters, and local residents. "Members from Deale and North Beach Volunteer Fire Departments, braved gale force winds, and high treacherous seas, risking their lives in small boats to rescue as many passengers off the doomed ship as possible."

The survivors drifted through tumultuous seas for as long as eight hours This brief observation does nothing to describe the harrowing experience of drifting in the water for a third of a day, struggling to stay afloat, never knowing if you were going to survive. Some survivors remained adrift after darkness fell. Imagine what it must have been like to have six-foot waves splashing over your head for a period of time that must have seemed interminable. Remember that fourteen people drowned under these same dreadful circumstances.

As they passed a point of land, Meckling grabbed onto a disintegrating duck blind. Madden: "The captain personally got us into the duck blind, how I'll never know because he had had terrible cramps. But he stood up there and pulled us in. . . . I think the captain did everything he could."

According to another description, deck hand Stephen Morton "and five others, all lashed together, made it to a duck blind a mile downwind and 200 yards offshore." These six survivors were rescued "by two men who went down to the beach 'to see if we could lend a hand' and stayed to ferry them two at a time in a 14-foot skiff through waves as high as a man." Morton was a 17-year-old high school senior. The two rescuers were volunteer firefighters George Kellum and William McWilliams. They received commendations for their heroism.

Other survivors drifted to shore one by one, very much the worse for wear.

Four days passed before all the bodies were recovered.

In the aftermath of the catastrophe and the consequent investigation, the Coast Guard bemoaned the fact that they did not have the authority to conduct safety inspections on sailing vessels under 700 tons, and to prevent such vessels from carrying passengers if they deemed the vessel to be unsafe. The *Levin J. Marvel* was documented as a "freight vessel for the coasting trade." The Coast Guard "tried without success last summer to make John Meckling, owner of the schooner, discontinue using it as a vacation cruiser around Chesapeake Bay."

The Coast Guard called passengers, crewmembers, and other parties to testify during the three-day investigative hearing that was held a week after the incident. Testimony disclosed several functional deficiencies with the ram, particularly with some of the twenty-two portholes "which were located below the main deck in the messroom, cabins and toilets." The crew was successful in closing some, but "a large number of them had dogs missing, latch bolts frozen, or both, or were warped, all of which factors precluded the portlights' being watertight. . . . large quantities of water entered the hull through the defective portlights."

One of the gasoline-driven bilge pumps was "carried down into the dining room and put into operation, but this proved unsuccessful due to the fact that the debris in the space concerned repeatedly clogged the suction."

Nancy Madden averred that she heard the radio in operation prior to the emergency. Yet when Meckling transmitted a call for help, the Coast Guard did not intercept his transmission, leading them to believe that the radio was not operational.

The Coast Guard called attention to the fact that the *Levin J. Marvel* was an uninspected vessel, yet was advertised as meeting "all requirements of maritime safety and standards."

The vessel "was not equipped with any lifeboats, life rafts, life floats or other lifesaving devices except for life preservers and a few rubber play rafts." The latter were used for watersport and for swimming.

Most damning of all, "Neither the Master nor any of the crew members possessed any license, validated Merchant Mariner's Document or Port Security Card issued by the U.S. Coast Guard. . . . The crew of the vessel was not adequate to operate the vessel with safety. . . . The vessel did not carry a proper lookout as required by Article 29 of the Rules of the Road." In layman's terms, the Coast Guard castigated the *Levin J. Marvel* cruises as fly-by-night or seat-of-the-pants operations.

Furthermore, "Portions of the wreckage which were recovered indicate an excessive amount of rot in structural members of the vessel."

In conclusion, "The casualty was directly caused by the unseaworthy condition of the *Levin J. Marvel*. . . . The unseaworthiness was due to the poor physical condition of the essential hull structures and fittings, which had been neglected by the managing owner.... A contributing cause was the poor judgment used by Mr. Meckling in taking his vessel from a safe mooring in the face of known bad-weather warnings....

"In spite of directives issued by the Coast Guard setting forth conditions with which the vessel must comply to be exempt from inspection, the Master continued to operate contrary to said directives by propelling his vessel with the yawl boat as an auxiliary means of propulsion, thus removing the *Marvel* from the category of 'uninspected sailing vessel.'..."

"The responsible owners resorted to misleading and false advertising by implying that the vessel met requirements of safety standards, such standards being in fact nonexistent."

The Coast Guard deliberated for five months before issuing the final report, on January 24, 1956. Their recommendations were severe. They recommended that "this case be referred to the U.S. Attorney General for prosecution."

In the meantime, some newspapers riled public sentiment by publishing unsubstantiated "facts" – or pseudofacts – about the condition of the schooner, claiming, for example, that she was "breaking up fast" when the passengers and crew abandoned ship; that she had been "pounded to bits" or "pounded to pieces;" and making statements such as, "There was nothing left of the boat, the *Levin J. Marvel* out of Annapolis, Md., except a fragment of her cabin and debris which littered the spongy sand." An unnamed police officer was "quoted" as stating, "I didn't see a bit of wreckage bigger than a door."

Such slanted comments and constant reiteration of the number of fatalities (which included two children aged 9 and 13) did much to alienate Meckling in the public eye. Nowhere – not once – was it suggested that the loss of the schooner could have been an "act of God;" that perhaps she had been overwhelmed by circumstances that were beyond human control. There was no doubt that the unfortunate loss of life was a terrible tragedy. Right from the beginning, there was little to no doubt that the press was making Meckling the scapegoat for the tragedy.

In his defense, Meckling claimed that the radio *was* in fact operational, and that his SOS was intercepted by a "Mr. Marshall," even if the Coast Guard failed to intercept it. He sent the SOS at 1 p.m., when the schooner's anchor first started to drag. The *Levin J. Marvel* did not sink until three hours later. Had the Coast Guard been monitoring their radios, they would have intercepted his call for help, and could have dispatched a cutter to save everyone onboard before the schooner rolled over onto her side.

In this light, it might seem to some that the Coast Guard had a vested interest in casting blame on Meckling, in order to cover up its own deficiencies.

In its report – which was not released until January 24, 1956 – the Coast Guard wrote, "Although testimony was given to the effect that a Mr. Marshall received a 'May Day' message, the Board is unable to locate such a Mr. Marshall, supposed to be an amateur radio operator in the North Beach, Md., area; and that, upon contacting the Federal Communications Commission, it was learned that they had no record of such an amateur station."

This condemnation made it appear that Meckling had lied in order to save his reputation. This did not endear him to the members of the investigative board. They raked him over the coals despite the grudging admission that when he departed Cambridge on the penultimate day, despite the forecast that the meandering hurricane might impact the Chesapeake Bay, the weather was "fine and clear with a gentle northeasterly breeze, slight sea and swell" when the *Levin J. Marvel* entered the broad waters of the bay.

The public was further piqued by another Chesapeake Bay shipping loss: *La Forrest L. Simmons* sank on the same day on which the *Levin J. Marvel* was lost, although without loss of life.

At the same time, newspapers were rife with articles and editorials that bemoaned the inadequacy of boating laws that were designed to protect a naïve and unsuspecting public. Each of these pieces mentioned the loss of the *Levin J. Marvel* as a prime example of the need for strengthening such laws or passing new ones. More blame accrued to Meckling by this censure than accrued to the lawmaking system that was ultimately responsible for the legal shortfalls. Each heap of additional censure attacked Meckling by means of collateral damage.

As soon as the Coast Guard released its report, Meckling was called to testify before the House Merchant Marine Committee. The salient point that the Committee wanted addressed was the state of the schooner's hull rot. This stemmed from the testimony of Elias Bartholow, the manager of the Booz Marine Railway, where the *Levin J. Marvel* was repaired after she ran aground in the Wicomico River in 1954.

Bartholow testified to the Coast Guard board, "Her seams were very slack and she needed caulking very badly. What we did as a temporary job was satisfactory. There was a lot that needed to be done." He added his opinion, "I think in fair weather she would have been fine. But I wouldn't have wanted to be out in the bay in her in bad weather."

This may have been precisely what the Coast Guard wanted to hear, and what it wanted to have leaked to the newspapers for sensationalizing. Yet cooler heads would have seen through the cover-up that Booz charged Meckling $4,490 for repair work which the company representative now admitted under oath was substandard. If the Coast Guard wanted Congress to grant the agency greater control over small-boat activities – by itself not a dishonest aspiration – then using the loss of the *Levin J. Marvel* was a means to an end, but one that ensured that Meckling would receive short shrift in the process.

After a day-long session on February 7, 1956, Meckling was indicted by a federal grand jury on charges of (1) misconduct, negligence and inattention to duty, and (2) operating a vessel in a reckless or negligent manner so as to endanger the lives and property of passengers and crew. "Conviction on the first charge carries a maximum penalty of 10 years imprisonment and $10,000 in fines. The second offense is punishable by one year in prison and a fine of $2,000."

Meckling was released on bail of $2,500.

Before Meckling came up for trial, local public sentiment was well roused against him. His attorneys initially sought a change of venue on the basis that bad press from bay area newspapers made it impossible for Meckling to receive a fair trial in Maryland, whose prospective jurors were likely to associate Meckling with nonexistent boating laws, and possibly to blame him for the very nonexistence of such laws. They thought that he could get a fairer jury trial in Pittsburgh, Pennsylvania.

His attorneys also requested a trial without a jury. This petition was based on the premise that a judge could be non-prejudicial with regard to published Coast Guard conclusions that were reached without full disclosure of the facts. When federal court judge Dorsey Watkins agreed to hear the case without a jury, Meckling's attorneys dropped their plea for a change of venue.

Meckling's best defense was that the *Levin J. Marvel* had not violated any laws that were then in existence, and that the conditions under which the schooner sailed on the fateful day were ideal for sailing. After all, a sailing schooner cannot sail without adequate wind. The prosecution went after Meckling rather than his vessel, claiming that he knew that the vessel was in defective condition and was ill equipped.

Whereas the prosecution relied heavily on Coast Guard "findings," the defense was able to contradict their so-called conclusions. For example, the Coast Guard claimed the Meckling did not have a barometer onboard. Meckling proved that he did.

One of the prosecution's witnesses was Elias Bartholow. He repeated his previous testimony, adding that the schooner's hull was excessively hogged, meaning that the bow and stern drooped so that the midship had a hump. "Can you imagine how weak she must have been?" Bartholow asked.

Defense attorney Harry Katz demanded to know why the shipyard did not "communicate that information to the Coast Guard."

In his eagerness to castigate Meckling, Bartholow put himself on the spot. He impugned his own character by replying, "It's not my business."

Passenger Harry Nathanson testified that he had been on two *Levin J. Marvel* cruises prior to surviving the one in which the schooner was lost. He stated that the vessel was "ill kempt, old and beaten up compared with the other two times." Yet he did not refuse to go on the cruise.

Nathanson stated that the anchor snagged on piles while docking and "pulled several planks apart so that some rotten timbers in the ship's hull were exposed." Still he did not disembark.

Meckling countered that although there was some rot on deck planks, there was no rot on hull timbers (which, in any case, Booz Marine Railway was supposed to have replaced for the money that Meckling paid.)

Cambridge city dockmaster Paul Herman testified that the warning flag was flying when the *Levin J. Marvel* left the dock. U.S. Weather Bureau forecaster Herbert Alkire countered this assertion by stating that the hurricane alert was cancelled an hour prior to that time. He stated furthermore that a hurricane "alert" meant "only that the public should pay sharp attention to weather forecasts in case a hurricane warning is actually called." He confirmed Meckling's contention that the *actual* forecast called for winds of 15 to 25 miles per hours. This was not adverse weather for a sailing vessel.

Passenger Perry Schwartz was an electrical engineer. He testified that when he examined the radio after Meckling began broadcasting his call for assistance, he found that the shaft of the tuning knob was corroded and that wires were "just twisted" together. It was his opinion that either there was no antenna or no power for transmitting. Voices could be heard on the receiver, but there was no indication that Meckling's emergency call was received.

Meckling countered this assertion in two ways. First, he stated that he left the tuning knob in one place after he had the transmitter properly tuned, then deliberately loosened the set screw in the knob so that passengers could not change the tuning.

Second, he produced a surprise witness: one 19-year-old Thomas Marshall, who testified that he intercepted the *Levin J. Marvel's* distress call on the short wave band of his radio at home in Deale, Maryland, at 1 p.m. on the day of her loss – just as Meckling had told the Coast Guard investigation board. Deale was located some fifty miles from the spot where the schooner foundered. He told his parents that he clearly heard the name, but did not notify authorities because the signal was so "loud and clear" that he thought that everyone must have heard it, including the Coast Guard. He chose not to interfere by cluttering the radio waves any more than acknowledging interception.

This must certainly have put egg on the Coast Guard's face for not intercepting Meckling's SOS and responding to an emergency in which fourteen persons including two juveniles lost their lives.

Passenger Nanette Lee testified that she overheard the forecast over Meckling's radio prior to passing into open water. She and another passenger urged Meckling to proceed by saying, "Come on. Let's go." Despite their enthusiasm, Meckling demurred until he heard a later and more favorable forecast.

Nancy Madden reiterated her view that Meckling was responsible for saving her life, and did everything in his power to save the lives of the other passengers. "He seemed to have superhuman strength to get around."

Finally, to put paid to unseen presumptions that the schooner's hull was rotten, William Verge testified that he and his partner Steve MacDougald had intended to purchase the *Levin J. Marvel* on August 13 – the day after she was supposed to complete her cruise by docking at Annapolis. Verge had been a deckhand on the ram. According to him, the sails were in good shape, the pumps operated smoothly, and the portholes opened and closed readily.

Furthermore, in anticipation of purchasing the ram, he personally donned diving gear and examined the hull below the waterline. He tried to pierce the hull timbers with an ice pick, "but broke the pick." This put paid to spurious allegations of rot. Thus ended a week of contradictory testimony.

After both sides rested their cases, Judge Watkins asked Meckling why he did not release the anchors in order to let the schooner drift closer to shore. Meckling replied that the situation shifted so fast from "not in immediate trouble" to "in extremis" that when he recognized the latter condition, the foredeck was under several feet of water. At that time his priority was getting his passengers and crew to don life vests.

After a fortnight of deliberation, on June 5, 1956, the judge found Meckling innocent of the most serious charge of "negligent to the point of *causing* loss of life and property." He found Meckling guilty of the lesser charge of "negligence so as to *endanger* life and property." He gave Meckling a one year suspended sentence and did not impose any fine.

A conspiracy theorist might declare that the Coast Guard altered or obfuscated its findings because it had an axe to grind against Meckling, especially as he had ignored Coast Guard captain Alfred Kabernagel's 1954 suggestion that he retire the schooner and go out of business. One might also declare that the Coast Guard suppressed crucial evidence in order to make its point. At the very least one could declare that the Coast Guard inquiry established prejudice against uncontrolled pleasure boating.

Meckling's case is perhaps classic in that it underscores the truism that partial truths often lead to erroneous conclusions. Listening to *all* the witnesses and entering *all* the facts is the only fair way to conduct a trial. Judge Watkins found that Meckling's decision to proceed despite inconsistent storm warnings was merely a "calculated risk," not a criminally negligent act.

More long-reaching was the Coast Guard recommendation that "Legislation be sought placing all boats, and vessels, of any type, size or means of propulsion which carry one or more passengers for hire, under Federal inspection." Long before Meckling's trial ended – indeed, even before it started – the gears were set in motion to propose such legislation.

The Coast Guard's damning findings, conclusions, and recommendations, along with the hue and cry of constituents who deplored the inexcusable loss of life, first reached the ears of local county commissioners in Maryland, then ascended the political hierarchy to Congressional representatives who for once decided to take action – perhaps not immediate action, but action that was as fast as Congress could take, in consideration of the complexity of the laws to be enacted.

The *Levin J. Marvel* was not the sole marine casualty that was responsible for the drafting of small-boat safety legislation, but it certainly was the final straw that led to its proposal and passage. Previous losses that were cited were the *Pelican* (45 lives lost) and the *Jack* (11 lives lost); both losses occurred off Montauk Point, New York in 1951.

According to an editorial in 1956, "Proposed new regulations for safety inspection of more than 3,000 excursion boats will be published by the Coast Guard in about three weeks, it was learned today.

"Inspection is required by a new law which Congress passed in the wake of a pleasure boat disaster on Chesapeake Bay last summer, which cost the lives of 14 vacationers.

"There will be no inspections under the law this year, and probably none before July 1. Officials hope to have funds for an inspection force by that time.

"The new law covers vessels not previously subject to examination. If they carry more than six passengers for hire. They are chiefly party fishing motorboats, excursion sailboats and ferry barges."

This editorial was more hopeful than practical; it jumped the gun by a couple of years. Stopgap bills and resolutions were enacted, the first of which was signed by President Dwight Eisenhower on May 19, 1956. It left a lot to be desired, but it was at least a step in the right direction.

There was a lot of wrangling in Congress before strict safety regulations could be imposed on the passenger vessel industry that objected to being regulated. The chief Congressional wrangler was Herbert Bonner of North Carolina. He helped to draft the first comprehensive legislation, and he was the loudest spokesperson for its passage. Because of his initiative, the Federal Boating Act of 1958 came to be known as the Bonner Act.

The Coast Guard was tasked with overall supervision and enforcement of the Act, and was handed the job of conducting vessel examinations on more than *one hundred thousand* small boats. The transition did not go smoothly because Congress, in its all-too-common lack of wisdom and foresight, neglected to provide funding for hiring new Coast Guard personnel, for training examiners, and for paying their wages. The Act languished until the Capitol made up the capital deficit.

Since then the Federal Boating Act has been amended a number of times as deficiencies were uncovered. More restrictive legislation led to the Federal Boat Safety Act of 1971. This Act addressed small-boat construction and safety standards, particularly the requirement for a collision bulkhead and additional compartmentalization. The latter Act was a tough Act to follow because more examiners had to be hired and trained in order to oversee every stage of a vessel's construction. But it was done, and done well, so that present-day passengers are safer than they have ever been in the history of boating.

Today, thanks to the loss of the *Levin J. Marvel*, every boat that carries more than six paying passengers – sightseers, whale watchers, anglers, divers, and so on – must prominently display a Coast Guard certification on an interior partition.

On March 15, 1956, the U.S. Army Corps of Engineers investigated the wreck site. Their examination "reveals wreck has broken up and 16 ft. is over wreck at MLW [mean low water]. Wreck not considered an 'unreasonable' menace to general navigation and removal is in the interests of navigation not considered necessary."

In 1987, the NOAA survey vessel *Heck* put divers on the wreck. The maximum depth was recorded by pneumatic depth gauge to be 22 feet. They found the wreck "to be in latter stages of decomposition but, hull ribbing and planking could be distinguished on several large pieces of the vessel. Several porcelain sinks with brass plumbing were also found. The least depth was taken on the remains of an interior bulkhead protruding approximately 6 to 8 feet above the bottom."

According to the survey recommendation, "The location and physical description of the wreck found by ship's divers confirms [sic] its identification as the schooner *Levin J Marvel*. It is recommended that the charted wreck symbol be annotated 'PA [position approximate] 17 ft. reported 1963'."

A 1998 side-scan sonar survey determined that the least depth over the wreck had not changed. The wreck symbol is still shown unchanged on the chart.

From the collection of Mike Moore

MARY A. DeKNIGHT

Built: ?
Previous names: ?
Gross tonnage: ?
Type of vessel: Schooner
Builder: ?
Owner: ?
Port of registry: New Jersey
Cause of sinking: Foundered
Location: Kent Island, opposite Annapolis

Sunk: April 3, 1879
Depth: 95 feet
Dimensions: 150' x 23' x 7'
Power: Sail

GPS: 38-56-27.57 / 76-23-11.89

Not every vessel possesses a fascinating history, or sinks under mysterious or dramatic circumstances, or is attended by great loss of life, or measures large enough to attract the interest of news hounds, or garners investigation by government authorities. Like the death of a homeless person, some vessels simply fade away: condemned by a cloak of virtual anonymity. The *Mary A. DeKnight* was one such vessel.

She received short shrift in local newspapers: a single sentence that read, "The schooner *Mary A. DeKnight*, of New Jersey, was capsized in the Chesapeake Bay, and the Captain, Howard Hagar, and crew were drowned."

Although the item might not have been newsworthy, it was certainly of ultimate importance to those who died in what to them was a monumental catastrophe; and to those loved ones who missed them sorely.

A weekly maritime newspaper added a tad more detail: "Mary A De Knight (of New Jersey), was capsized in the Chesapeake Bay on April 3d, and the captain - Howard Hagar - and crew consisting of Sandford Fobbings and Samuel Bass of New Jersey, and John Johnson, of Wilmington, Del, drowned. She capsized about thirty miles south of Baltimore, while bound for Annapolis."

Skip one hundred eighteen years to this slender notice on the AWOIS list: "Investigation of wreck. GAI Consultants surveyed this item for the Maryland Port Administration. Believed to be the wreck of *Mary A. DeKnight*."

Despite the paucity of information concerning the circumstances of loss, I include the wreck here – sandwiched between two chapters of far greater historical interest – in order to bring it to the attention of recreational divers who seek new and interesting sites to explore: qualities which the *Levin J. Marvel* and the *Medora* seriously lack. The wreck lies only half a mile from the *Herbert D. Maxwell*. Check it out.

MEDORA

Built: 1842
Previous names: None
Gross tonnage: 394
Type of vessel: Wooden-hulled side-wheel steamer
Builder: Virginia and Maryland Steamboat Navigation Company, Baltimore, Maryland
Owner: Baltimore Steam Packet Company (Old Bay Line), Baltimore, Maryland
Port of registry: Baltimore, Maryland
Cause of sinking: Boiler explosion
Location: Baltimore Harbor

Sunk: April 14, 1842
Depth: Not applicable
Dimensions: 180' x 23' x 9'
Power: Wood-fired steam

In one sense it can be said that the *Medora* had the shortest time in service of any vessel in history. In another sense it can be said that she had one of the longest.

In the history of ocean navigation, several vessels are known to have been sunk on their maiden voyage. The freighter *Washingtonian* first comes to mind, not only because of her proximity to the *Medora* (about 100 miles), but because I covered her collision with the schooner *Elizabeth Palmer* in *Shipwrecks of Delaware and Maryland*. Another is the Liberty Ship *John Morgan*, which I covered in *Shipwrecks of Virginia*; in the same book I wrote about the battleship *Washington*, whose construction was halted prior to completion, and whose sleek new hull was then towed offshore and scuttled without ever being commissioned into the U.S. Navy.

A number of German U-boats were lost on their first war patrol in both world wars. I covered some of these in *The Kaiser's U-boats in American Waters* and *The Fuhrer's U-boats in American Waters*. Such first-patrol losses were not uncommon in light of the massive number of Allied warships that were actively seeking to sink by any means such world-domination warmongers that intentionally put themselves in harm's way.

Everyone over the age of four knows about the *Titanic* striking an iceberg because her stubborn skipper refused to reduce the speed of his vessel after he was warned about a nearby ice field.

The popular perception may be that the shortest cruise ever taken was that of the warship *Vasa*. Only minutes after her departure, and only a mile from her dock in Sweden, she foundered precipitately when a strong gust of wind blew her over. The date was August 10, 1628.

Yet when it comes to the length of a maiden voyage, the *Medora* beats them all. She blew up and sank without ever leaving the dock!

The side-wheel steamer *Medora* was built specifically to transport freight and passengers along the Chesapeake Bay and its tributaries. On the day after her eagerly anticipated first departure – April 15, 1842 – the following article appeared in the *Baltimore Sun* under the headline AWFUL DISASTER! EXPLOSION OF THE STEAMBOAT MEDORA!:

"Great Loss of Life!! One of the most melancholy occurrences with which our city has for a long time been visited, took place yesterday afternoon, at about half past two o'clock – an occurrence which sent a thrill of horror through the general heart, and carried the woe consequent on violent and unexpected death, into the bosoms of many families.

"The steamboat *Medora*, recently built by the Virginia and Maryland Steam Navigation Company, and intended to ply between this city and Norfolk, was about to leave Cully's Wharf upon an excursion down the bay, for the purpose of testing its qualities. A number of respectable citizens were invited to witness her performance; but how many were actually on board when the heart-rending occurrence of her explosion took place, we have, as yet, no means of ascertaining.

"All things, however, being prepared for her departure, the bell rung and the [paddle] wheels made three revolutions, when the boiler burst with a tremendous report, throwing up clouds of vapor, attended by fragments of the vessel and by the bodies of unfortunate human beings who were on board – the whole presenting to the spectators a scene of indescribable and terrific sublimity.

"As the smoke cleared away, the effects of the calamity became visible. The vessel was made, in an instant, an entire wreck – all her timbers, from the engine forward, being rent away. She sank immediately to her guards, and now lies 'a sheer hulk' in the basin.

"Hundreds of persons on the wharf, at the time, displayed the utmost alacrity in rescuing from the water the dead and dying. News of the disaster soon brought a large number of persons to the spot, agitated by the dread of finding relatives or friends involved in the calamity, and among the rest, many mothers, who told, by their tears and cries, the fearful apprehensions they entertained for the safety of their children. Their fate was, from the circumstances of the case, a mystery, and this idea created, for a short time, a scene of unutterable agony and terror.

"Immediately after the occurrence, the mayor of the city, Solomon Hillen, Esq., and the high constable, together with the police of the city, arrived, and were actively engaged in assisting, by every possible means, the wretched survivors, or in searching for those who had sunk into the water unnoticed, or were yet in the cabin of the boat.

"Simultaneously with their arrival, a large number of surgeons and physicians also arrived, ready to exert their professional skill. In addition to others whose names we have not learned, we noticed Doctors Miller, Smith, Whitridge, Hintze, Monkur, McGuire, Dunbar, Riley, Kinneman, Albers, Baker, the two Doctors Riche, and the two Doctors Roberts.

"Under the circumstances, and in the absence of any investigation, it is of course impossible to say what was the direct and immediate cause of this fatal calamity. It is generally supposed, however, that as the boat had been some time ready for departure and the steam up, that the boiler must have been nearly exhausted, and had become hot, and that in this state water was turned in; it is certain that at the moment of the explosion, steam was letting off with constant force.

"A gentleman who witnessed the event from the deck of the *Georgia*, directly opposite, remarks that a dense smoke for an instant obscured the immediate part of the boat at which the explosion took place, and as the report which, though as loud as a small field piece, had a dull and heavy sound, reached the ear, the smoke stack was seen darting like an arrow out of the cloud a hundred feet into the air, and on each side were thrown the bodies of human beings with the arms and legs extended by their whirling motion through the air.

"The *Medora*, at the moment, was immediately abaft of the steamboat *Constitution*, and almost in contact with her, a fact which it is necessary to name as explanatory of several circumstances detailed below. We annex a list of the persons killed and wounded, the latter either suffering from contusion, fracture or scalding."

What followed was a list of victims and the manner in which they had been injured or killed. For instance, John Vickers "was blown from the boat completely over the stern of the *Constitution*, and fell on the wharf; he was taken up dead, his head being awfully fractured."

John Speedy "was thrown on board the *Constitution*, and fell upon a stout handrail, which was broken in two; the scalp of his head was cut in three or four directions from the crown, each cut being as many inches in length. He suffered, in a state of apparent insensibility for about an hour, when he was removed, but died before he reached his residence. He leaves a wife and two children."

John Young "was taken out of the water from a piece of the wreck, one or two of his limbs were fractured, and he was so much hurt internally, that he died at the house to which he was taken, within a couple of hours. He leaves a wife and child."

Benjamin French "was so much hurt and scalded that he died within an hour after the accident."

"The body of John Harper, the second mate, was dragged from the fore part of the *Medora*, which was gunwale down, a short time before night."

"A man named Hoofnagle was thrown by the explosion on board the *Constitution*, but escaped uninjured. Thomas Wildley, Esq., was on board the *Medora*, but stood aft, his hat was blown off, but he sustained no injury."

As always, the difference between who lived and who died, between who was injured and who escape injury, was a matter of chance. To ascribe this agency of luck, the newspaper credited "the inscrutable hand of a mysterious Providence."

Samuel Boone was one of the luckiest. He was standing on the deck above the boiler when the explosion occurred. He was flung some fifty feet into the air, "among the flying fragments of the shattered boat. He fell in the water 30 or 40 yards from the boat, and sunk to the bottom; then raising under a part of the deck, he with difficulty found his way out the edge, by means of a cabin. He then assisted an unfortunate sufferer to get on the floating fragment, in company with two others, who were all taken off by a boat. After remaining awhile on the wharf, surveying the heart-rending scene, he was landed on the north side of the basin, and assisted by a friend to his boarding house. He received only a few bruises and scratches, was scalded a little about the arms and face, and on Saturday night was able to visit his employer, complaining however of soreness in the right thigh and shoulders."

The number of people who were onboard at the time of the explosion was estimated to have been between fifty and one hundred.

Later it was reported that John Speedy had made a miraculous recovery: he was quite literally raised from the dead.

The next day the mayor posted the following notice: "One Hundred Men Wanted.– In consequence of the dreadful accident that happened to the steamboat *Medora*, on last evening, one hundred men are wanted, to clear away the wreck of said boat, and collect the bodies of our citizens that are now missing."

In those days, when government agencies had not yet reached the stage at which

From *Dixon's Letter*.

paid personnel were permanently employed to provide emergency services, catastrophes such as this relied upon volunteers to aid those in distress. The injured were cared for in private homes instead of in hospitals. Neighbors helped by furnishing food and drink to survivors. These Good Samaritans did the work that is done today by police, fire fighters, and medical technicians. On the other hand, there was no federal income tax to provide money for government services.

Generosity was the watchword. "The residents in the vicinity exerted their utmost efforts for the comfort of the wounded, and did all they were able to render proper respect to the unfortunate dead. The houses were opened freely, and attention was bestowed without stint. Indeed too much praise cannot be awarded to the householders for the great and unwearied application to the relief of all."

The gruesome task of extricating bodies from the wreckage continued for several days. The list of the deceased grew longer as more bodies were recovered and as seriously scalded or injured victims succumbed to pain and mutilation.

"The most affecting, though not the most startling part of such tragedies as that which it has pained us to record for two days past, is to be found in the funerals of the deceased. The friends of the departed are there – the relatives – the widow it may be, and the orphan children, or the bereaved parents, or altogether; and all prepared to take a last look at the beloved deceased, untimely snatched from the embrace of their affections, and consign him to the last earthly home appointed to man.

"Many circumstances combine to render the scene deeply affecting. We are shocked at the violent death, we are melted and solemnized at the funeral; and if we visit the late residence of the deceased, and witness the effect of the sudden bereavement of the survivors – but here we pause; we may not draw aside the curtain, and expose to the public the scene sacred to such grief, such unutterable woe and misery, as we witnessed yesterday – the young widow and her only child, just old enough to articulate its father's name, and to ask for him repeatedly; and while too young to understand what death is, yet sufficiently old to pierce its mother's heart with inquiries, which it were next to death to answer."

Modern day reporters do not write such exquisite and emotional prose.

"Yesterday afternoon, the bodies of George Enly and Robert Doyle, two of the persons killed by the explosion of the *Medora*, were interred in the Methodist burying ground on Light street, Federal Hill, the Rev. Mr. Guest officiating on the occasion. The deep interest excited by the disastrous occurrence which caused their death, was evinced by the presence in Light street of about ten thousand persons, of all ages and both sexes, merely as spectators of the funeral procession, which was itself composed of some two or three thousand persons. The deceased were both members of the Watchman Fire Company, and in addition to their personal friends, immediate relatives and near connexions, they were attended to the grave by thirteen fire companies, the members of which, on very short notice, turned out in large numbers, most of them with banners, and accompanied by a band of music, together with the music of the United States recruiting party, under Sergeant Twist."

So much has American society changed in the last one hundred seventy years that I can hardly imagine so many people turning out today for a funeral of less than Presidential proportions. Even if that many citizens were concerned about the demise of a pair of firemen, they are more likely to watch a procession on television in the comfort of their temperature-controlled homes. This sentiment does not necessarily reflect indifference; it merely demonstrates the cultural transformations that have accrued as a result of technological progress.

The mayor convened an inquest two days after the catastrophe. Today such an investigation would be held in a fancy courtroom, but in those days official procedure was much less formal – although the undertaking was *not* less serious. The inquest was held in the house of the mother of one of the deceased: John Boon. Coroner William Rice presided over the proceedings. Twelve male jurors were selected to ask questions and listen to testimony. The purpose of the inquest was to determine the cause of the explosion. No one doubted that the boiler exploded; unknown were how and why.

The first witness to be sworn in was John Watchman. He was the proprietor of the Watchman Fire Company, the outfit that built the engine. He was onboard the *Medora* at the time of the explosion. According to Watchman, steam was raised and the engine turned over five days prior to the *Medora's* planned departure. "She worked well with 30 inches of steam on, and on Wednesday evening [the day before departure] for about an hour, with 27 inches; and as they did not intend to work her with no more than 25 inches, he felt satisfied that all was safe" for the *Medora's* trial run the following day.

(Note that in this instance "inches" refers to engineering shorthand for "pounds per square inch," or p.s.i., a unit of pressure.)

"At three o'clock in the afternoon, Andrew Henderson, president of the Baltimore and Norfolk Steam Packet Company, boarded the *Medora* half an hour before her planned departure. He took charge of inspecting the machinery. He gave the order to "put down the damper to prevent the steam from being raised too high, they not being yet ready to start. He then made the necessary examination, and found that there were but about 10 inches of steam on, and deemed all right. Soon after he came on board, he tried to raise the safety valve, but found it too heavy; he could not raise it, and thinking the chord might have slipped off the pulley, he examined and found it had not. On trial of the cocks, the third included, he found plenty of water; he then tried the fourth, or steam cock, and thought the steam was too high; he then went round to the boiler to [Duncan] Ferguson [an engineer in Watchman's employ], who told him there were but 22 inches on. In answer to a question, he said that he would not, under ordinary circumstances, have been afraid of fifty inches.

"By reason of a crowd around the engine, he [Watchman] was unable to approach sufficiently near to see the steam gauge; but having confidence in Ferguson, he turned to go aft, though not exactly at ease in his mind." At this point Watchman went aft to obtain some paper on which 'to time the boat.' He had nearly reached the lady's cabin 'when the explosion took place, which felt to him like a gust of wind, and knocked him down against the cabin.'"

Watchman "thought it singular that he could not raise the valve. It had been regulated to be raised by the steam at 27 inches – would bear 45 and he would not be afraid of 50. He was, however, satisfied that there must have been much more than that on her; that there must have been some tampering with the safety valve, seeing she lifted the night before with 27 inches. An extra weight might have been put on the lever, or it might have been fastened so as to prevent the raising of the valve, which would cause an explosion. He believes the valve must have been in some way tampered with. . . . His impression is that there must have been a pressure of more than sixty, as much perhaps as one hundred, to have burst her. He was satisfied there was plenty of water, and that the explosion was caused by an influx of cold water. She had made but one and a half or two revolutions, and this could have thrown in but a very small quantity by the force pump, not enough to do any injury with so much water as was then in the boiler.

"Whoever may have tampered with the valve, did not properly know the consequences that must ensue; it might have been done by some of the men, from an ambitious desire to show up the speed of the boat to do the best advantage, without any design to do mischief. Witness stated that [Samuel] Smith [ship's carpenter], who was too severely injured to be present, informed him that while standing near, he saw the gauge stick run suddenly up to the upper deck, when he, being frightened, instantly turned and ran, and the explosion immediately occurred."

The next witness the coroner called was Gideon Brown. He was part owner of Brown & Collyer, the outfit that built the boiler. When he boarded the *Medora* at 3 o'clock, "there was then very little fire. He examined the boiler with a view to discover leakage, if any, but could find none; [he] opened the fire doors and saw but a few sticks of wood in, and at that time there was less than three inches of steam on – not so much – the gauge showed less. Ferguson ordered a light fire to be made, which was done. He examined the third cock, and found plenty of water and also saw Mr. Watchman do the same. Mr. [John] Moale [steamboat company agent] came on board but a few minutes before the explosion. Witness examined the fourth steam cock, and thought there was not then much steam on; and from the appearance of the boiler, when he made his examination, but for the heat 'he wouldn't have been afraid to go to sleep on it.' . . .

"He thinks and will always think, that there was some tampering by someone who had no business there. When the water is heated, steam generates very rapidly. Fifteen minutes before the explosion there was but very little fire; more was made by Ferguson's order; witness saw it done, and one of the men remarked that she burned wood very fast. The witness described the construction of the boiler, especially as to its braces, with much minuteness, and with a readiness and facility that proved him a perfect master of this subject. He showed that it was braced fore and aft in the best possible manner, and stated that it was utterly impossible for it to explode under ordinary circumstances. He did not examine the valve – it was out of his line, but he examined the boiler to see if it leaked by any of the rivets, as new boilers sometimes do, but found no leak, and he was certain there was plenty of water in it."

David Harvester, an engineer of the *Constitution*, which lay alongside the *Medora*, saw some steam escape from a connecting pipe. He described the color of this steam as very blue: "as blue as indigo." He testified that if the steam pressure were low, "it would be of a light color and vapory appearance. On looking up he saw the steam passing slowly out of the blow pipe. He became apprehensive of danger, turned to run, saw the boiler rising, flung himself behind the wheel-house, and escaped unhurt; after which he made a fruitless effort to save a man whom he saw in the water, by throwing him a piece of plank, which the drowning man failed to secure, and sank. He thought the safety valve had been fastened down, and described the way in which it could be done, by extra weight and otherwise. If the lever was propped to the upper deck, the valve could not be raised; or the stick of the steam-gauge might have been broken off unseen by any person, and as the steam would not then be indicated correctly, this might lead to an explosion."

Captain Tripp, of the George Washington Philadelphia Steamboat line, witnessed the explosion from a distance of one hundred fifty feet. He "thought she had but little steam on, she having blown off such a small quantity. The motion of the engine was slow, but the action of the engine is not indicative of the quantity of steam. She had made but one or two revolutions, before the explosion. He thinks the cause of the explosion, from the testimony he had heard, was not an insufficiency of water, but an excessive pressure of steam, which might have resulted from either a wrong estimate of the strength of the boiler, or of the quantity of steam generated."

Seven other witnesses were called, but none added materially to the evidence in hand. When all was said and done, all of those who had the most direct knowledge of the circumstances that preceded the explosion, had been killed. This included Andrew Henderson, president of the shipping company.

By the way, Captain Sutton, skipper of the *Medora*, "was blown high in the air, and fell among the wreck of timber in the water. He received a severe wound on his head, had his face and arms bruised and mutilated in the most shocking manner. He appeared to be doing well."

The jury duly found that John Boon "came to his death by injuries sustained by the explosion of the boiler of the *Medora*; and from the evidence before us, we are of opinion that the accident was not occasioned by raising the steam too high, and greatly above the gauge intended to be used in the ordinary use of said machinery on board of said steamer. Whether this excess as owing to carelessness or tampering with the safety valve, the jury cannot undertake to say."

The jury's verdict was far from the end of the story. According to the *Baltimore Sun*, the day after the inquest, Joseph Cragg "confessed that he caused the explosion, by removing the weight on the lever of the safety valve to its further extremity, and then putting on additional weight; and that Ramsay and Ferguson were cognizant of his doing so – that it was in fact the act of all three by agreement, though actually done by him; and that they did not intend to do mischief, but had intended, as conjectured by Mr. Watchman, to display the qualities of the boat to best advantage."

Cragg had not attended the inquest due to the extent of his injuries. His confession was corroborated by Thomas Smith, who "was on board at the time – was standing near the steam gauge – saw Cragg run out the weight to the extreme end of the lever – the steam being then at 20 or 22 inches. In a few minutes he observed the steam rise rapidly, and finally saw the stick fly out, followed by the mercury which was in the gauge. This alarmed him, and he turned away, when the explosion took place."

However, the first that Cragg knew of his confession was when he read it in the newspaper. He hastened to obtain council in the guise of Justice of the Peace A.H. Pennington, in order to swear an affidavit that contradicted the published account. In his sworn testimony, "deponent now positively denies ever having made any such confession, other than that of removing, by order of Ferguson, the weight of the safety valve. As to an agreement between Ferguson, Ramsay and himself, during that time he had not spoken to Ramsay, nor at any previous time, in relation to the subject; and that as to Ferguson, no other conversation took place than what is already related, in regard to the engine, I did not put any additional weight on the safety valve, nor do I know of any having been put on. I cannot imagine any cause for the explosion, having considered that every thing was correct and safe about the engine and boiler."

This was not the first time in recorded history that an overzealous correspondent filled in the gaps between facts with flights of fancy from an overactive imagination. Nor would it be the last – not as long as such tactics sell newspapers to an eager but unsuspecting public.

As a case in point, Albert Ramsay also went to the trouble to swear out an affidavit in front of Pennington. "Mr. Cragg and deponent had no conversation during the evening nor had any arrangement or understanding been made between Ferguson, Cragg or himself, as is reported in the papers of the 19th of April, nor does he know any thing about the changing of the weights on the lever, as therein stated, or of any additional weight having been added."

By dint of these affidavits, *if* any extra weights had been placed on the lever of the safety valve, only Ferguson could have placed them there – and Ferguson was not alive to defend his actions. In fact, Ferguson's demise and the two denials imply that an irresponsible reporter must have created the fiction of extra weights from whole cloth.

Not until April 21 was the body of Francis McAlear discovered "partially concealed by a remnant of the boiler." His funeral was attended by a long procession. "Archbishop Eccleston and the Rev. Mr. Koskery occupied the first carriage; in the second carriage were three Reverend gentlemen, corpse included, immediately followed by the family and relatives of the deceased. A train of eighteen hacks, filled, were next observed. This was succeeded by the Calvert Beneficial Society, with music and a beautiful banner in mourning. With this society was associated in the procession the St. Joseph's Beneficial Society, and both together numbered 300. The Watchman, Liberty and New Market fire companies were each out in considerable strength, with their appropriate banners and music.

"Thus arranged the line moved slowly to the 'narrow house' of the deceased, where suitable services were performed, and where the Archbishop addressed the vast assemblage. He spoke feelingly of the deceased of his virtues, and of his preparation for death, though snatched so suddenly from life. The ceremonies being closed, the procession re-formed in the same order and returned."

After lingering in pain from bad scalding and broken ribs, George Hyde, John Watchman's apprentice, succumbed to his injuries on April 26. This brought the tally of fatalities to twenty-six, twenty-seven, or twenty-eight (accounts differ). A greater than equal number were either scalded or injured, or both. According to one estimate, at least fifteen persons escaped unscathed.

Many individuals and benevolent societies both donated and collected funds for the relief of those who were deprived of their loved ones, especially wives and children who relied on them for financial support. Human nature being what it is, one Thomas Sparks went about the city "obtaining money under the false pretense of aiding the sufferers of the *Medora*."

This latest act of infamy is *still* far from the end of the story. Samuel Buckingham, "U.S. inspector of steamboat machinery, was not on board when the accident occurred; but he had frequently seen her machinery during the progress of her construction, and he thought it was about the best he ever saw. It was not his duty to go on board without orders, and if he had gone, he would not have been officially recognized. The owners of the boat were not bound by law to have her inspected before a trial trip, but they were so bound before taking freight or passengers."

The paragraph above harkens to deficiencies of the Steamboat Act of 1838.

Boiler explosions were a common occurrence in the early 1800's. The generation of steam to turn an engine that would produce locomotion was a concept that commenced in the 1780's, by William Murdock in England and by John Fitch in the United States. Murdoch invented the first steam locomotive, while Fitch focused his inventive genius on steamboats.

Steam engines soon became the major product of the industrial revolution. Within years the so-called iron horse rode rails at speeds that could never be obtained by means of the original horsepower; and steamboats plied the inland waterways independent of wind and current. The unfortunate byproduct of the glamour of steam was the failure of materials that contained the steam in vessels. By 1838, the number of fatalities that resulted from boiler explosions numbered in the thousands.

The public clamored for protection from these steam-filled bombs whose high-temperature H_2O scalded human skin worse than that of a chicken that was broiled in an oven, and whose shrapnel shredded bodies as if they were made of tissue paper.

Mechanical engineers wrote reams of articles about the material construction of pressure vessels with regard to the strength of metals that existed at the time.

Congress eventually, albeit ponderously, discussed legislation as the first step toward pledging – if not ensuring – safety for the passengers and crews of steamboats. Like most first steps, this one was faltering and prone to falling down – but it was a start in the right direction. The proposed bill promised "to provide for the better security of the lives of passengers on board of vessels propelled in whole or in part by steam."

Disgruntled historians are prone to castigating this bill because part of one sentence was deleted before the final draft was voted into law. In the following extract, the deleted portion is placed within brackets. Italics were part of the original bill. "Sec. 7. *And be it further enacted*, That whenever the master of any boat or vessel, or the person or persons charged with navigating said boat or vessel, which is propelled in whole or in part by steam, shall stop the motion or headway of said boat or vessel, or when the said boat or vessel shall be stopped for the purpose of discharging or taking in cargo, fuel, or passengers, he or they [*(in all cases where the structure of said boat will permit it)* shall keep the engine of said boat or vessel in motion sufficient to work the pump and give the necessary supply of water, and to keep the steam down in said boiler to what it is when the said boat is under headway, and, at the same time, *in all cases,*] shall open the safety-valve, so as to keep the steam down in said boiler to what it is when the said boat or vessel is under headway, under the penalty of two hundred dollars for each and every offense."

It seems to me that keeping the engine in motion was superfluous as long as the safety valve was opened in order to let excess steam escape, thus reducing pressure in the boiler, and consequently, preventing excess pressure from developing. Yet historians with a grudge against this seminal piece of legislation claim that the deleted part of the sentence badly flawed the intent of the law. I disagree.

Congress fine-tuned the law in 1852, and has continued to do so every decade or so ever since, as new and unanticipated hazards beset transoceanic travel. New laws for the safety of life at sea are still being enacted today. It does not necessarily follow that new laws are needed because the old ones were defective.

In addition to lawmakers and the general public at risk, those who professed the greatest concern about pressure vessel containment were the mechanical engineers who designed and built boilers for steamboats and railroad locomotives. Experimentation was an ongoing process, and the examination of failures was part of the learning process. For decades prior to and following the *Medora* disaster, these engineers published the results of their studies in the *Journal of the Franklin Institute*. At least three articles focused solely on the failure of the *Medora's* boiler.

These articles were highly technical and loaded with mathematical formulas: precisely the information that fellow engineers needed in order to build stronger and more efficient boilers. Much of the detailed technical description is lost upon the lay reader because of its esoteric language and mechanical terminology. Therefore I will jump to the conclusions.

After seven pages of description and stress calculations, Benjamin Latrobe opined, "The strength of the boiler, in its weakest places . . . amounted to just three times the extreme pressure which the engine builder appears to have intended it should be called upon to bear, and in proportioning the strength of his work to the duty it was to perform, he would seem to have been sufficiently prudent. How, then, did the boiler explode, when guarded by a safety valve of such ample dimensions, designed to give way at one third of the bursting strain?

"That the free action of the valve must have been interfered with, would be a natural conclusion, and is corroborated by the testimony of one of the assistant enginemen, as be presently mentioned. That the valve had been before loaded to produce a pressure greater than the limit prescribed by its own construction, may be inferred."

The fallacy in the above statement derives from the fact that Latrobe's source of information originated from newspaper accounts, including the published summation of the inquest. While it is true that Sherlock Holmes obtained the bulk of the "facts" of his cases in the identical fashion, he was a fictional character, and Arthur Conan Doyle employed London newspaper articles as a quick and easy plot device which, as I have shown above, in reality is grossly defective. God forbid that we should decide the guilt or innocence of a person on trial on what we read in modern newspapers!

Latrobe seemed not to be aware that the so-called testimony of valve interference was retracted. In any case, he calculated that the weight required to raise the pressure to the explosive threshold "must have amounted to 580 pounds. Now it seems very unlikely that a weight, or weights, of such size or number, were in fact hung upon the valve lever, as that could scarcely have been done without detection, and it was manifestly intended to be a concealed act on the part of those engaged in it. The extra stress upon the valve, necessary to cause explosion, was then, most probably, produced by another mode than the suspension of weights from the lever – such as tying it down by its cord, or bracing it down by a strut between it and the upper deck."

He decided that this scenario was extremely unlikely; no knowledgeable or self-respecting engineer would have done such a thing; nor, being well aware of the danger, would he have allowed it to be done in his presence.

Latrobe's second source of information was his personal examination of the remains of the *Medora's* boiler. After seven more pages of description and calculations, he determined, "the boiler may have been in fact weaker than it has been estimated, from a deficiency of strength in the iron of which it was made." However, he stated categorically that the iron was not of "bad quality." Instead, he concluded that iron sheet of quarter-inch thickness, while sufficient for the casing of a small-diameter boiler such as that used in locomotives (commonly from three to four feet in diameter), was insufficient for a large-diameter boiler like the one installed in the *Medora*, which measured eleven feet in diameter.

He based this conclusion on new calculations which showed that "at the high temperature accompanying high pressures, a given increase in the temperature causes a more rapid rise in the pressure than at the low temperatures of the lower pressures." In other words, the volumetric ratio of pressure to temperature increased geometrically rather than arithmetically. The increase in pressure was so dramatic that excess steam could not escape from the safety valve fast enough to reduce the internal pressure to a containable level.

To compensate for this bold and innovative concept, he made several suggestions: the metallic casing could be made thicker; the boiler could be strengthened by means of internal braces; or, his best recommendation, install two small boilers instead of one large boiler: "The one large boiler will, perhaps, cost less in the manufacture, and occupy less room in the boat, but it will be much more difficult to move, in placing and displacing it; while with more than a single boiler, each of which can be insulated from the other, it may be kept up, and the engine worked at a lower speed, till the injured boiler is repaired."

Latrobe's reasoned approach ignored the possibility that stronger iron alloys might one day be produced. There was no way for him to predict such a discovery.

Latrobe also recommended that "frequent trials of the state of the safety valve should be made, and it should not be left to *blow of its own accord*, at a safe pressure, but should be raised by force, and the surplus steam permitted to escape. This would prevent the valve from *adhering to the seat*, as it has been known to do, in consequence of the rusting of the iron, or the introduction of some glutinous, or cohesive, matter thereto."

After Joseph Cragg learned that he had once again been maligned with regard to his putative action of adding another weight to the safety valve lever, he visited Latrobe, informed him of the true circumstances, and requested that he publish a retraction and recount the true events. Latrobe was appalled by his initial misinformation, and wrote a four-page apology that included some additional information.

With regard to the weight on the lever, Cragg told Latrobe that at the inquest, Watchman meant the weight that belonged there, not an additional weight. Watchman told Cragg that the jury misinterpreted his explanation.

Ramsay also spoke with Latrobe, and informed him "that end of the lever came close up to, or rather *just through*, the boarding of the boiler-house; so that there was no room upon it to hang weights outside of the large one, and any such weights must have been seen, had they been so suspended."

Thus did Latrobe's addendum article clear up some misconceptions for other engineers, if not for the general public.

Subsequent to the publication of Latrobe's conclusions and recommendations, Charles Reeder was tasked with repairing the *Medora's* machinery after the hull had been raised from the bottom. He determined that "the iron of the *Medora's* boiler must have been *of an inferior quality*." He substantiated his contention by experimenting with five strips of metal from the damaged boiler casing, then comparing those strength tests to a strip of No. 3 wrought iron boiler plate "from the manufactory of Brooks & Co., of Pennsylvania." He also supported his conclusions with diagrams and calculations.

In short, "there was evidently not sufficient surplus strength to compensate for the imperfections in materials and workmanship."

In building a new boiler of the same design, he strengthened those areas that he thought were weak points in the original construction. He also reached another conclusion: that when John Watchman tried "to raise the safety valve, when the steam gauge showed ten inches of steam, might impress some persons with the belief of its being fastened down.

"His mode of raising the valve was by a small cord attached to the end of the lever, and running over a small pulley directly above it, thence to a similar pulley, and finally down to a place convenient to the engineer.

"Under a pressure of 10 lbs. by the gauge, if the weights were out to, or near, the end of the lever, a man would have to overcome a weight of about 170 lbs., (in addition to the friction of those pulleys,) by pulling down upon the cord.

"Now, the reason that he could not life the safety valve, was not because it was fastened down, but simply because, being of less weight himself, he was not able to overcome that which he had to lift."

By these considerations the reader must be given to understand that at the time of the *Medora* catastrophe, the physics of steam pressure and the metallurgical knowledge of boiler construction were in their infancy.

The *Medora* was reborn and renamed *Herald*. Reeder's new boiler was duly installed to replace the one that exploded. It provided safe and reliable steam for the next forty-three years, until the *Herald* was abandoned, in 1885.

NELLY WHITE

Built: 1866
Previous names: None
Gross tonnage: 444
Type of vessel: Wooden-hulled side-wheel steamer
Builder: Brooklyn, New York
Owner: St. Michael's Steamboat Company, Baltimore, Maryland
Port of registry: Baltimore, Maryland
Cause of sinking: Collision with *Ida G. Farren*
Location: Sandy Point

Sunk: August 5, 1886
Depth: Unknown
Dimensions: 185' x 29' x 9'
Power: Coal-fired steam

As a passenger and excursion vessel, the *Nelly White* had a long and various career before she met her end ignominiously on a lonely strand of beach on the western shore of the Chesapeake Bay.

Her construction was completed in the year after the end of the Civil War. When she was first placed in service, she took over the route of the *Sea Bird* while that vessel was undergoing repairs. She operated along the Shrewsbury River: a short length of navigable water that was connected to Sandy Hook Bay via the inside passage behind the barrier islands in northern New Jersey.

In 1867, the *Nelly White's* base of operations was shifted to the Long Island Sound. Witness this advertisement: "For Norwalk, connecting with Danbury Railroad.–The new and fast steamer *Nelly White* leaves Pier No. 37, East River, foot of Market st.[New York City], Every Afternoon, at 2-1/2 o'clock. Fare, 75 cents. Excursion tickets, $1.25." Excursion rates have increased astronomically since then. The cost for an equivalent ferry ride now exceeds $50, although that does include the driver's vehicle.

The *Nelly White's* route was often changed in accordance with need. Sometimes she was shifted from her regularly scheduled route in order to work as a relief boat.

On March 18, 1869, the *Nelly White* had an accident that in today's world would have put her out of commission for weeks, perhaps for months, while the Coast Guard examined her hull in dry dock, forced the performance of unnecessary repairs, and created so many reams of paperwork that whole forests would have been denuded of trees, while lawyers from multiple States both sued and countersued everyone who stood within shotgun range in a gross attempt to find someone to blame – that is, someone to pay and make a few people rich at the expense of others – before the issuance of a new certificate of documentation would permit the vessel to resume her ordinary business. Life was simpler in those halcyon days before lawsuits ran rampant and a litigious society went wild and totally out of control:

"The steamboat *Nellie White*, which has recently been running to Harlem and Astoria in place of the *Sylvan Grove*, yesterday morning came in collision with the dock at Astoria with sufficient force to carry away the forward guards and break in the lower cabin forward of and nearly to the paddle-wheel. Two or three persons were struck by flying splinters, but no one was seriously injured. Much excitement was caused among the passengers until the extent of the damage was fully known.

From the collection of Mike Moore.

"The wind and tide were both in favor of the steamboat, and the signal to reverse the engine was not given soon enough to prevent the collision. The passengers considered the pilot to blame. The same pilot had the command of the *Sylvan Grove* at the time of the collision with the *Providence* last summer."

Undoubtedly, the "excitement" among the passengers today would be manifested by their eagerness to view the collision as an opportunity to take advantage of the situation by calling their attorneys and laying claim to exaggerated injuries that they never suffered.

The *Nelly White* had another mishap on November 2, 1874. The way the incident was reported, "Yesterday forenoon, at 10:45 o'clock, the Sound steamer *Nelly White*, while coming through Hell Gate, on her return trip from Norwalk, at the rate of fourteen knots an hour, struck upon a sunken wreck or spar, and although there was scarcely any perceptible shock, a hole fully six inches in diameter was made in her bottom on the port side, about forty-five feet from the bow. Capt. Raymond Hoyt, who was at the wheel when she was struck, immediately went to ascertain whether any damage had been done, and discovered that water was rushing into the vessel with alarming rapidity. He at once cut through the deck of the fore cabin, directly over the leak, and by placing a mattress, and a number of blankets over the aperture partially succeeded in preventing the entrance of the water. As there was about forty passengers and a large quantity of freight on board, it was deemed best to land at Hunter's Point, and upon arrival there it was found that there were eighteen inches of water in the hold. The passengers were then landed and the pumps set to work, and at 1 o'clock the steamer was taken to her regular landing at the foot of Market street, where the cargo, which was only slightly damaged, was discharged. The steamer was then taken to the 'Box' dock at the foot of White street, where she will be repaired in time to resume her regular trips this afternoon. Capt. Hoyt, who has been a pilot on the river for the last thirty years, says that the vessel was on the west side of Woolsey Point and in the ship channel in four and a half fathoms of water when she struck, and thinks from the nature of the injury that it was caused by a spar attached to the wreck of some sunken vessel. As the *Nelly White* draws but four feet and a half of water when loaded, and was fully seventy-five feet from the shore when the accident occurred, he says the accident could have arisen from no other cause. The damage done to the steamer, which is not insured, will not exceed $50 besides the expense of docking."

This "hull hole" was the nautical equivalent of a fender bender.

In the spring of 1876, the *Nelly White* moved her base of operations to the Delaware River. She established a regular excursion route between Philadelphia, Pennsylvania (on the west side of the river) and Bordentown, New Jersey (on the east side), with seven stops in between. As this was the year of the Centennial, the steamer enabled huge numbers of people to visit Philadelphia from neighboring communities (in an era when private means of transportation were few).

The *Nelly White* stayed on the Delaware River route for the next five years, until she fell on hard times, at which time she was put up for auction. The following notice, which was published in New York newspapers on April 23, 1881, is self-explanatory: "Receiver's sale of the steamboat *Nelly White*.–Pursuant to an order of the Chancellor of the State of New Jersey, the undersigned Receiver of the Bordentown and Philadelphia Steamboat Company, will sell at public sale, at 1 o'clock P.M. on Monday, the 25th day of April, A.D. 1881, the Steamboat *Nelly White*, Tackle and Equipments, now lying in the Morris Canal Basin, Jersey City, N.J. The sale, which will be positive, will take place on board of the boat. Conditions at sale. The steamer will be open for inspection every day prior to and on the 24th. Apply on board to Captain Ludlam. For descriptive circulars address Wm. R. Flynn, Receiver, Bordentown, N.J."

It seems to me that the sale lacked much in the way of advance notice. The auction was published on April 23, the vessel was open for inspection on April 24, and the sale was consummated on April 25 – not more than forty-eight hours from notice to sale, with the notice appearing in small print among hundreds of similar notices.

Notwithstanding the above, the lucky high bidder was the St. Michael's Steamboat Company, one of several subsidiaries of the Tolchester Steamboat Company. Before placing her in service on the Chesapeake Bay, her new owners ordered a complete overhaul of the vessel at the Skinner Shipbuilding yard in Baltimore. She received a new boiler that was built by Jas. Clarke & Company, of Baltimore, Maryland, and her interior was renovated in order to accommodate more than a thousand daytime passengers. The *Nelly White* then became a favorite excursion vessel, making daily passages between Baltimore and Tolchester Beach: an enormous resort, amusement park, and picnic ground on the eastern shore of the Chesapeake Bay, and a favorite holiday spa for families that wanted to get away from the grime and grind of everyday life.

After two decades of faithful service, the career of the *Nelly White* ended suddenly on August 2, 1886: "The steamer *Nelly White*, which was beached Thursday morning off Sandy Point, after a collision with the schooner *Ida G. Farren*, is said to be a total wreck. The steamer was in a dangerous position when beached, and the rough weather of Thursday night completed the work of destruction. A part of the furniture, etc., has been saved.... She was valued at $30,000, and owned by the St. Michael's Steamboat Company. She was not insured. The *Nelly White* has been in Baltimore for five years. For two years she ran on the Tolchester route. Capt. Eliason said that though the steamer was a total loss, he was very glad that when the collision occurred there was no excursion party on board."

Other sources stated that the value of the *Nelly White* was $20,000.

The *Nelly White* was abandoned where she lay. Although the vessel's shallow draft left the hulk hugging shore, the wreck was considered a potential hazard to safe navigation. The site was marked with a spar buoy for the next eight years. The buoy was discontinued for two years, then re-established in 1896 by the Lighthouse Board. Nowadays no portion of the once-elegant excursion steamer is in evidence above the waves.

This is not to declare that the wreck is totally gone. It is possible that the hull still lies buried under shifting sand and accumulated mud. But only the hull and a few appurtenances might remain, because everything of value was salvaged by the Baltimore Wrecking Company. The generator and electric lights were installed in the *Emma Giles*, as that vessel was then under construction. Likewise the engine, which has a curious and coincidental relationship to the present volume: it was built by Wilson Small, owner of the West Street Foundry, after whom the *Wilson Small* (which see) was named.

This old advertisement shows the *Nelly White* approaching the loading pier at Tolchester Beach.

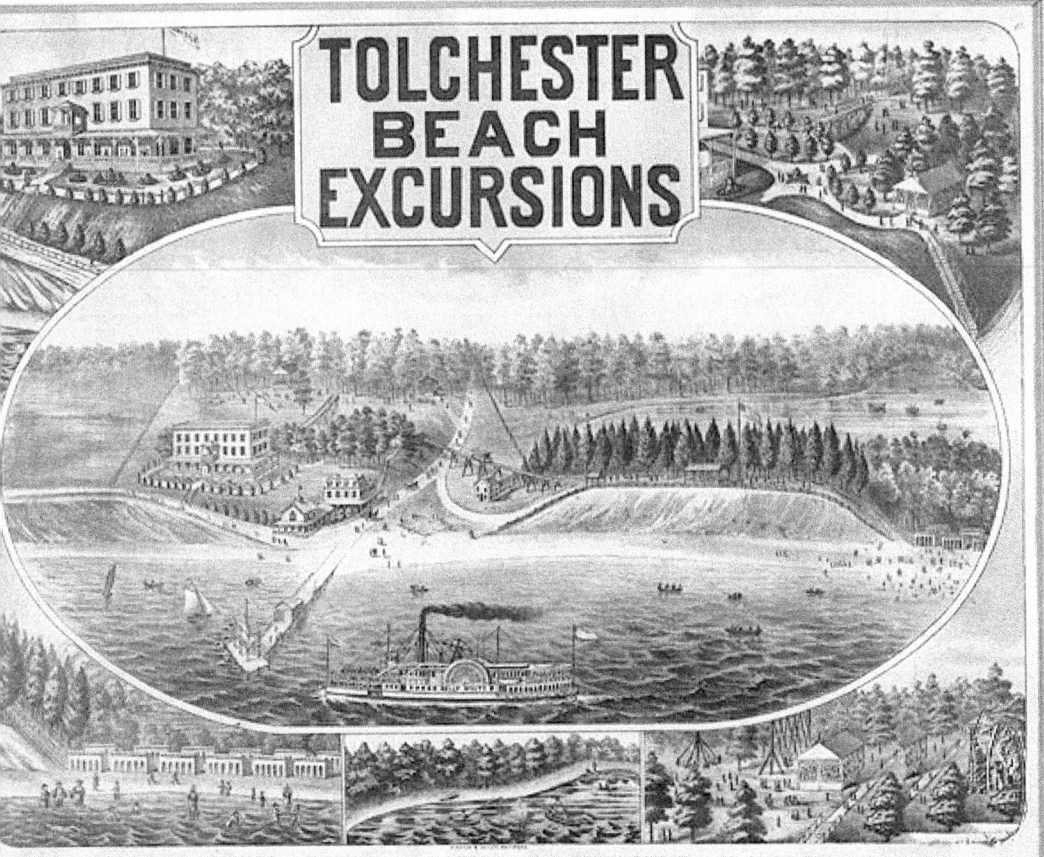

NEW JERSEY

Built: 1862
Previous names: None
Gross tonnage: 324
Type of vessel: Wooden-hulled screw freighter
Builder: John T. Fardy, Brothers and Company, Baltimore, Maryland
Owner: Baltimore Steam Packet Company (Old Bay Line), Baltimore, Maryland
Port of registry: Baltimore, Maryland
Cause of sinking: Fire
Location: Between Plum Point and Trippe Bay
Sunk: February 26, 1870
Depth: 50 feet
Dimensions: 166' x 23' x 8'
Power: Coal-fired steam
GPS: 38-37-03.20 / 76-24-35.90

When the packet freighter *New Jersey* was first put in service, in December of 1862, she was issued a temporary registration in Baltimore: the city in which she was built. The owner of record was Michael Garrett, representing the Commercial Transportation Company, which was based in Trenton, New Jersey.

In short order the *New Jersey's* registration was transferred to her intended home port: Lamberton, New Jersey. You will not find Lamberton on modern maps because the town has since been subsumed by Trenton. Trenton is located on the left bank of the Delaware River about twenty-five miles upstream of Philadelphia and Camden. It is the farthest upstream port on the river before shallow water and rocky rapids make steamship travel impossible.

By intentional design, the *New Jersey's* beam measured twenty-three feet. This was narrow enough to permit the vessel to fit through the Chesapeake and Delaware Canal, which at that time had a width of twenty-four feet. Thus the *New Jersey* had six inches to spare on either side of her hull when she transited from one bay to the other.

In case of engine failure – which was common in the early days of steam propulsion – the *New Jersey* sported three masts which could be rigged with sails fore and aft, as a schooner.

As happened to many vessel owners during the Civil War, the company lost control of the *New Jersey* when she was taken over by the U.S. government for use as an army transport. The *New Jersey* was returned after the cessation of hostilities, much the worse for wear.

After the Civil War, the Baltimore Steam Packet Company (better known as the Old Bay Line) sought to enlarge and modernize its small and struggling fleet. One of its vessels – the *Thomas A. Morgan* – was clearly aging, having been built in 1854. The Old Bay Line had paid nearly $57,000 for her in 1862. In 1867, the line acquired the five-year-old *New Jersey* by trading in their thirteen-year-old *Thomas A. Morgan* and paying an additional $2,000.

The *New Jersey's* service for the Old Bay Line was short-lived. She burned and sank off Sharps Island on February 26, 1870. Unlike the *Wawaset* (which see), which received nearly as much press as a Presidential assassination, the *New Jersey* got no more than a paragraph in passing from out-of-state newspapers. The difference in coverage between the two incidents was loss of life: more than seventy on the *Wawaset*,

Courtesy of the National Archives.

none on the *New Jersey*. The price of fame is death.

Here are all three sentences verbatim: "The propellor *New-Jersey*, which left here [Baltimore] on Friday for Norfolk with a large freight, was burned to the water's edge and sunk in ten fathoms of water, off Sharp's Island in Chesapeake Bay. The Captain and crew escaped in the boats and were picked up and brought to this city by the propellor *Transit*. The *New-Jersey* was valued at $56,000, and insured for half that sum."

The Steamboat Inspection Service conducted an investigation. This also contrasts unfavorably with that of the *Wawaset*, which was many pages in length and which sought blame for the large number of fatalities. As in the newspaper reportage, the remarks consisted of only a single paragraph comprising but two sentences.

Verbatim: "In the district of Baltimore, the burning of the steamer *New Jersey*, which took place on the night of the 26th of February, 1870, in the Chesapeake Bay, involving the loss of steamer and cargo. From the testimony obtained from the officers of the steamer, it is quite evident that the fire originated from the ignition of some dangerous freight shipped on board, and marked, contrary to law, as ordinary merchandise; this opinion is further confirmed by the subsequent discovery of shipments of freights of a dangerous character on some line of steamers marked merchandise."

And that's all she wrote!

In actuality, the full report was undoubtedly much longer, but the original nineteenth-century steamboat investigations were not archived for posterity. Unless they were reprinted in contemporary newspapers, the details have been lost and only the curt summaries remain.

Most of the cargo consisted of flour, corn, bacon, jars of fruit, and pitchers of molasses. The dangerous portion was petroleum carried in wooden barrels.

Although there was no loss of life, there was a great loss of freight that was owned by those who paid the Old Bay Line to transport it. One company in particular was Headrick & Brother of Tunnel Hill, Georgia. The value of the freight they lost amounted to $265,000. Headrick & Brother hired the Virginia and Tennessee Air Line Railway company to collect the product in Baltimore and deliver it to Tunnel Hill. The way the transit company elected to arrange for transportation was by consigning the product first to the *New Jersey* for transportation to Norfolk, then by way of land travel to Tunnel Hill. Headrick & Brother sued the transit company for non-delivery. This suit made the Old Bay Company liable by way of subrogation.

The defense adopted the position that it was exempt from liability pursuant to an 1851 Act of Congress: 9 U.S. Stat. at Large, 635. Because this Act placed a limitation of liability on the part of ship owners, it has come to be called the Limitation Act. This Act stipulated that in case of loss or damage to cargo, the liability of the owner of the vessel was limited by the value of that vessel after the loss.

For example, let's say that the *New Jersey* was worth $56,000 when she departed from Baltimore on that fateful morning. That means that although Headrick & Brother lost $265,000 worth of product, the liability of the Old Bay Line was limited to $56,000. But wait! It gets worse. According to the Act, the ship owner was liable for the value of the vessel *after* the loss. Since the value of the *New Jersey* on the bottom of the bay was zero, the liability of the ship owner was the same.

To put this Act into modern perspective, let's say that today's Congress passed a similar Act for road vehicles: all cars, trucks, vans, buses, SUV's, motorcycles, and eighteen wheelers. A kid who owns a $500 jalopy goes for a joyride, loses control of the wheel, crashes into a Rolls-Royce and kills everyone inside, but survives the collision. The most amount of money for which he could be held accountable would be

$500 – *unless* the jalopy was totaled, in which case he would be accountable for nothing.

It may come as no surprise to my readers that many of the Congressional representatives who voted to pass the Limitation Act in 1851 held major interests in shipping lines. The passage of the Act was a way of feathering their own nests and protecting their personal financial interests.

The transit company evoked the Limitation Act as its defense. After the presentation of evidence, the judge charged the jury as follows: "That the Act of Congress, passed in 1851, excepts sea-going vessels or vessels used upon the ocean from the provisions of our Code and of the common law prescribing the liability of common carriers. That if the evidence shows that plaintiffs' goods were destroyed by fire, on a vessel, such as is described in the Act of Congress, unless it is shown by the proof that the fire was caused by the design or neglect of the owner or owners of said vessel, the design or neglect of agents, under the Act, would not entitle the plaintiffs to recover in such case. Under said Act of Congress, the shipper and the owner may make a contract extending or limiting the liability of the carrier. If you have before you a shipper's receipt or bill of lading specifying the terms upon which plaintiffs' goods were to be shipped, made by the ship owner or carrier and accepted by the plaintiffs or their agent, the jury will be authorized to consider said receipt as a contract under said Act, under which said goods were to be shipped.

"With reference to the kind of vessel embraced within the provisions of the first section, it is proper to state that no canal boat, lighter or other vessel used in inland waters, is included within the provisions of said statute. But, if the vessel is shown to have been such as is usually used as a seagoing vessel, and suited to transportation of

Opposite page: a saucer and heavy-duty mug. Left: an ironstone china shard that is typical of those that are found on the wreck. Much of the *New Jersey's* cargo of china was imported from England. This item is the product of W. & E. Corn, of Burslem. The particular style with the Royal Coat of Arms was manufactured between 1864 and 1891. Difficult to read is the incising beneath the emblem, which reads "Versailles Shape."

freights from one port to another, along the coast of the United States, loss occurring on her by fire, not shown to be caused by the design or neglect of the owner, will not fall upon owner."

Don't feel bad if this verbose charge sounds confusing. I find it not only confusing but contradictory. In fact, so did the attorneys for the plaintiff. After the jury found for the defendant, thus allowing the Old Bay Line to get off scot-free, attorneys for the plaintiff moved for a new trial: "1st. Because the Court erred in the charge to the jury in reference to the effect of the Act of Congress of March, 1851, on the liability of the defendant. 2d. Because the Court erred in failing to instruct the jury as to the effect of the presence of matches and other combustibles with the freight, in changing the burden of proof."

The motion was overruled – possibly because no judge likes to be told that he was wrong and made a mistake.

The plaintiff appealed.

The appeals court explained the 1851 Act thus: "No owner of any ship or vessel shall be liable to answer for any loss or damage which may happen to any goods or merchandise which shall be shipped on board any such ship or vessel, by reason of any fire happening on board the same, unless such fire is caused by design or neglect of such owner. The seventh section provides that the Act 'shall not apply to the owners of any canal boat, barge or lighter, or to any vessel of any description whatsoever, used in rivers or inland navigation.'

"The defendant was an association composed of several transportation companies, including the Baltimore Steam Packet Company, who were owners of the steamer *New Jersey*, a first-class freight boat, and a sea-going vessel, engaged in the carrying trade between Baltimore, Norfolk and Portsmouth. The suit was brought by plaintiffs for goods which were put on board said steamboat in Baltimore, for transportation through the Chesapeake Bay to Norfolk, and thence to Tunnel Hill in this State. The vessel and the goods were destroyed by fire on the night of the same day it left Baltimore, and from the finding of the jury, the loss occurred without design or neglect of the owners. Defendants claim they are not liable, under the provisions of the Act of Congress above quoted. Plaintiffs insist that the case is within the exceptions of the seventh section of the Act and the common law rule of liability applies."

It seems clear to me that the *New Jersey* was not a sea-going vessel when she traveled only across the bay and not into the ocean; that she was used solely on rivers and for inland navigation. Nonetheless, after some spacious argument and irrelevant allusion to other cases, the appeals court affirmed the earlier decision.

Headrick & Brother was out $265,000. The Old Bay Line was out one freighter. There the matter rested.

The first report of the discovery of the wreck was published in 1978. That was when the hydrographic survey vessels *Rude* and *Heck* – belonging to the National Oceanographic and Atmospheric Administration – conducted a routine wire-drag survey in the Chesapeake Bay and snagged their gear on an obstruction that "cleared to 40.5 feet." They sent NOAA divers down to obtain more information. The divers found a wooden-hulled wreck that measured – as best they could determine in poor visibility – about one hundred feet in length and eighteen feet in width.

NOAA identified the wreck as the *New Jersey*. The identity and coordinates were duly entered on the Automated Wreck and Obstruction Information System (AWOIS).

It was not long before the National Diving Center in Washington, DC started organizing charters to the wreck. Divers found a trove which I will let my friend Mike Moore describe: "Her cargo at the time of sinking has been the chief source of artifacts. Among the cargo found so far are canned (in glass) peaches (the pits are still inside), glass molasses pitchers with the metal lids preserved very well below the mud, chinaware that unfortunately was badly burned in the fire, and fire hose clamps. The clamps (we assume they were for fire hoses) were destined for the Washington Navy Yard for, again, we assume, a ship under construction there. Each clamp is a two piece affair engraved 'U.S.N.Y.W.D.C. 1870'."

The abbreviation stands for United States Navy Yard, Washington, District of Columbia, dated 1870. Due to the abundance of molasses pitchers that early divers found, the *New Jersey* is often called the Pitcher Wreck.

Mike has made more dives on the wreck than I have, so I will let him describe it the way it was in the early 1980's: "Except for the boiler, the engine and two anchors near the bow, the *New Jersey* lies very close to the bottom. The starboard side of the hull is almost totally buried while the port side comes up about 4-5 feet off the bottom. The stem of the bow is intact and comes up quite a bit higher. The major landmarks of the wreck are the boiler, the engine and two crossed anchors up in the bow. The wreck lies with her bow facing East. . . .

"Since the port side is the higher it also seems to be the best area to look for goodies. Starting at about the after end of the engine investigate the mud between the centerline of the wreck and the port side. China and fire hose clamps tend to be on top or very shallow in the mud while the glassware tends to be buried rather deep. To reach the glassware plunge your arm down into the mud up to the shoulder and feel around. You may get lucky and hit a piece directly. A better find, however, is to hit smooth wood. It's a packing crate that might contain a concentration of glassware."

Maximum depth is 50 feet. The boiler stands nine feet off the bottom. Due to the possibility of encountering a strong current, it is best to dive during slack tide.

Mike introduced me to Chesapeake Bay shipwrecks. He first took me to the *New*

This side-view drawing was made by NOAA divers in 1987 (see following page for details). The cylindrical object on the extreme left represents the boiler. The brick-shaped object to the right of it represents the engine. The slender uprights represent ribs.

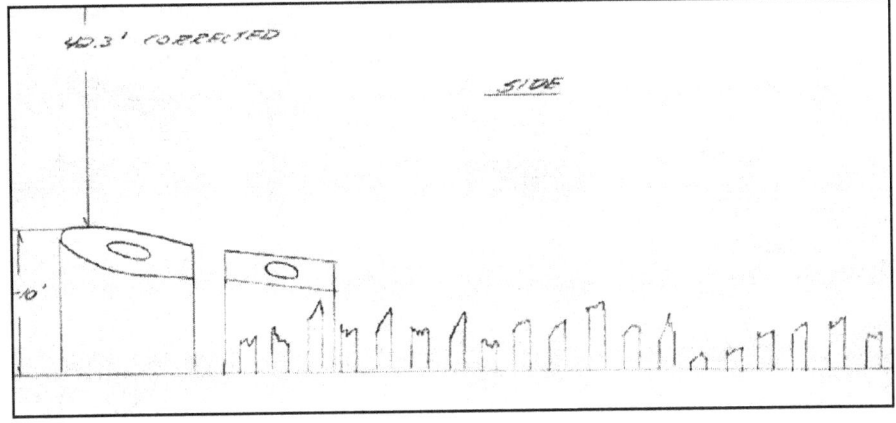

Jersey in July 1987. There is little that I can add to his description. With only three feet of visibility, I clambered over beams, timbers, and copper pipes as I circumnavigated and crisscrossed the wreck. On that dive I spent an hour and three quarters on the bottom, plus fifteen minutes decompressing. What I found most enthralling was crawling into what I believe must have been a cargo hold. An area that measured approximately six feet by twelve feet was literally paved with white china shards. I could see nothing but white no matter where I looked. Sadly, most of this exposed china was broken. Undoubtedly there must have been some intact china beneath the overburden.

Ironically, NOAA conducted another survey of the *New Jersey* three months later, in October. This time the *Heck* was alone. She located the wreck by means of side-scan sonar, dropped a weighted line to which a search buoy was attached, then deployed a pair of divers. According to the survey report:

"The divers search buoy fell next to the object of the search. The divers discovered the remains of a large wooden vessel approximately 100 feet long and 20 feet wide. The search buoy landed next to some of the wooden ribbing of the hull. The divers followed the ribbing for nearly 100 feet at which point they discovered the remains of a large boiler. Further investigation concluded that the boiler was the shoalest point and a least depth was taken. The old boiler and remains of the ship's hull ribbing were all that remained of the vessel. . . . Although little remains of the wooden hull, the boiler protrudes 9 to 10 feet off the bottom."

It is interesting to note the difference between Mike's and my descriptions, and the description made by the NOAA divers. They made no mention of china. This is not to say that they passed over the pile and didn't see it; rather, it demonstrates the differences in attitude and the reportage of key features between experienced wreck-divers who dive on shipwrecks as a matter of pure exploration, and survey divers to whom china must not have been an important feature, because their purpose was to determine if the wreck presented a hazard to navigation.

I should also note that the NOAA divers spent only twenty minutes in the water, whereas I spent two hours. That must be the difference between work and play.

In February 1987, the National Geographic Society sponsored a survey trip to the *New Jersey*. It was supposed to utilize a sonic imaging system to draw a picture of the wreck, much like a pen and ink sketch. They made the mistake of choosing the worst weather month of the year, foredooming the trip to dismal failure. The poorly planned survey of the *New Jersey* was canceled due to high winds.

As a further perversion for the record, in May of 2000, I contacted Susan Langley at the Maryland Historical Trust for historical information about the *New Jersey*. She duly informed me that she had a data file for the wreck site, but refused to let me see it. Instead of providing me with primary source documentation that she had in hand, she suggested that I seek information from secondary sources. I do not like to use secondary source material because it only perpetuates mistakes that the previous researcher might have made if he was careless or less than thorough.

Whatever information Langley has in her possession, she is staunchly keeping to herself and keeping it away from the public that paid her through their tax dollars to obtain.

S-49

Built: 1922
Previous names: *C*
Displacement tonnage: 993 (surfaced), 1230 (submerged)
Type of vessel: S-class submarine
Builder: Lake Torpedo Boat Company, Bridgeport, Connecticut
Owner: None
Cause of sinking: Disposed (either scuttled or foundered)
Location: Off Point Patience in the Patuxent River

Sunk: December 16, 1942
Depth: 130 feet
Dimensions: 240' x 21' x 13'
Power: 2 diesel engines, 2 electric motors
Navy designation: SS-160
GPS: 38-19.898 / 76-29.269

The Patuxent River does not look exactly like a cup of coffee – unless you like your brew leavened with a touch of cream; or unless you go all the way to the bottom. At 130 feet the river is suffused with a Stygian blackness that is the ultimate in sensory deprivation, like floating at the bottom of an ink well.

In recreational diving, this is known as a braille dive.

In order to savor the full effect of darkness, I purposely dropped down the anchor line with my light switched off. As I descended through the upper layers of brine, the shadowy outline of yellowed braided rope disappeared just beyond the reach of my next grab. It was like sliding down a thin ghostly barber pole into the pit of Hell.

At 50 feet I had my last look at my gauges. After that, even the luminescent dials did not glow brightly enough for me to see the readouts. Now I reached out blindly, grappling with one hand, feeling the taut rope, gripping tightly so as not to be swept into limbo by the downstream current, pulling forward, reaching out with the other hand. My hold on the anchor line was my only touch with reality.

I could estimate my descent only by the increased pressure on my ears. I lost all sense of time, all sense of depth, all sense of physical contact. The drysuit protected me from the temperature, the mitts from actual feeling with the rope. There was nothing before me, nothing behind. There was just my mind, floating in a black endless expanse.

Sea trial. (Courtesy of the Naval Photographic Center.)

My fin tips were like cat whiskers, sensing beyond the nerve endings of my toes. They brushed against something. I exhaled, and rushing bubbles skittered past my ears. The loss of air changed my buoyancy. I fell slowly, like a feather on the moon. My bent knees touched a resilient cushion. Was I sinking into soft river ooze?

My face mask banged into something solid. I clutched the anchor line as if my life depended on it. With my free hand I grappled for the light that was secured to my wrist by a lanyard. I worked my fingers along the waterproof casing until I felt the switch.

And then there was light! But precious little of it.

In front of me was a red, drooling wall, like some surrealistic painting by Salvadore Dali. Rusted steel bulged as if the surface had been blistered by heat. I followed the hull downward. Crouched on my knees, bent at the waist, with my face close to the river bed, I could barely make out an off-white bottom of shell hash covered with a layer of soft silt that swirled around my legs like dust in a windstorm. Curious eyes peered up from a bed of empty oyster shells: small fish that lived in tubelike holes in the sand.

I punched the inflator button on my drysuit and rose gently away from the bottom. My light beam was not strong enough to reach anything, and for a long moment I was back in that ethereal world of dark limbo. My light carved a short tunnel through swiftly moving, free-floating plankton.

The anchor line curved upward. I moved along it until I reached the linked chain. I found the grapnel snagged on the top of the wreck, at 115 feet. The steel hull was heavily overgrown with plush, colorless polyps, like giant bunches of grapes hanging inverted from a metal vine. They appeared to grow in patches, here piled over a foot thick, there leaving bare, reddish steel.

What kind of wreck I was on I could not fathom. I left the anchor line and inched my way along the upper deck, following the parallel pattern of protruding beams. Only a few feet away I came upon a mushroomlike protuberance, like a two-foot-tall morel. It was a capstan. Half the top was covered with polyps; the other half was swept clean right down to bare metal.

As I cleaned the clinging marine growth off the top, an intricate floral design appeared. A Navy anchor was embossed on the circular cover plate, surrounded by stems of foliage leading to a three-petaled flower.

I moved aft without yet knowing it. Soon I

found a strange contrivance, like a huge garbage disposal with a brass handle and a worm gear that went through the steel decking: a device that later proved to be a ready-access ammunition trunk.

A little farther aft I ran into – quite literally – the conning tower.

When Mike Moore first told me about a U.S. submarine lying at the bottom of the Patuxent River, I was skeptical. I mentally scoffed at a seemingly outrageous circumstance. He said that he had snagged the wreck the year before, but had not been able to dive on it. This time he wanted to verify that it was in fact an S-class submarine, as it was rumored to be, that was shown on the nautical chart as an obstruction.

To me, it sounded too improbable to be true, but I knew from a long diving career that many strange tales lie under the water, waiting to have their stories told. So, despite my misgivings, I leaped at the opportunity to accompany him in his small boat. He trailered it to Solomons, Maryland, and offloaded it at the public launch that is located practically under the Route 4 bridge on the downstream side of the north shore. From there it was only a five minute high-speed ride to the site, which lies off-center near the south shore.

With a dive light, visibility stretched to three feet. I traced the bulkhead upward from the conning tower to the protruding bridge. It bulged forward exactly as it should have bulged. I had been on two other S-class subs: the *S-5* off Cape May, New Jersey, and the *S-16* off Key West, Florida. I had also studied deck plans and photographs, so I was very familiar with the contours of the upper works. One feature that I noticed right away, as I was specifically looking for it, was the line of portholes. They had been blanked and welded over.

When I was a kid, my father used to tell me fantastic stories. One that I remembered now was that he got kicked out of submarine duty in the Navy for sleeping with his porthole open. I used to laugh because everyone knew that submarines didn't have portholes. Even kids knew that. But truth is often stranger than fiction. Some early submarines *did* have portholes . . . but the portholes didn't pierce the main pressure hull.

These portholes ringed the lower level of the two-story conning tower: a streamlined steel structure that was similar to a gun tub in that the upper level had no roof; the surrounding fairwater offered protection for the watch crew against the elements, especially crashing seas, when the sub was being "conned," or controlled, in surface mode. The chariot bridge filled with water when the submarine submerged.

The lower level contained the conning tower proper, with a control station that was encased in a watertight pressure vessel. Portholes enabled lookouts in the lower level to peer ahead through the spume and spray without getting wet. The thickness of the glass in these portholes limited the submarine's diving depth to 200 feet; if the sub went deeper than that, external water pressure would punch in the glass.

The lower level of the conning tower was sealed from above and below by watertight hatches. The hatch above led to the chariot bridge and atmosphere. The hatch below led to the control room inside the main pressure hull. In the event a porthole glass was broken, the lower hatched could be closed in order to seal the main pressure hull against flooding.

Under water, I saw that the chariot bridge was topped with a wooden handrail that hugged the steel coaming. Inside, by placing the light next to my head and moving inch by inch along the interior, I saw that the navigational equipment was nonexistent. The submarine appeared to have been stripped.

I worked my way in the direction that I now knew to be aft. I noticed the absence of periscope shears. The after end of the bridge was open, so I rolled right out and down to deck level. I traced the flattened deck back until it ended in a downward sweep that terminated on the rounded outer skin. Again, it was identical to the layout that I knew was featured on S-class subs.

As the stern narrowed to an end like a ball point pen, I dropped off the side and over the starboard plane. Abaft the plane, the stub of the propeller shaft ended abruptly, as if it had been hacked off. At the very tip of the stern was a rounded opening, like the ovipositor of a colossal insect: the stern torpedo tube.

The fifty-one S-class subs were actually divided into three types, but within the

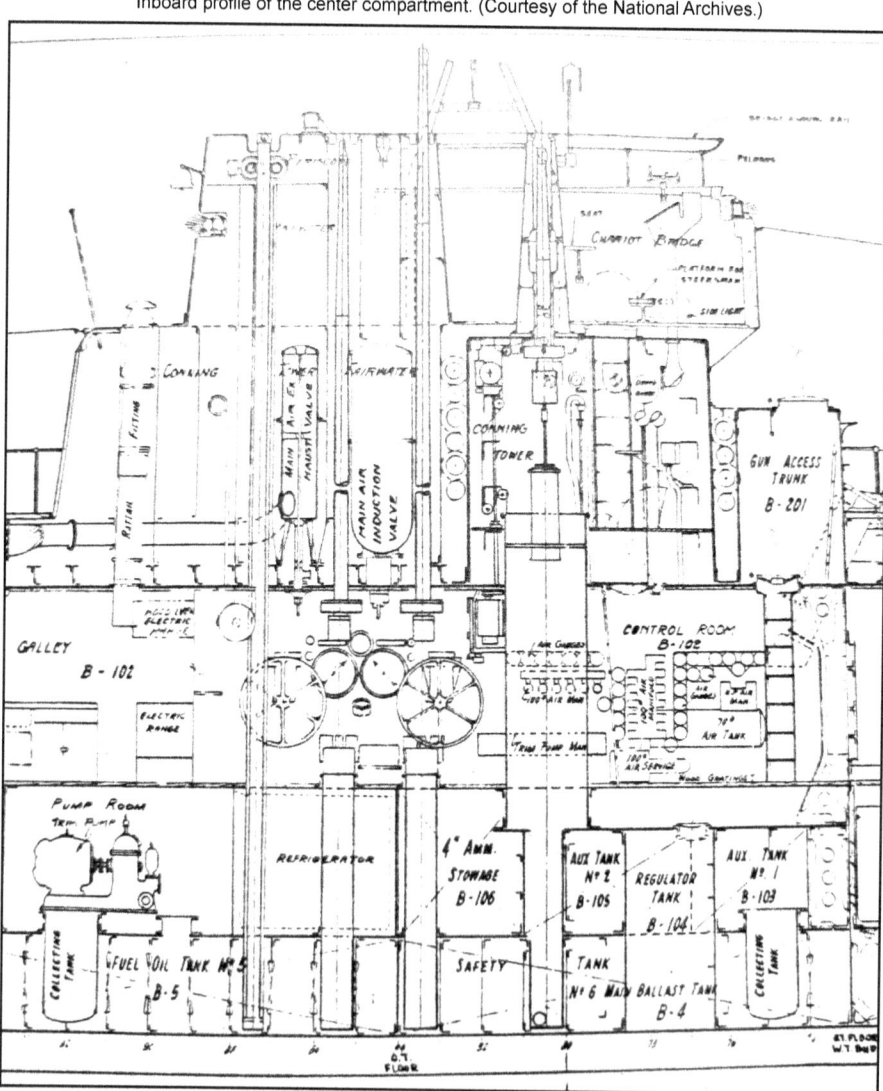

Inboard profile of the center compartment. (Courtesy of the National Archives.)

types quite a bit of individualizing was engineered, both initially and during subsequent refits. The S-class subs were powered by different engine types, operated by different kinds of machinery, armed with guns of varying sizes, and weighed in with different displacement tonnages. In short, no two S-class subs were identical.

Three prototypes were built. Generally, *S-4* through *S-17* followed the government design of the *S-3*, which measured 231 feet in length. *S-4* through *S-13* were built by the Portsmouth Naval Shipyard; *S-14* through *S-17* by the Lake Torpedo Boat Company.

S-18 through *S-41*, and *S-42* through *S-47*, were designed and constructed by the Electric Boat Company, after their *S-1* prototype. The length of the former group measured 219 feet; the length of the latter group measured 225 feet.

Lake Torpedo Boat Company designed the *S-2*, but the design was abandoned in favor of the other two types.

Then, the Lake Torpedo Boat Company received a contract to build four boats in a similar mold, but longer and with increased power. These were *S-48* through *S-51*. At 240 feet in length, they could have been called a stretch-class submarine. They were the only S-class subs to possess a stern torpedo tube in addition to the four in the bow. No matter how big their external dimensions, S-class submarines were cramped and crowded inside. The men who served in them called them "pigboats."

If you want to know what an S-class submarine was like, read the 1931 Edward Ellsberg classic entitled *Pigboats*. Ellsberg was a Navy commander at the time he wrote the book; he continued his career throughout World War Two, and retired as a rear admiral. Although he never actually served on an S-class sub, he was a hard-hat diver and salvage master who was the senior officer in charge of raising both the *S-4* and *S-51*. These operations gave him first-hand knowledge of their interior layout and workings.

For a more visual representation, view the 1933 movie that was based on *Pigboats*: it was called *Hell Below*, and starred Robert Montgomery, Walter Huston, Jimmy Durante, Robert Young, and Sterling Holloway. It is every bit as thrilling as the book, and set the trend for the submarine movies that followed after World War Two.

The war for which the *S-49* had been designed was long over by the time she was launched, on April 12, 1921. Her hull was designated SS-160; that is, the one-hundred sixtieth submarine that was ordered for construction since the inception of the program in 1900. The *S-49* was commissioned on June 5, 1922, at her home port of Bridgeport, Connecticut. Her usual complement was forty-two officers and men.

The extended-length submarine could maintain a surface speed of 14.5 knots with her diesel engines running to the stops, and could proceed under water on battery power at 11 knots. In addition to sixteen 21-inch torpedoes, she sported a 4-inch deck gun.

For the next four years the *S-49* led a relatively mild career that involved submarine research and development; she never strayed far from New London, Connecticut. Then, on April 20, 1926, disaster struck. She was tied up at her dock just as on any other day. The men were just finishing breakfast when a terrific explosion rocked the boat.

"The steel plates of the flooring blew upward, flattening the men against the top of the compartment. Following the explosion, smoke of greenish hue was blown high through the hatchways."

An alarm was sounded throughout the base, bringing hundreds of sailors on the run. As some of the crew stumbled out of the hatches, coughing and gasping, a rescue party donned gas masks and descended into the smoking hull to bring out the injured. The battery room was forward of the control room, and a fierce fire was raging among the 120 cells. The connecting hatch was sealed so that the fire was contained forward. It was hoped that the conflagration could be starved by cutting off the oxygen.

Meanwhile, four men died from hydrogen gas inhalation, and eight others were hospitalized.

In midafternoon, an outboard battery vent was opened in order to relieve the internal pressure. "During the night, the submarine took on a

slight list to port and air pressure was used to keep ballast." But the influx of air caused further undoing, and another explosion occurred early the next morning. Eventually, the fire was contained, and the *S-49* went into dry dock for extensive repairs.

An inquiry blamed the catastrophe on overcharging the batteries, which caused hydrogen to leak out of the cells. The hydrogen combined with oxygen in the air, and a spark from a dropped deck plate ignited the mixture. This was not an uncommon occurrence in the submarine fleet.

In January 1927, the newly refurbished submarine went on extensive maneuvers with her sister boat, the *S-50*, and got as far away from home as the Dry Tortugas. They were back at New London by March.

Soon afterward, the *S-49* was sent on her last cruise for the U.S. Navy – to Philadelphia for deactivation. The *S-49* took up residence at the Navy Yard on League Island. She was decommissioned on August 2, and joined the reserve fleet. By this time newer and larger submarines were plying the seas: the 341-foot-long V-class.

The Navy decided to get rid of most of the obsolescent S-class subs. Several had been lost with great loss of life. Their sluggish response and shallow design depth of 200 feet were considered inadequate in light of advancing technology. The *S-49* was among the first to go. She was struck from the Navy list on March 31, 1931. The submarine that had cost the government $2.5 million dollars to build, was sold for scrap to the Boston Iron & Metal Company, of Baltimore, Maryland, for $7,666: phenomenal depreciation even in light of the nationwide depression that was in progress.

From this point onward the records become vague, and the exact chronology and course of events must be stitched together in a sequence that is less than precise and often lacking in detail. The folks at the Naval Historical Center do not have a clue about the *S-49's* subsequent history. The entry in the *Dictionary of American Naval Fighting Ships* is all too brief: "*S-49* was sold to the Boston Iron and Metal Co., Baltimore, Md., on 25 May 1931. Reduced to a hulk by that company in 1936, but not scrapped, the hulk was apparently reacquired seven years later, 'as equipment,' for use in experimental work at the Naval Mine Warfare Proving Ground, Solomons, Md."

While this entry contains no incorrect information, it passes over the most fascinating decade of the submarine's history without a mention. Although primary archival documentation sometimes contradicts itself, I will do my best to reconstruct the continuation of the *S-49's* activities before and during the "lost" years when the Naval Historical Center relegated her status to limbo.

Unlike the other four submarines that the Boston Iron & Metal Company purchased, the *S-49* was not immediately disassembled to have its parts melted down. Instead, she was partially dismembered in accordance with stipulations of the London Naval Arms Limitation Treaty, which called for a reduction in the warship tonnage of the navies of the signatory nations. Her armament was removed, and her torpedo tubes were plated over and welded shut.

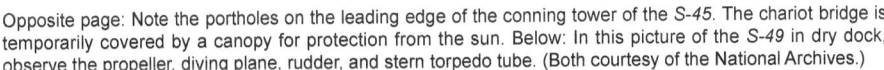

Opposite page: Note the portholes on the leading edge of the conning tower of the *S-45*. The chariot bridge is temporarily covered by a canopy for protection from the sun. Below: In this picture of the *S-49* in dry dock, observe the propeller, diving plane, rudder, and stern torpedo tube. (Both courtesy of the National Archives.)

In addition, the removal of her batteries made it impossible for her to proceed submerged. Pre-nuclear submarines were outfitted with two types of engines: diesel engines for topside propulsion, and electric motors for underwater propulsion. Diesel engines could not be employed under water because the combustion of fuel consumed vast quantities of oxygen; these engines could be run only when the intake valve was open to the atmosphere. Once submerged, when obviously the intake valve and hatches were closed, a running diesel engine would quickly suck all the oxygen out of the air inside the pressure hull, thus suffocating the crewmembers. Instead, electric motors were switched on for propulsion; these motors drew electricity from storage cells.

Therefore, although the *S-49* continued to exist in the shape of a submarine, and was technically available for military reactivation – that is, she had not been scrapped or sunk in water beyond the depth of then-current salvage capability – she was no longer considered a machine of war.

The *S-49* then took a turn that is unique in the annals of U.S. Navy submarine disposition: she became the only privately owned excursion submarine in American history.

Purists might take exception to the above paragraph by citing the nonmilitary career of the obsolete *O-12*. In 1930, when the U.S. Navy had no further use for that submarine, she was converted for civilian use at the Philadelphia Navy Yard, after which she was turned over to the United States Shipping Board for her previously arranged assignment: leasing to Hubert Wilkins at the rate of one dollar per year for his upcoming Arctic oceanographic expedition. The *O-12* was renamed *Nautilus*.

Wilkens planned to dive the submarine under the ice in order to explore the polar sea. He did manage to submerge under the ice, but the upper works were severely damaged in the process. Subsequently, the *Nautilus* suffered so many mechanical breakdowns that Wilkins reluctantly turned back after reaching 82° north latitude: a record that was not passed until 1958, when the U.S. nuclear submarine *Nautilus* (SSN-571) surfaced at the geographical North Pole.

It was fortunate that Wilkens turned back when he did, for the *Nautilus* encountered a fierce storm in which both engines were damaged. The hull leaked badly. The fresh water tanks were frozen. The radio was broken beyond repair. The *Nautilus* barely limped back to civilization. In retrospect, Wilkens was a global explorer who accomplished much during a long life of adventure. The failure of his Arctic expedition was due to mechanical difficulties, not to poor planning or conduct.

Like the *O-12*, the *S-49* was renamed when she entered civilian service. Captain Francis J. Chrestensen bought her from the Boston Iron & Metals Company for a reported $25,000 (which was quite a markup from the sale price; elsewhere the purchase price was quoted as $3,000; neither source is reliable but the latter is more likely). He registered the submarine as a yacht and named her *C*. He then took the newly christened submarine on a tour of the Great Lakes and, later, along the eastern seaboard. Highlights of her ten-year odyssey were occasionally reported in local newspapers.

According to Chrestensen's advertising brochure, "Since 1931, the *S-49* has been used as an educational exhibit, giving to millions of people an opportunity of seeing and inspecting a submarine. It has brought to thousands of people a better appreciation of the Navy. After viewing the intricate workings of the *S-49* anyone must realize that only men of the highest ability would be competent to operate such boats. Also the rea-

Note the letter "C" painted in black on the bow. The letter and numerals of the original name are barely visible, having been painted over in white so as to match the hull. (From a picture postcard.)

son for high Naval appropriations is apparent for the construction of such ships. Remember, if you help to preserve your Navy's strength in time of peace, it will protect you in time of war."

Chrestensen's words were woefully prescient. In the 1930's, diminishing military appropriations reduced the Navy's manpower and warship construction so much that the service was acutely unprepared to meet the U-boat threat when Hitler dispatched his killer fleet to the American eastern seaboard in 1942.

The first major exhibit of the *S-49* commenced in 1933, at the Century of Progress Exhibition (also known as the Chicago World's Fair). This exhibition opened on May 27, 1933, and lasted until October 31, 1934 (although it was closed during the fierce winter months.) The submarine was a late arrival, not appearing on site until June. By that time, nearly a million visitors had thronged through the exhibits – but millions more passed through the gates during the next year and a half. The crowds far surpassed the expectations of the Exhibition's planners.

Coincidental with the *S-49's* arrival in Chicago was the release of the motion picture *Hell Below*. These two attractions – one in the water on Lake Michigan and the other on big screens throughout theaters around the country – went a long way toward inciting enthusiasm in the American populace for the acceptance of newer and larger submarines, some of which were fortuitously built before the end of the decade. Even though "hulls" were lacking by the time war broke out, at least the Navy had perfected the design, so that production could proceed apace when necessity arrived.

The ex-Navy submarine had prominent waterfront dockage (as did the *City of New*

One of Chrestensen's advertising postcards, depicting the forward torpedo room.

York, the steam barque that had transported Admiral Richard Byrd to the South Pole on his first Antarctic expedition, in 1928). After paying an entry fee at a dockside kiosk, visitors were funneled through a gateway onto the forward deck. The ladders below the fore and after hatches had been replaced with metal staircases, permitting easy access to the well-lighted interior. During this year-and-a-half gig, tour guides led many thousands of curiosity seekers through the pressure hull, where they learned what it was like to live in a submarine.

Not everyone was thrilled by all the forms of progressive Exhibition. Two vocal dissidents were Phillip Yarrow and Mary Spencer. Yarrow was the president of the Illinois Vigilance Association, which, among other suppressions, was justifiably opposed to white slave traffic: the luring of naïve girls into a life of prostitution or enforced "marriage" in other countries.

Spencer was an attorney with a puritanical nature. She objected to the expansive display of flesh that was exposed by the dancers at the French pavilion. "Not only is Miss Spencer seeking an injunction to close Paris [the descriptive name of the French pavilion], but she has protested to Washington. Reminding that soldiers are quartered at Camp John Whistler inside the grounds and that a submarine is tied up nearby, she is demanding enforcement of a federal law which provides that no lewd exhibition shall be given within half a mile of a military reservation.

"To be sure, the submarine is no longer in service. Formerly the *S-49*, it has been privately owned since the government, in accordance with the disarmament conference, scrapped it three years ago. But Miss Spencer defends her action on the grounds that the four wind-browned men, explaining the mysteries of its escape hatches and torpedo tubes, were members of the war-time crew."

These protests were either ignored or overruled, as nothing ever came of them. The exhibition of the submarine and nearly naked women continued unabated, and no doubt pleased more of the fair's visitors than it displeased.

After leaving Illinois, August 1935 found the *S-49* at Manitowoc, Wisconsin (also on Lake Michigan), under somewhat controversial circumstances. Chrestensen sent a promoter in advance of the submarine's arrival. The promoter paid for an advertisement to be placed in the *Herald-Times*. The ad read, in capitals: "MR. F.C. SCHOCH, MANAGER OF THE BENEVOLENT AND PROTECTIVE ORDER OF ELKS, ANNOUNCES THAT THE ELKS HAVE SUCCEEDED IN MAKING ARRANGEMENTS WITH THE NATIONAL MARINE EXHIBITING COMPANY OF BOSTON TO HAVE THE WORLD'S FAIR SUBMARINE *S-49* STOP AT MANITOWOC."

The newspaper accepted the promoter's money for the ad and promised to publish it. However, when the mock-up was shown to the newspaper's business manager, he entertained suspicions about the alleged connection with the Elks Club. He doubted the likelihood that the club would associate itself with a commercial enterprise. He called Fred Schoch. Schoch told him "that he had given no one authority to use the club sponsorship but had merely given permission for the gate leading from the street through the Elks dock to be opened for the public's convenience to get to the Land & Fuel docks where the sub was docked. It appeared to this newspaper that this submarine fellow was clearly attempting to use the Elks name under false pretenses."

Chrestensen's mercurial personality shone through when he arrived in Manitowoc two days later, learned that his ad had not been published, and descended upon the newspaper's headquarters with all the aplomb of a Midwest tornado. He demanded to know why his ad had not been published, along with two large photographs of the submarine that the promoter had furnished. The business manager explained the matter of the Elks Club, and added that Chrestensen's promoter had purchased space for the text but not for photographs.

Another of Chrestensen's promotional postcards, depicting the aft torpedo room.

At a wharf in Lorain, Ohio in 1936. Note the change in the color scheme, with no "C" and with the Navy designation painted in white against a dark background. (Courtesy of the Institute for Great Lakes Research.)

Chrestensen was miffed, no doubt expecting the same kind of front-page publicity that newspapers had given to the submarine during the Century of Progress Exhibition.

Under a page-2 boldface headline that read "**Submarine Visit Here Flops; Captain Vents Spleen When Refused Free Newspaper Ads**," the *Herald-Times* reported subsequent events pertaining to Chrestensen's initial appeasement and surly turnabout attitude with regard to his failed publicity campaign:

"After having blown off a lot of steam, Chrestensen admitted that perhaps a mistake had been made with reference to the Elks, and told about his coming into port and the difficulties he had in gaining the harbor in the fog. This was news, and, though the paper was about ready to go to press, a bordered feature story was rushed into print. In addition to that, a small free reader was given because of the lack of advance publicity. This was a free-will offering since the situation seemed to warrant it and the paper, after all, did not want to take a hard-boiled attitude.

"The fellow, because he had not gotten over his Elks sponsorship, appeared to be up against it for news of his coming. That was satisfactory but yesterday [August 27, 1935] when another demand was made for "free" pictures the request was again denied and in a plug-ugly voice the Captain berated the paper, its manager and its policies, and stalked out of the newspaper office in high dudgeon. To get even, he wrote up a personal attack against the paper's business manager, whose name he used in bold headlines, and gave his side of the story in the text. Then he essayed to find a job office to print the attack. In this he was unsuccessful until he reached a certain printing office, whose identity need not be stated, where, apparently, it was received with acclaim.

"The tirade was printed on a yellow sheet and circulated downtown yesterday where it had just the opposite reaction its authors designed.

"It might be said, just in passing, that the *Herald-Times* will continue to treat any 'fly-by-night' amusement enterprise in the same manner as it has done in this instance. We owe a certain allegiance to our legitimate advertisers and believe they should be given consideration over submarine shows or any other undertaking that comes to Manitowoc to take money out of town.

"Perhaps you cannot blame a 'promoter' who comes into Manitowoc for a 'soft touch' for venting his spleen when the public refused to be ballyhooed into paying twenty-five cents a throw to see an antiquated war machine. Someone had to be made the goat."

It would seem that Chrestensen's publicity scheme lost this bout with the Fourth Estate.

There is irony in Chrestensen's city of choice for the early public exhibition of the *S-49*. The Manitowoc Shipbuilding Company was located, appropriately, in Manitowoc. The company had been building vessels for Great Lakes shipping companies since 1902. With World War Two looming on the horizon, the company accepted contracts from the U.S. government for the construction of – you guessed it – submarines. Twenty-eight were completed before the end of the war. Of these, twenty-five saw action in the Pacific Theater. Collectively they sank 132 Japanese vessels. Four Manitowoc subs were lost in action.

The reach the sea, the Manitowoc-built subs were barged up the Chicago River, along the Chicago Drainage Canal to the Illinois River, then down the Mississippi past New Orleans, Louisiana, and into the Gulf of Mexico.

Nowadays the Wisconsin Maritime Museum is located in Manitowoc. In 1970, the U.S. Navy donated the *Gato*-class submarine *Cobia* (SS-245) to the museum. The *Cobia* is similar to the subs that were built in Manitowoc during the war. The submarine is on permanent display, and is available for touring much the same as the *S-49* during its occupancy in that city.

As a matter of interest, the *S-49* was not the first submarine to ply the fresh waters of Lake Michigan. That honor belongs to the German unterseeboote *UC-97*. It was one of six U-boats that were commissioned into the U.S. Navy after World War One, then brought to the United States for study and to tour the country as a way to promote the drive for Victory Bonds for a country that was broke. The *UC-97* was selected to proceed up the St. Lawrence River and into the Great Lakes. In 1919 it stopped at American and Canadian ports in Lakes Ontario, Erie, Huron, and Michigan. On July 7, 1921, it

16. SUBMARINE AND STREET SCENE — GREAT LAKES EXPOSITION, CLEVELAND, OHIO

Souvenir postcard.

Top right: One of Chrestensen's promotional postcards, picturing how the ladder beneath the after hatch was replaced with a staircase for the convenience of visitors.

Middle right: In this construction photo of sister ship *S-48* prior to completion, some of the gauges in the central control room have been blanked. (Courtesy of the National Archives.)

Bottom right: Control panel in the electric motor room. (Courtesy of the Submarine Force Library and Museum.)

was scuttled some twenty-five miles off Chicago, Illinois. (For complete details, see *The Kaiser's U-boats in American Waters*, by this author.)

A month after departing from Lake Michigan, The *S-49* received more favorable newspaper treatment in Sandusky, Ohio. On September 27, 1935, the *Sandusky Star Journal* published a photograph of the "monster" submarine along with seven paragraphs of descriptive text (although not on the front page). Here is one paragraph: "*The S-49* will be docked at the Big Four Dock and will be open to the general public for inspection. Competent guides will escort parties through the entire boat and will explain everything in detail. A small admission fee will be charged to defray part of the expenses of bringing the boat here."

It is possible that, having learned his lesson in Manitowoc, Chrestensen authorized his promoter to purchase sufficient space in the newspaper to include the photograph.

The *S-49* also made stops at the Ohio cities of Toledo and Lorain which, like Sandusky, were situated on the southern shore of Lake Erie.

The next big event for the *S-49* was the Great Lakes Exposition in Cleveland, Ohio (her home port) during 1936-1937. Once again she shared the waterfront with the *City of New York*. It was estimated that seven *million* visitors paid homage to the exposition. Untold thousands of tourists paid 25 cents each to duck through the submarine's low hatches and slink claustrophobically through her cramped compartments.

In dock, the *C* was "decked out with a string of colored lights, liberally coated with bright aluminum paint and, of all things, a pay-as-you-enter turnstile set up on the forward deck."

After the successful exposition in Cleveland, the *S-49* was reported at Oswego, New York (on Lake Ontario) in June 1938. She was then slated to proceed up the Oswego River to Syracuse, New York, but "Captain Christensen was unable to bring the craft to Syracuse because of the draft of 12 and one-half feet and requirement of 26 feet overhead clearance."

The next big notice of the *S-49* occurred in August 1938, after Chresentsen's wife sued for possession of the submarine. Anna had a long list of grievances which, unfortunately for Francis, received more newspaper coverage than the *S-49* ever did. The Texas tabloid *San Antonio Light* devoted a full page to the couple's embarrassing marriage travails – not on page 1, but on page 3.

The anonymous correspondent wrote somewhat tongue in cheek. Here are some samples:

"In her complaint before the Superior Court of Montreal, which didn't do her any good, the frustrated wife says that she married the captain in September, 1934, and that his income is $100,000 a year. Where all this wealth comes from she does not reveal. . . .

"The captain must have owned the *S49* [sic] for some three years before they were married and therefore, unless he concealed that material fact from his bride, she can hardly hold it against him. The trouble was that it became their home and legal residence. A submersible sounds so much more romantic than an ivy-covered cottage that it is surprising someone has not written a song about it. But, in reality, Mrs. Chrestensen found it full of unpleasant disadvantages. For one thing, the meanest tumble-down shack is sure to be where the housewife left it when she returns from the beauty parlor, unless there has been a fire or earthquake, and, in any event the ruins will remain. . . .

"If the house is a trailer, it can be traced, but the *S49* [sic] could efface itself without leaving a hole in the water to show where it had been. Another annoyance was the captain's alleged custom of permitting the public to prowl all over their submersible home, at fifty cents a prowl. Considering the cost of keeping a submarine in commission including a skeleton crew of eight men, it seems unlikely there was any great profit in these exhibitions, hardly $100,000 a year. Perhaps these were some of the reasons which caused Dame Anna Ramel Chrestensen to say in the second line of her complaint:

"2 – That ever since the marriage life in common with him has been impossible.

"Nevertheless Mrs. Chrestensen seems to have achieved the impossible by living in common with him until something more than six months ago when they parted at Buffalo [New York]. Whether Mrs. Chrestensen left the captain's submersible bed and board or the said bed and board left her, has not been stated. . . .

" 'Never let your husband buy a submarine,' warned Mrs. R. F. Chrestensen, of some American port, she isn't sure which. 'He may make it his residence and then you are just sunk if you need to collect alimony for separation or divorce. You might as well try to collect from a turtle at the bottom of a lake.'

"Mrs. Chrestensen knows because, fortified with court papers, court officials and a lawyer, she tried it the other day at Montreal, Canada, only to see her husband, Captain Chrestensen, thumb his nose at them and the whole landlubber world in general. Then he boarded his private submarine, the *S49* [sic], ran down the St. Lawrence River and out to the depths of the Atlantic Ocean [an obvious exaggeration].

"It was only a moral victory for the captain who, having attained it, was moved by sentiment or some other prompting to return to Montreal, go into court and settle the dispute with his wife with a reconciliation, after which the two resumed their life on the ocean waves. Perhaps Captain Chrestensen only wanted to establish a precedent regarding the legal status of a private submarine in connection with domestic litigation, or probably he wanted to go on record with a brand new trick of alimony dodging."

The *S-49* continued her peregrinations after this marital distraction and break in domestic bliss. The San Antonio pundit may have embroidered the case of establishing a precedent with regard to connubial litigation, but the next case clearly established a very important precedent – one that is still being argued today by students of American jurisprudence. This was a case involving First Amendment rights (freedom of speech and freedom of the press): a case that Chrestensen argued all the way to the Supreme Court of the United States.

It began innocuously after Chrestensen decided to exhibit his submarine in New York City. It was the summer of 1940, when the Nazis were invading European countries left and right. America remained politically neutral despite popular Allied sympathy. Although America's entry into the war was not yet inevitable, Congress commenced to think about making appropriations for the construction of modern submarines. What better allegiance could there be than to promote the *S-49* in the country's largest city?

Chrestensen wanted to dock the submarine at Battery Park, within view of the Statue of Liberty. City officials refused to grant permission for him to do so by invoking sanitation codes, proclaiming in their protest that proximate toilet facilities were inadequate to handle the anticipated crowds. So he moved the submarine to a public dock on the East River.

The situation was satisfactory until Chrestensen started to hand out leaflets that advertised guided tours through the cramped interior: "See how men live in a hell diver. Popular prices: adults 25 cents and children 15 cents."

No sooner had he begun to solicit visitors in this manner than the police department informed him that he was now breaking a different municipal ordinance of the Big Apple's sanitary code, one that pertained to littering. Paragraph 318 of the code read, "No person shall throw, cast or distribute, or cause or permit to be thrown, cast or distributed, any handbill, circular, card, booklet, placard or other advertising matter whatsoever in or upon any street or public place, or in a front yard or court yard, or on any stoop, or in the vestibule of any hall of any building, or in a letterbox therein; provided that nothing herein contained shall be deemed to prohibit or otherwise regulate the delivery of any such matter by the United States postal service, or prohibit the distribution of sample copies of newspapers regularly sold by the copy or by annual subscription. This section is not intended to prevent the lawful distribution of anything other than commercial and business advertising matter."

The invocation of this code was questionable. While the written legalese sounds impressive, it was largely irrelevant in the instant case because Chrestensen did not intend to throw or cast his leaflets as if he were delivering newspapers to household subscribers. He intended to hand them to pedestrians. As everyone knows, codes of this nature are selectively enforced, depending upon which side of the political fence an individual or business resides. The police department took a hardboiled stance and stuck by the letter of the code.

When Chrestensen complained to the police commissioner, Lewis Valentine, the commissioner remained adamant. In conversation, Valentine explained that the code pertained only to commercial advertising matter, and not to leaflets that were informational in nature: public protest, candidates for political office, and so on. Chrestensen seized upon this technicality by creating a double-sided handbill whose obverse side protested the City Dock Department's refusal to permit "wharfage facilities at a city pier for the exhibition of his submarine, but not commercial advertising," while the re-

A picture postcard showing the *S-49* in Cleveland.

verse side was revised from the original by deleting the admission fee, which, in his mind, converted the text from an advertisement to straightforward information.

Valentine disagreed. He allowed that "distribution of a bill containing only the protest would not violate paragraph 318, and would not be restrained, but that distribution of the double faced bill was prohibited. The respondent, nevertheless, proceeded with the printing of his proposed bill and started to distribute it. He was restrained by police. Respondent then brought this suit to enjoin the petitioner from interfering with the distribution."

It is difficult to accept that so slight a difference in interpretation of a sanitary code would eventually become a federal case, but it did. Chrestensen filed a lawsuit against the police commissioner. In Valentine v. Chrestensen, Chrestensen argued that his First Amendment rights had been violated. The First Amendment makes no distinction between commercial speech and non-commercial speech. It guarantees freedom of *all* speech, no matter in what form that speech is expressed.

Yet the court found otherwise by upholding the City's right to limit an individual's or a business's freedom of speech with regard to handbills. Chrestensen tenaciously stuck to his guns and appealed the lower court's ruling. The case eventually landed in the lap of the United States Supreme Court.

Although the justices admitted, "This court has unequivocally held that the streets are proper places for the exercise of the freedom of communicating information and disseminating opinion, and that, though the states and municipalities may appropriately regulate the privilege in the public interest, they may not unduly burden or proscribe its employment in these public thoroughfares. We are equally clear that the Constitution imposes no such restraint on government as respects purely commercial advertising."

Amazingly, in their opinion, the justices did not even mention the Bill of Rights or the First Amendment. They simply concluded, "It is enough for the present purpose that the stipulated facts justify the conclusion that the affixing of the protest against official conduct to the advertising circular was with the intent, and for the purpose, of evading the prohibition of the ordinance. If that evasion were successful, every merchant who desires to broadcast advertising leaflets in the streets need only append a civic appeal, or a moral platitude, to achieve immunity from the law's command."

This 1942 Supreme Court decision was a bold nullification of the freedom of speech. This precedent-setting decision has been cited in numerous cases, argued forward and backward, and sometimes reversed or overruled by subsequent courts: not only lower courts but even later Supreme Courts.

Freedom of speech is the backbone of democracy: a freedom that is guaranteed by the Constitution, but one that unfortunately has been eroded by later decisions. Certainly the framers never intended the freedom of speech to be parsed in order to suit political agendas. Freedom is either total or nonexistent; there is no middle ground.

Chrestensen moved onward, and the *S-49* was moved to other venues. September 1940 found her on the Hudson River in Kingston, New York, where her turnstiles were open from ten o'clock in the morning until ten o'clock at night. She was still on the Hudson River in July 1941, this time docked at Albany, New York; the same visiting hours applied, and she was even open on Sunday.

The *C* was still registered as a yacht in the 1944 edition of the *Merchant Vessels of the United States*. Yet, official records indicate that she was reacquired by the U.S.

Navy on January 29, 1943: "Accepted by Comfour from War Shipping Administration for use in experimental work at Naval Mine Warfare Proving Ground, Solomons," Maryland. (Comfour is Navy shorthand for Commandant of the Fourth Naval District.) The operations officer of experimentation was given as Commander Higgit.

The *S-49* was not recommissioned as a Navy vessel; rather, she became nothing more than a hulk or an odd piece of equipment such as a desk or filing cabinet. What this means in terms of historical narrative is that her daily activities were not recorded in a deck log and signed by a watch officer. Indeed, I could not find any official documentation to establish that her name reverted from *C* to *S-49*, although communiques referred to her in the latter designation.

The Navy did not keep a written record of daily events on vessels that were not listed on the active naval register, any more than it kept a diary of proceedings in a building. If anything, SS-160 can be compared to a vehicle, which was used by anyone who held the proper authority, but not necessarily requiring written permission. It was simply a piece of property that could be used in accordance with military necessity, or discarded as trash when it was worn out or no longer of any use.

Rumor rather than documentation has it that the hull was employed in training exercises in the use of the McCann Rescue Chamber: an airtight vessel that was lowered to a sunken submarine and attached to an escape hatch, so that trapped submariners could be rescued from their flooded craft. Rumor also has it that the hull was rerigged so it could be submerged remotely, without anyone on board, and subsequently refloated in similar fashion. Additional rumor claims that the hull was purposely placed at the bottom of the Patuxent River in order to serve as a target for testing underwater acoustical detection devices such as sonar.

Adding to the confusion of this rather nebulous and phoenixlike later career is this cryptic memorandum from Commander Robert Sminkey: "Shortly after being towed to Solomons from Baltimore, *S-49* foundered off Point Patience in the Patuxent River on 16 December 1942 and sank in 102 feet of water."

You have undoubtedly noticed that this date is six weeks prior to the date on which Comfour was supposed to have acquired the hulk. Hopefully, the mystery of SS-160 will someday be unraveled by the emergence of files that my extensive correspondence with the Navy, and my personal inspection at the Naval Historical Center, have been unable to locate. In any case, there it remained, sunken but not forgotten.

For years afterward the hull was reportedly used as a training ground by the Navy hard-hat school, by underwater demolition teams, and for teaching welding and torching and familiarization with working by feel. SS-160 certainly filled these bills admirably. Jon Hulburt substantiated these allegations circumstantially when he found a brass-and-canvas diving boot on the wreck.

As late as the 1970's, Vietnam-era divers reportedly used the site for similar exercises. In addition, it might still have found use as a sonar target in order to test newer and more sophisticated equipment.

Recreational divers began to visit the hull in the late 1970's. Andy Whitehouse told me that at that time the wreck lay only 150 feet from the south shore, that the bow was pointed upstream at a depth of 80 feet, and that the stern angled down to 130 feet. The way he and his buddies accessed the site was by swimming out from the beach to a depth that was greater than 80 feet, then letting the current carry them to the hull. I have no reason to disbelieve him.

Yet Whitehouse's description is inconsistent with the present position and depth of the wreck: by my observation the bow points *downstream* and sits on an even keel with about a ten degree list to starboard, at a constant depth of 132 feet. All I can say is: this is how it lies now, that was how it lay then. What happened in between is anyone's guess.

On subsequent dives I found verification that extensive modifications had been made to the wreck. While groping around the conning tower in near-zero visibility, I discovered a bulkhead on which were mounted gauges and speaking tubes. I was at a loss to explain why they were bolted onto the outboard side when they should have been mounted *inside* the conning tower, until Hulburt convinced me that the port side of the conning tower had been cut away, and that the gauges were actually located at their original location on the inboard side of the existing starboard bulkhead, which at one time *was* inside the conning tower.

The overhead or ceiling of the conning tower was still in place, although due to the virtual blackness I had never noticed the overhang from underneath. Afterward, with more ambient light and better visibility, I confirmed Hulburt's suspicions. The metal was so heavily overgrown with marine encrustation that the cutaway edges appeared smooth and natural.

It seems likely that the port bulkhead of the conning tower was torched off for some reason. Whether that was done before the submarine made its final plunge, or afterward by Navy divers in training, remains another mystery.

Add to this the fact that one speaking tube had copper electrical wires protruding from it – a condition that would have compromised the watertight integrity of the hull – and we can form a picture of a submarine that could not possibly have dived with any hope of resurfacing if half the conning tower had previously been removed.

Also in this partially exposed conning tower were an engine-order telegraph with controls for both engines, and a torpedo firing selector switch for all five torpedo tubes. I took close-up pictures of these items. I added these images to slide presentations that I gave at dive club meetings and underwater symposiums; I incorporated the images in my wreck photography workshop as examples of how to procure suitable images in poor visibility conditions.

After a while, I began to hear whispered grapevine talk about how bold or crazy Jon Hulburt and I were, because divers had mistakenly gained the impression that we had doffed our tanks in order to crawl down hatch openings into the dark, cramped interior of the now-famous Black Water Submarine, where visibility rarely exceeded two to three feet, and where one touch of an encrusted surface resulted in an eruption of silt that reduced visibility to zero. I corrected this undeserved adulation by proclaiming the truth loud and clear whenever I heard such praiseworthy gossip. I also made certain to emphasize how I had taken the photographs from outside a conning tower that had been carved in two down the middle. In the meantime, Hulburt and I had a good laugh about our superhuman reputations.

Continued exploration has yielded other data about the submarine's condition. The plating over the bow torpedo tube outer doors is not obvious: it is distinguishable more by the absence of indents than by actual observation. Whether the tubes have been removed is impossible to determine without examining the forward torpedo room from

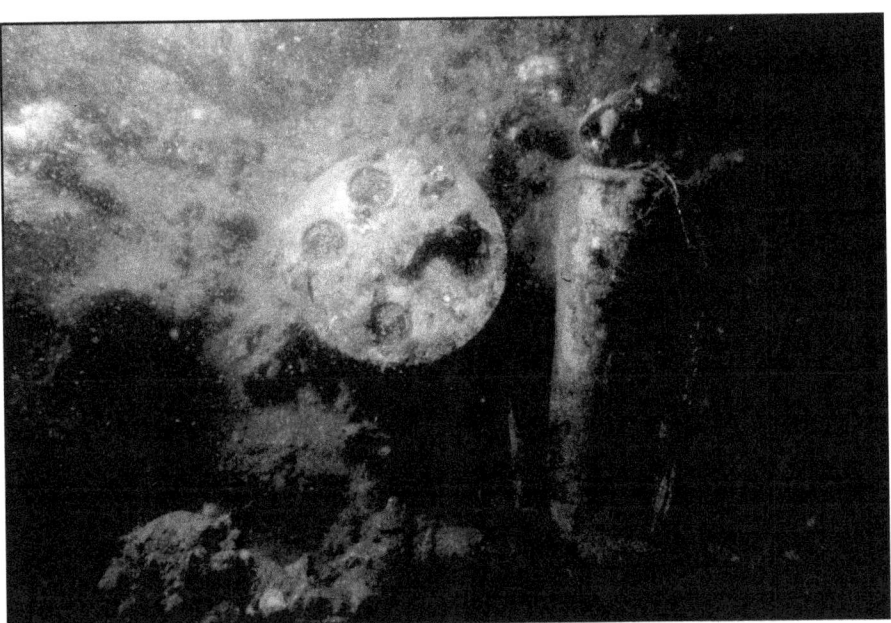

Torpedo firing selector switch and speaking tube in the lower level of the conning tower, from which the port bulkhead has been torched off or cut away. Note the wire extending out of the speaking tube.

inside. The external opening of the stern tube is partially plugged; a circular steel plate is bolted over top of it.

I have not seen the hatch at the bottom of the conning tower due to a copious layer of mud. Nowhere is it easy to determine what the wreck actually looks like under the thick carpet of marine growth.

There is some environmental concern that the polyps that grow so profusely on the hull, and in the Chesapeake Bay in general, are consuming too much oxygen from the water, and are consequently harming the oyster beds. If the preponderance of empty oyster shells on the bottom of the river is any guide, the once-thriving oyster industry has much to worry about.

I thought at first that the resultant deoxygenation might be responsible for decelerating the deterioration process of the steel hull: visually, the wreck appears to be in good condition. However, succeeding dives have proven otherwise. On one dive I made during an incoming tide, the wreck literally came apart in my hands. First, as I gripped the top of the bridge coaming, a great sheet of metal tore free. Then, as I was swept along the hull I grabbed a thick stanchion, which broke in two. I tumbled backward, ricocheting and grabbing for something solid, and ripped off two sections of steel decking before I found a secure handhold. I felt like the Hulk, tearing the wreck apart piece by piece. Only with great difficulty did I make my way back to the anchor line.

On another occasion, a diver got ripped off the anchor line after the slack tide ended, and we had to chase him for half a mile downstream as the current and outgoing tide conspired to shoot him into the bay and out to sea.

The water runs faster on the outgoing tide when the tidal flow assists the river current instead of bucking it. Diving is impossible during the outgoing tide. The best time to get into the water is just before slack tide. The slight current will sweep away stirred-up silt. To avoid the distress of the diver in the preceding paragraph, splash at the end of the slack that is followed by the incoming tide instead of the slack that is followed by the outgoing tide. That way, if you get caught by the turn of the tide, the water flow will not be as strong.

The structural integrity of the hull is an illusion. The steel looks good and feels strong, but I suspect that on the atomic scale it has degenerated badly. The wreck is more like a fractured eggshell, waiting for the least little nudge to make it crumble.

In this it is no different from any other shipwreck. Only for a short time will it maintain its delicate balance at the bottom of the river. Eventually the hull will become pockmarked with rust holes; later, as openings appear in the pressure hull, the influx of water will accelerate deterioration. Access to the interior will become possible, perhaps even easy.

Only for the most serious diver is the *S-49* at all appealing. Decompressing under conditions in which you can touch your buddy but not see him, while hanging onto an anchor line in a stiff current in which the farthest you can see is your dirt-covered kneepads, may not be your cup of cold tea.

But then, a hot lunch is only five minutes away.

Yet another of Chrestensen's promotional postcards, showing the many gauges, valves, wheels, and controls in the aptly named control room, inside the main pressure hull and directly beneath the conning tower. The two large hand wheels were used to regulate the submarine's depth and trim.

THREE RIVERS

Built: 1910
Previous names: None
Gross tonnage: 1,110
Type of vessel: Steel-hulled side-wheel steamer
Builder: Maryland Steel Company, Sparrows Point, Maryland
Owner: Baltimore & Virginia Steamboat Company, Baltimore, Maryland
Port of registry: Baltimore, Maryland
Cause of sinking: Fire
Location: Cove Point

Sunk: July 4, 1924
Depth: Raised
Dimensions: 180' x 36' x 9'
Power: Coal-fired steam

The *Three Rivers* was built as a passenger vessel in 1910. She was propelled by a single-cylinder engine that turned two paddle wheels which were cleverly concealed in a paddle box whose outer beams were even with the outer bulkhead of the superstructure. She normally carried a crew of thirty-four.

For all of her unremarkable career except for the final two months, the *Three Rivers* was operated under the aegis of the Maryland, Delaware and Virginia Railway Company (which was in partnership with the Baltimore, Chesapeake and Atlantic Railway Company, as well as with the Baltimore and Eastern Shore Railroad Company). For fourteen years she provided fast and reliable passenger service on the Chesapeake Bay.

On April 2, 1924, she was sold to the Baltimore & Virginia Steamboat Company. This change of ownership proved fortuitous for the former owner, disastrous for the latter.

The major reason – indeed, perhaps the only reason – that the *Three Rivers* catastrophe is remembered today is because five newsboys who worked for the *Baltimore Evening Sun*, and who played in the paper's newsboy band, died in the conflagration that overtook the vessel.

July 4, 1924 found the *Three Rivers* on a passage from Crisfield to Baltimore. She was returning from the fourth annual Chesapeake Bay championship workboat races. Shortly after midnight, flames were discovered in the saloon when the vessel was steaming northward off Cove Point. Because the blaze occurred at night, nearly everyone except duty personnel was asleep. According to official records, at that time there were 139 persons onboard, of whom 59 were band members; newspaper accounts claimed the number of passengers was as high as 350.

According to one (possibly exaggerated) newspaper account: "So rapidly did the flames spread and so thick was the smoke that many were forced to jump into the water. They dropped from the sides of the burning steamer like flies, some without life preservers.

"Panic spread among the passengers. Some ran screaming from their staterooms, leaving their children and belongings, and clad only in nightclothes. They either jumped overboard or ran screaming about the deck until taken aboard the lifeboats.

"Several passengers and members of the crew were injured. Some of them were burned fighting the fire. Others were cut by glass broken in their frenzy to climb through

stateroom windows. Still others were hurt by falls.

"Some of the newsboys heroically ran from stateroom to stateroom arousing passengers, took care of smaller members of the band and helped the crew to quiet passengers.

"Two of the lifeboats were launched and took many passengers to the steamer *Middlesex*, which arrived here [Baltimore] this afternoon with survivors. Many persons were picked up from the water. The gangplanks, boards, chicken coops, a life raft and even two coffin boxes were thrown overboard to help support those who were driven into the water by the flames.

"Steamers bound down the bay and going to Baltimore heard the frantic blasts of the whistle of the *Three Rivers*, or saw the mounting flames, and put on full steam for the vessel. The *Middlesex* of the Baltimore & Virginia Steamboat Company, the *Allegany* of the Merchants' and Miners' Transportation Company, the *Plankatank* of the Baltimore, Chesapeake & Atlantic Railway Company, an unidentified vessel of the Dollar Line, one of the Chesapeake Line and one of the Bay Line stood by and helped in the rescue.

"Survivors taken aboard the *Middlesex*, which was the first boat to reach the burning ship, received first-aid treatment and were provided with clothing and put to bed. Other survivors are believed to be aboard one of the other boats."

According to bandleader Frank Morse, "Many of the boys were among the last to leave the burning boat. They threw life preservers to those struggling in the water. Some manned fire hoses and fought the flames."

The *Three Rivers* burned nearly to the waterline. The smoldering steel hull grounded, but the wooden superstructure was completely consumed. The heat was so intense that metal lifeboats were buckled like corrugated tin, and the glass in the portholes melted like butter so that some of the glass had the appearance of icicles.

In retrospect, it is amazing that, with so many people adrift in the water in the dark, fatalities were so few: ten confirmed dead. A dozen others were injured from cuts and burns.

Five members of the Newsboys Band were found in the burned-out remains of the hull: Vernon Jefferson, Nelson Miles, Walter Millikin, Thomas Pilker, and Lester Seligman; they were aged from thirteen to seventeen. Also found in the hull was the body of a Negro. "The body of a white man believed to be James Truitt, of Baltimore, was found floating in the Bay off Cove Point late yesterday [July 6] and shortly before the body of a negro around which was strapped a life preserver of the *Three Rivers* was washed ashore on Hooper's Island. The bodies of two other negroes had been found shortly after the disaster."

Elsewhere it was noted that passengers James Mack and Evelyn Parker (also given as Evelyn Crocker) died in the calamity, as did pantryman Elijah Brogden. The astute reader will have noticed that the unofficial count of persons who perished, either in the blaze or by drowning, exceeds the official body count, but I am reporting precisely what contemporary accounts recorded in the absence of the investigation of the steamboat inspectors, most of whose investigative reports are not extant. A one paragraph summary in the annual report estimated the monetary loss at $90,000.

Opposite page: Three views of the *Three Rivers*. From top to bottom: Before the fire, during the fire, and after the fire. (From the collection of Mike Moore.)

The deceased newsboys were buried side by side in the Loudon Park Cemetery, in Baltimore. The *Baltimore Evening Sun* erected a stone memorial so their deaths would not be forgotten by future generations. The memorial and gravesites are still maintained.

Normally the saga of a shipwreck would end at this point. Not so in the case of the *Three Rivers*. The burned-out hull was raised and towed to safe harbor. During the following year its title was transferred three times: first to the Tolchester Beach Improvement Company, then to Charles Jording, and finally to the Richmond Cedar Works.

The machinery was removed in the process of converting the vessel to a barge, which was then renamed *Richmond Cedar Works No. 6*. According to an article written by Ernest Imhoff, and published in the *Baltimore Sun* in 1994, the barge "carried wood for three decades in coastal Virginia waters until abandoned in 1958."

Even then the story does not end, for I came across an interesting anecdote in *A Personal History of Nuclear Medicine*, by Henry N. Wagner, Jr. He related an account that was handed down through his family memoirs. Wagner's mother and grandmother planned a family visit by taking the *Three Rivers* on what turned out to be her fatal voyage. At the last minute, Wagner's mother begged off the trip because of a head cold. His grandmother proceeded on her own.

Wagner: "Not only do the fittest survive, but also the luckiest. Grandmother's luck was that among the newsboys was a 17-year-old newsboy, William Elkins, who played the bass horn in the newsboy band. He heard grandmother's cries for help, and broke into her cabin through the single porthole facing the deck. Throwing her arms over his shoulders, he crawled back out on deck, grabbing two life jackets. He tried unsuccessfully to launch a life raft, and then, giving up, threw a rope down the side of the boat, and descended from the third deck down into the water. Grandmother was hanging on with her arms over his shoulders. With her crying but not struggling, he swam two hundred yards with her still clinging to his back. They reached a lifeboat launched by another boat, the *Middlesex*, which had responded to the SOS and raced to the rescue of the *Three Rivers*. They were hauled aboard the *Middlesex* to join the other survivors. . . . . A few days later, my grandmother and parents-to-be invited William to a celebratory dinner at their 1919 W. Fayette St. home, where they presented him with a gold watch to express their gratitude for his heroism."

Wagner also wrote that his mother's decision not to accompany *her* mother "saved her life (and made possible mine)." Wagner was not born until three years later. On such seemingly meaningless vagaries of fate does life and survival sometimes depend.

TULIP

Built: 1863
Previous names: *Chih Kiang*
Gross tonnage: 183
Type of vessel: Wooden-hulled fourth-rate gunboat
Builder: Jewett & Company or Fincourt & Company, Brooklyn, New York
Owner: U.S. Navy
Cause of sinking: Boiler explosion
Location: Ragged Point, Potomac River

Sunk: November 11, 1864
Depth: 45 feet
Dimensions: 97' x 21' x 9'
Power: Coal-fired steam

GPS: 38-10.038 / 76-35.981

U.S. Navy sources differ as to the *Tulip's* origination. Some documents claim that she was built by James C. Jewett; other documents state that the builder was Fincourt and Company. Her length measured either 101 feet or 97 feet, with the latter measurement cited more often. She was constructed either as a tug or a lighthouse tender.

All documents agree that the screw steamer was built for the Chinese navy in 1863, and that she was named *Chih Kiang*. They also agree that the *Chih Kiang* never reached her intended buyer. It appears that Chinese mandarin Henry G. Ward died before he could take possession. The U.S. Navy paid $30,000 to add the wooden-hulled vessel to its beleaguered fleet. The Navy purchasing agent was given as Admiral H. Paulding.

On August 24, the Navy added a battery to enable the newly ordained gunboat to protect herself from Confederate onslaught during her towing operations along the Potomac River. The initial battery consisted of two 24-pound howitzers and one 20-pound Parrott rifle. To this was added two heavy smoothbore 12-pounders, on September 30, 1864.

Another modification that was made in 1864 (on June 4) was a cabin.

"Initially engaged in towing duties at the Washington Navy Yard, the gunboat/tug saw service with the [Potomac River] flotilla, in its operations against Confederate forces in the Rappahannock [River]. In the latter duties, the ship aided in the transportation of Federal troops and took part in supporting naval landing parties and interdicting Confederate supply and communications traffic.

"Continuing these wartime riverine activities through the end of 1863 and into 1864, *Tulip* developed a defective starboard boiler as time went on. Commander Foxhall A. Parker, commanding the Union Potomac Flotilla, ordered the ship home to the Washington Navy Yard so that repairs could be effected to the vital half of her propulsion plant, and *Tulip* accordingly set out on 11 November with orders restricting her steaming to the port boiler only."

On board at that time were 57 officers and men. The commanding officer was Acting Master William H. Smith.

What happened next was described by one of the survivors, Acting Ensign and Executive Officer R.N. Wagstaff, in his succinct report to Commander Parker: "I have to report to you the loss of the U.S.S. *Tulip* on the evening of the 11th inst. In obedience to orders we steamed with one boiler from St. Inigoes Creek at about 3 o'clock P.M.

bound for Washington. At about 5 o'clock Act'g 3rd Ass't Engineer Geo. Parks, in charge of the engines of the vessel said to us – Captain Smith and myself – that if we would stop at Piney Point about two hours he would have steam on the starboard boiler – which was the damaged one – before we reached Piney Point, Act'g 3rd Ass't Engineer John Gordon then on watch said to me, that 'there was no use of stopping at Piney Point for he had already got steam on the other boiler'. I then reported to Capt. Smith, what Mr. Gordon had said and he directed me to proceed on up the river. At about 6 o'clock and 20 minutes when abreast of Ragged Point, I was sitting in the wardroom with Act'g 3rd Ass't Engineer Geo. Parks when I heard Act'g 3rd Ass't Engineer John Gordon call over to haul fire's. Act'g 3rd Ass't Engineer Parks ran on deck and I followed – I saw steam coming from the Engine room – Act'g 3rd Ass't Engineer Parks jumped down into the Engine room and immediately returned – Act'g 3rd Ass't Engineer Gordon called out 'For God sake some one raise the safety valve.' Act'g 3rd Ass't Engineer Parks again jumped down into the Engine room and at this moment the explosion took place. The vessel to the best of my belief sunk within three minutes from the time of the explosion. We, ten in number, were picked up at 7 o'clock by the Tug boat *Hudson* and brought to this place [on the USS *Wyandunk* at St. Inigoes Creek]."

Newspaper accounts added gory detail that was lacking in Wagstaff's meager official report. The *Tulip's* "boiler exploded with a terrible crash, rending the upper portion of the vessel to atoms, scalding the officers and crew, and hurling them in all directions. Several of those who escaped without serious injury ran immediately to lower the gig, but before they could get it down, the wreck of the *Tulip* sank, carrying down with it most all on board. Some of the officers and men seized what they could lay their hands on and succeeded in keeping afloat for over an hour until their position was discovered by the tug boat *Hudson*. The *Hudson's* officers searched diligently among the floating pieces of wreck, but succeeded in finding no others than those mentioned, and steamed on to St. Inigoes."

According to another graphic newspaper account, "Captain Smith, the pilot James, Master's Mate Hammond and the Quartermaster were on the bridge over the boilers,

Tulip lookalike *Fuschia*. (Courtesy of the Naval Photographic Center.)

and must have been blown to atoms. The only trace left of Capt. Smith was his hat."

Two of the survivors died later of their injuries.

Wagstaff's report implied that Smith either ordered steam on the defective boiler, or at the very least approved of the boiler's use when he was informed about it.

A faded memory and a family letter appear to clarify this point, although with some reservation due to faulty recall. J.M. Ellicott was a youngster when the *Tulip* exploded. According to him, "The *Tulip* was a converted lighthouse tender gunboat attached to the Potomac Flotilla under Commodore Foxhall Parker, based at my home on St. Inigoes Creek in 1864. One of her two boilers was condemned, and she was ordered to Washington for a new one. He (Parker) dined with us that evening before sailing and in the course of the conversation said that as soon as he was out of signal distance he was going to get up steam on the condemned boiler, as he did not intend to go creeping up the Potomac under the fire of the Confederate batteries.

"Members of the family postulated vigorously and begged him not to do it. Their warnings frightened me and I could not sleep that night. About 9 o'clock we heard a dull explosion and I sat up in bed exclaiming, 'The *Tulip*!' And so it was. She had blown up and sunk off Piney Point."

The fallacy in this recollection is that the captain of the *Tulip* was Smith, not Parker. The accuracy of the rest of the reminiscence may therefore be suspect. Be that as it may, the way Ellicott remembered events that were related to him as a child, "Most of the officers were in the messroom, directly above the boiler, but when the engineer reported that steam was pouring from the boiler, the purser walked out. A few moments later he was blown overboard by the explosion. He swam ashore." Official records are lacking in this regard.

Upon hearing about the accident, Foxhall dispatched Philip Sheridan, captain of the USS *Juniper*, to investigate. Sheridan reported, "In obedience to your orders of the 12th instant, I proceeded to Raggy Point in search of the bodies and remains of the U.S. Str. *Tulip* which was blown up by steam on the eve of the 11th instant off that point. I sent our two boats and landed on the beach where I found large fragments of her remains. I found a trunk belonging to A.M. Mate Reynolds of that vessel, a valise belonging to the pilot, a coat, bag and several blue shirts and a number of officers' caps. I also found two sponges, a lot of signal flags and a package of letters marked U.S. Str. *Tulip*. Large portions of her deck, the top of her pilot house, and her 1st cutter lay on the beach but up to the present time I have not been able to find any bodies."

Sheridan appended a postscript: "I should have mentioned that the cutter referred to above, was entirely stove, and that I found some of the ribs and knees of the *Tulip* on shore, showing that that vessel was completely blown to pieces."

Like many shipwrecks, the *Tulip* was largely forgotten or ignored after the horror of the catastrophe yielded to worse ongoing events in war-torn America. A generation earlier, the loss of 49 people from a shipboard boiler explosion would have resulted in Congressional investigation. Now the episode was reduced to a footnote that was incidental to the overall conflict between the North and the South. Compared to 600,000 soldiers who were killed in combat, 49 fatalities were relatively insignificant. So many vessels were sunk during the War between the States that the demise of a fourth-rate gunboat did not garner much attention.

However, the naval rating of the gunboat did not reflect upon the rating of the men who were killed on her. Eight unidentified bodies were buried at the Potomac Flotilla Base. After the war, the temporary base reverted to civilian hands. The deceased patriots and their erstwhile companions might have been overlooked forever had it not been for one man who took it upon himself to advocate a "Memorial to sailors killed on U.S.S. *Tulip* during Civil War": U.S. Navy Captain J.M. Ellicott, retired, and the same person who is noted above as remembering the incident from his childhood. He petitioned the Secretary of the Navy to commemorate those men who died in the sinking."

According to his letter, dated September 15, 1929, "Toward the end of the Civil War the Potomac Flotilla had a coaling base on Saint Inigoes Creek, a branch of the Saint Mary's River, on property owned by my grandfather, Dr. C.M. Jones. One evening the U.S.S. *Tulip*, a converted lighthouse tender, left the base for Washington, D.C., with a condemned boiler. When off Piney Point in the Potomac River the boiler exploded and, I think, the *Tulip* sank, and nearly all on board were lost.

"The following day about a dozen bodies of sailors, possibly individually unrecognizable, were buried in a thicket on the bank of Saint Inigoes Creek almost due north of Dr. Jones' residence, which is known as Cross Manor. This property now belongs to me and my sister, Mrs. Chas. S. Grason, who makes her home upon it. The burial site has remained undisturbed ever since, but during a recent visit I found the graves of the sailors completely indistinguishable and the site, as it has always been, unmarked.

"I suggest that the records of the Potomac Flotilla be searched to obtain whatever identity is possible of the sailors buried there, and that a monument or memorial tablet be erected on the spot. It can be unmistakably identified by its direction (North) from Cross Manor, on a low bank at the water's edge and under a large ash tree, much larger than any other tree in its vicinity. The site is also known to my sister, Mrs. Chas. S. Grason, living on the premises."

When government works at all, it usually works slowly. Not until eight years later – on June 15, 1937 – did Congress pass an Act to authorize the purchase of the burial site and the erection of a monument to honor the dead crewmembers. In 1939, the government purchased a half-acre plot on the bank of St. Inigoes Creek, in St. Inigoes, Maryland. On June 15, 1940, a granite monument was erected in this small and newly designated cemetery. The ornate stele stood some seven feet tall. This monument ensured that the dismembered and disremembered gunboat would no longer be relegated to the history books and musty archives that were out of sight and therefore out of mind.

The *Tulip* was next recalled to social consciousness on the one-hundredth anniversary of its sinking. By a strange coincidence, after Germany signed the Armistice that ended World War One (on November 11, 1918), the date of the *Tulip's* loss became Veterans Day. According to a 1964 newspaper account, "Tomorrow, Veterans Day, a delegation of local dignitaries will troop over dirt roads, through cornfields and down a dusty path about 10 miles from [Lexington Park] to commemorate the 100th anniversary of the loss of the *Tulip* and its 49 men."

Although the *Tulip's* grave site now had a marker, the site of the wreck did not. Its precise location was unknown.

Enter the Adventurers Dive Club. In the late 1960's, club members obtained the location of an unidentified shipwreck from a local fisherman. In those days before electronic navigation – at a time when loran was in its infancy and global positioning sys-

IN MEMORY OF
THOSE WHO PERISHED
IN THE EXPLOSION
OF THE U.S.S. TULIP
NOVEMBER 11, 1864

The *Tulip* graveyard/memorial is located on the eastern shore of St. Inigoes Creek. The GPS coordinates are 38-09.731 / 76-25.448. Tune in your travel GPS receiver to 47733 Cross Manor Road: the street address of the house whose fence lies behind the Maryland Civil War Trails sign, which points the way along the 100-yard dirt road that leads to the site.

Alternatively, from Point Lookout Road (Highway 5), turn southwest onto Villa Road; proceed for a mile and a quarter; turn north (right) onto Grayson Road; proceed for half a mile to the T; turn west (left) onto Cross Manor Road; proceed for a quarter mile to the end, which is marked by a white fence on which the house address is given. Park on the grass on the right, near the Maryland Civil War Trails sign. Walk a hundred yards along the dirt road to the end.

Top of this page: One of two descriptive plaques, headstone, and stone monument.

Left: Lettering on the monument.

Bottom of opposite page: The other descriptive plaque with Inigoes Creek in the background.

tems were unheard of – club members set out to locate the wreck by means of land ranges. The fisherman's ranges were accurate, enabling club members to find the wreck and dive on it.

The wreck lay at a depth of 45 feet. No superstructure remained, and the hull was mostly buried in soft mud. Only two to three feet of wood protruded from the silt-laden bottom. Furthermore, visibility could usually be measured in inches. The enterprising divers were certain that they had found the remaining timbers of the *Tulip's* hull.

Despite the awful conditions, they were not to be discouraged from disinterring the historical trove that the *Tulip* represented. They started to recover artifacts that could be put on display for future generations to see. They build a water jet to wash the mud out of the sunken hull. Working largely by feel, they burrowed down beneath the deck into the wreck's black interior. During the course of this stupendous volunteer project, they found and rescued hundreds of relics from a bygone era – relics that had not seen the light of day in more than a century.

Club members decided to seek exclusive salvage rights that would protect their tremendous efforts from encroachers. On December 17, 1968, club president James McCarson submitted a letter of intent to Congressman John Dingell, in which he asked what procedure should be followed in order to pursue the club's objective. Dingell contacted the federal government's Property Management and Disposal Service, in Washington, DC. He professed the club's interest in "the retrieval of artifacts that may be on board, rather than salvaging the wreck itself."

McCarson's simple request opened a Pandora's Box of administrative red tape that was released upon the world of naïve citizens. Not only does the government work slowly, as noted above, but it also works ponderously and often contrary to the good of the people it is supposed to serve.

Lewis Tuttle, the Assistant Commissioner for Personal Property Disposal, was noncommittal. Before he would make any determination about the acceptability of McCarson's proposal, he sought advice from the Army Corps of Engineers, the Department of the Interior, and the Department of the Navy. With that many government agencies involved – and with that many egos to soothe – there was little doubt that the proposal of the Adventurers Diving Club would encounter stiff competition from those blustering persons who were in authority to make denials.

The major objections were voiced by the Navy. Although the Navy was willing to let the Adventurers Diving Club raise the hulk and preserve it intact, naval advisors did not believe that this was possible because of the extensive damage that was suffered in the explosion. The Navy was not willing to let the divers salvage the wreck piecemeal. Two reasons were given for taking this view.

One: "It should be presumed that *Tulip* sank with a quantity of explosive ammunition on board. It is entirely conceivable that this ammunition, in spite of its long immersion, may still be dangerous and should not be handled by amateurs."

Two: "47 of *Tulip's* crew went down with the ship. Eight unidentified bodies were later recovered and buried ashore near the site of *Tulip's* loss; it may thus be presumed that remains of 39 of her crew may still be in the wreck."

Ultimately, the Judge Advocate General recommended that exclusivity be denied, and that the Property Management and Disposal Service "not enter into any contract for salvage rights with the Adventurers Diving Club."

There the matter rested . . .

. . . for another generation. Now enter Uwe Lovas: a diver, shipwreck researcher, and shipwreck locator. In 1985, Lovas discovered the final resting place of the *U-1105* (which see) in the Potomac River. One day in 1994 he visited the Montrose County

Museum in Montrose, Virginia. He was fascinated by the display of artifacts that had been recovered from the *Tulip*. Although the wreck lay only a few miles from the *U-1105*, he had never heard of it. With his curiosity aroused, he questioned a museum official about the provenance of the artifacts.

Lovas learned that they had been donated to the museum by one of the divers who had worked on the volunteer salvage project. He also learned the name of the individual. He contacted him and arranged a meeting. This individual – whose name Lovas cannot presently recall – told him how a fisherman had provided land ranges for the wreck, and described a peculiar V cut in the trees from which a straight line extended over the site.

Lovas then contacted the Maryland Historical Trust, with which he had previously worked after his discovery of the *U-1105*, and asked if they were interested in relocating the remains of the *Tulip*. They were.

The MHT furnished a boat and a side-scan sonar unit. Lovas and MHT staffers conducted a search operation in May of 1994. Lovas quickly located the V cut in the trees, exactly as it had been described to him. The boat towed the sonar unit across the Potomac River directly away from the V cut . . . and passed over the wreck on the very first pass! They dived on the wreck in June in order to confirm its identity.

According to Navy records, "In August 1995, under a department of Defense Legacy Resource Management Program Grant, the Maryland Maritime Archaeology Program crew returned to the site for a three-day reconnoiter to study site conditions and record the wreck's structure. The results of that brief visit were incorporated in to the planning of a full-scale sensing and video taping of the site in October of 1996."

And *there* the matter rests . . .

. . . until some enterprising individual in the *next* generation again stirs up interest in a fourth-rate gunboat that was sunk by human folly instead of by enemy action.

Bottom of opposite page: This descriptive plaque is located in Point Lookout State Park. Please note that the park has an entry fee. When I visited the park, none of the employees at the visitor center knew anything about the plaque: neither its location nor its existence. The GPS coordinates are 38-02.856 / 76-19.536.

To locate the plaque, proceed approximately a mile and a half past the park entrance. Look for a wooden signpost on the right (west) side of the road. The numbers 10440 and 10444 are painted in white in vertical format. Turn onto the gravel road. Park by the picnic pavilion and continue on foot. The road ends at an L. turn right (north); walk another two hundred yards and the plaque will be on your left (west). The body of water beyond the plaque is the Potomac River delta.

In addition to the *Tulip*, the plaque also commemorates the side-wheel steamer *Express* (which see) and the Coast Guard cutter *Cuyahoga*, both of which were sunk in the vicinity on the Chesapeake Bay.

Although the *Cuyahoga* sank nearby, it is not covered in the present volume because the wreck was raised, taken to sea, and scuttled off the coast, where it has become a popular fishing and diving site. See pages 194 and 195 for photographs of the hulk being salvaged. For details of the sinking, see *Shipwrecks of Virginia*, by this author.

U-1105

Built: 1944
Type of vessel: Modified Type VII-C U-boat (submarine)
Displacement tonnage: 761 (surfaced), 865 (submerged)
Power: Two diesel engines, two electric motors
Speed: 17 knots surfaced (on diesels), 7.6 knots submerged (on motors)
Armament: Five torpedo tubes (four bow, one stern), antiaircraft guns
Builder: Nordseewerke Shipyard, Emden, Germany
Cause of sinking: Scuttled in explosives test
Location: Potomac River delta

Sunk: September 18, 1949
Depth: 80 feet
Dimensions: 218' x 20' x 15'
Unofficial alias: Black Panther
GPS: 38-08.173 / 76-33.106

By the time the *U-1105* was commissioned into the German navy – on June 3, 1944 – the U-boat war was already lost. The so-called "happy days," when U-boats ruled the Atlantic Ocean and the Mediterranean Sea, were long since gone.

The Allies developed and implemented an electronic surveillance system which in England was known as Asdic (Anti-Submarine Detection Investigation Committee), and which in America was called sonar (SOund Navigation And Ranging). This device was able to detect the presence, distance, and depth of submerged U-boats.

Sonar works by the propagation of sound waves through water, the way radar works by transmitting radio waves through air. The sending/receiving device transmits a discrete quantum of sound that is known as a ping (or a sound bite in modern lingo). When the ping reflects or bounces off a hard object such as the hull of a submarine, the device receives a sharp return signal. In this manner U-boats were detected as soon as they got within range of the sonar unit. The effective range during World War Two was somewhat more than a mile.

The hunters became the hunted. The wolves became lambs. Wolf packs became flocks fleeing in terror.

As a countermeasure, Germany developed a material that absorbed and dispersed sound waves at the frequencies at which sonar operated. This synthetic rubber contained small voids or hollows which soaked up sound waves the way a sponge soaks up water. Sound was not totally eliminated, but it was attenuated to a degree that made a U-boat undetectable from more than a thousand feet.

The rubber was formed in the shape of flat rectangles that were known as anechoic tiles. The German code name for this process was Alberich. (Alberich was a mythological sorcerer who could render himself invisible.) The tiles were glued to the hull and conning tower by means of a strong adhesive, much in the way in which heat-resistant tiles are glued to the undercarriage and leading surfaces of space shuttles.

The process of gluing tiles was long and laborious, adding a large labor force and thousands of hours to the construction time of each U-boat. Because U-boats were being sunk in action faster than they could be replaced on the assembly lines, Germany abandoned rubberizing its U-boats after ten of them were coated.

The *U-1105* was one of the few that went into action with a soundproof integument. It was under the command of Oberleutnant zur see Hans-Joachim Schwarz. Sea trials and training missions proceeded over the winter of 1944-1945. Not until April did the *U-1105* depart on its first and only war patrol.

According to U.S. Navy records, "In the spring of 1945, the submarine patrolled Allied convoy routes near Black Rock, Ireland. In April, *U-1105* escaped detection by an Allied destroyer patrol. Days later [on April 27], the U-boat detected three British destroyers that were part of the second division of the 21st Escort Group. The submarine fired two acoustic torpedoes and then dove to 100 meters to escape counterattack. Fifty seconds passed before the first torpedo struck, with the second hitting just moments later. Thirty-two crewmen from *U-1105's* victim, HMS *Redmill*, were lost. The Allied search for *U-1105* and the search for *Redmill's* survivors began immediately. The submarine, unable to maintain its 330-foot depth, sank to the bottom at 570 feet, remaining motionless. For the next 31 hours, the Allied squadron searched for the U-boat without success. *U-1105* remained undetected for the remainder of the war."

The number of depth charges that were dropped in pursuit of the *U-1105* was recorded as 299.

Germany credited Schwarz with 1,300 tons for sinking the *Redmill*. Although thirty-two men were killed when the torpedoes blew sixty feet off the *Redmill's* stern, the frigate (as the British navy designated what the U.S. Navy called a destroyer) did not sink. She was successfully towed to Lisahally, Ireland. With the war winding down, and with Victory in Europe only days away, the frigate was never repaired. She was scrapped in 1947.

"On May 4, *U-1105* received the last order from Grossadmiral Karl Donitz: the war is over. Ironically, the submarine surrendered to the 21st Escort Group, the same escort group it attacked just a few weeks [sic] earlier. Ordered to the surface, the submarine proceeded to the Allied base at Loch Eriboll, Scotland on 10 May 1945 to sur-

From the collection of Mike Moore.

Courtesy of the National Archives.

render. *U-1105* sailed [sic] under armed frigate and air escort along with other surrendered U-boats, through the North Minch to the British naval base at Lock Alsh, then to Lishally [sic], Northern Ireland, via Londonderry. At Lishally [sic], *U-1105* was turned over to the United States as a war prize for study of its unique synthetic rubber skin."

The U-boat in question was not turned over at once. The Brits first conducted a series of tests that included submergence drills and propulsion trials. Most important, however, were experiments to determine the efficacy of the anechoic tiles with regard to sonar detection. The problem that the examiners faced was similar to that faced by NASA scientists half a century later, involving heat-resistant tiles on space shuttles: the adhesive weakened with use over time, causing the tiles to peel off the hull and leave the metal unprotected.

The *U-1105* nearly did not make the passage to the United States. In accordance with the terms of the Potsdam Agreement, Germany was not allowed to possess any U-boats ever again. Hundreds of U-boats remained afloat at war's end: some at dock and some at sea. Those at dock were quarantined. Those at sea were ordered to the nearest Allied port for internment. A number of U-boats surrendered to the American mainland. Each major Allied nation – the U.S, the U.K., and Russia – were allocated ten U-boats for testing purposes. The rest were taken to sea and scuttled.

As the U.S. already held in its possession most of the requisite number of U-boats – including Type VII's, Type IX's, and Type XXI's – the U.S. Navy was not too fussy about which additional ones to obtain from the eastern side of the Atlantic Ocean. After a while, though, someone woke up to the fact that the allocations did not include a U-boat whose hull was coated with anechoic tiles. This deficiency was soon rectified, and the *U-1105* was selected for American acquisition.

Then another problem arose: despite the fact that the *U-1105* had made but a single war patrol, it was found to be in such a sad state of disrepair that extensive overhaul was required to make it seaworthy. The Brits spent more than a month on the refit. Not until mid-December did the tainted U-boat depart for the American shore, manned by a U.S. Navy crew.

Foul weather hexed the transoceanic passage. Although the U-boat had been stripped of all her armament – torpedoes, deck guns, and ammunition – the 40-millimeter gun mount was still secured to the deck. The mount was torn off by a massive wave that rolled the U-boat onto its side. The radio was damaged beyond repair. One engine failed completely. After a week and a half of radio silence, those awaiting word from the U-boat feared that it had been lost at sea.

Communication was re-established off the coast of Newfoundland. The U-boat had been so damaged by the storm that it had to be towed ignominiously the rest of the way to the Portsmouth Navy Yard, New Hampshire. By the time of its arrival – on January 2, 1946 – the hull had been shorn of most of its anechoic tiles.

There is no record that the *U-1105* was ever commissioned into the U.S. Navy. Because it was never commissioned, it was not included in the official history of U.S. Navy vessels: the eight-volume *Dictionary of American Naval Fighting Ships*. It was merely a piece of property, like a jeep or a desk or a filing cabinet.

Some of the remaining anechoic tiles were removed so that their sonar deflecting capabilities could be studied in the laboratory. Tests on the tiles were conducted at the Acoustic Laboratory of the Massachusetts Institute of Technology, in Cambridge, Massachusetts; and at the Naval Research Laboratory, in Washington, DC.

The U.S. Navy learned a great deal by examining the German U-boats that were in its possession. Navy examiners were not loathe to admit that U-boats were superior in every way to U.S. submarines. Many post-war design and structural changes in U.S. submarines resulted directly from studies of U-boat electrical and mechanical innovations, some of which were later incorporated in the design and construction of America's nuclear submarine fleet.

After the exhaustive examinations were completed and the information was compiled for future reference, the American-held U-boats were scheduled for destruction by various means. Some were scrapped, while others were scuttled in deep seawater in explosives tests: most by torpedo, although the *U-2513* was sunk in a rocket attack. The purpose of the explosive tests was to determine the vulnerability of U-boat hulls to underwater explosions from different-sized charges.

The fate of the *U-1105* differed from that of its brethren in that, whereas the other U-boats were sunk only once, the *U-1105* was sunk several times. Before serving as an underwater pogo stick, it was laid up for a year and a half: first in Boston and then in Washington, DC. Finally, in 1947, it was towed to the Chesapeake Bay, where it was submerged in 70 feet of water off Piney Point, Maryland – a somewhat unusual place to dock or store a vessel for later experimentation. The precise location was recorded as 38° 7' 6" north latitude, and 76° 32' 40" west longitude.

On August 10, 1948, the salvage vessels *Windlass* and *Salvager* commenced diving operations on the submerged U-boat, in preparation for raising the hull. The *Windlass* established a four-point mooring directly over the *U-1105*. On August 24, the buoyancy and watertight integrity of the hull were tested. Additional tests were interrupted when

This is an inboard profile (or cutaway) of a Type VII U-boat. Numerous variations exist within the type, and among individual U-boats, moreso as the war progressed and tactics changed. (From the collection of Mike Moore.)

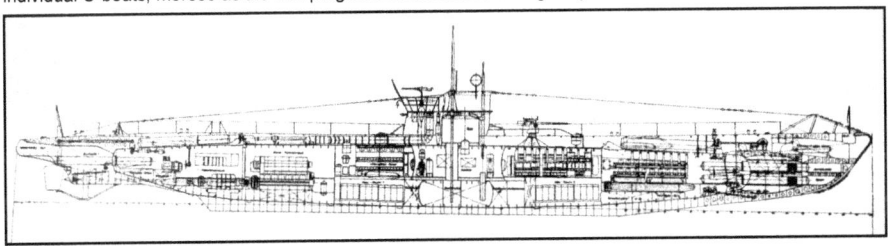

American sailors working on the *U-1105* before the ultimate depth-charge test. (Courtesy of the National Archives.)

hurricane Carol swept through the area on August 30-31. The *Windlass* and *Salvager* remained on site and rode out the tempest.

The *U-1105* was raised with the aid of pontoons on September 28, 1948. The *Windlass* got underway with the partially submerged U-boat streaming aft on an 8-inch tow line. The hawser was later transferred to the *Salvager*, which completed the tow to a nearby mooring site. Diving and salvage operations then continued throughout most of the month of October. These operations had less to do with the U-boat than with assessing salvage and towing techniques. These operations were secured in November. The U-boat was stripped of all experimental equipment, then it was resubmerged off Point No Point Light. Buoys were deployed to mark the spot, where the depth of water was recorded as 114 feet; the location was given as 113° true from Holland Island, 283° from Point-No-Point, and 226° from Point Lookout.

Windlass and *Salvager* returned to the site of the *U-1105* on July 11, 1949. For the next couple of months, they conducted experimental salvage operations by using the U-boat as a test vessel. On August 22, they towed the *U-1105* along the channel to a new location. Experimental salvage operations were not secured until nearly one month later.

The deck log of the *Windlass* recorded the U-boat's location as 38° 08' 10" north latitude, and 76° 33' 10" west longitude; and 272.5° true, 200 yards from Piney Point Light.

On September 16, the U.S. Navy Explosive Ordnance Disposal team commenced the emplacement of demolition charges on the still-floating hulk. Divers worked for two days to rig a 250-pound MK 6 depth charge some 30 feet beneath the keel of the hull. This depth charge was filled with HBX-2 (short for Hexahydro-1, 3, 5 Trinitro-8-Triazine). This high explosive was developed during World War Two. It was less shock sensitive than Torpex.

The charge was detonated on September 18. The explosion ruptured the hull forward of the conning tower. The U-boat went down like a rock, disappearing from view in just twenty seconds.

The scuttled U-boat was then abandoned and forgotten. Its location was misrecorded: the degrees of longitude were given as 67 instead of 76 (as recorded in the *Windlass's* deck log). This was likely a typographical error. The incorrect longitude placed the U-boat some 500 miles east of its actual location: far offshore and beyond the edge of the continental shelf, where the water was thousands of feet deep.

Compounding this error, the folks at the Naval Historical Center wrote that the *U-1105* was "towed out to sea where, in September, she was sunk in demolition tests."

In the 1980's, Uwe Lovas compiled a list of U-boats that were sunk off the U.S. eastern seaboard. He was primarily interested in U-boats that lay at depths that were reachable by means of conventional scuba. His goal was to discover a U-boat – any U-boat – that had not yet been discovered. When he read the account of the *U-1105*, he pondered about why the Navy would have towed the hulk so far offshore, when extreme depth existed much closer to the beach.

Lovas conducted primary research at the Naval Historical Center. When he found

In the top photo the Naval officer on the left appears to be timing the onset of explosion with his wristwatch. In the bottom photo he seems to be so disinterested in the outcome that he did not bother to watch the U-boat disappear from view. (Both courtesy of the National Archives.)

a photograph of the U-boat at the site of its destruction, he spotted trees on shore in the background. He concluded immediately that the longitude numbers had been transposed. Later he plotted the revised longitude on a chart of the Chesapeake Bay, and saw that the correct location was near the mouth of the Potomac River – precisely where a wreck symbol was shown.

And the rest is history, as they say.

Lovas told me that, after all the time that he spent conducting archival research, finding the wreck was deceptively easy. It was right where it was supposed to be.

In 1991, Lovas related the circumstances of his discovery and subsequent dive to fellow U-boat enthusiast Hank Keatts, who wrote the story for publication in *Discover Diving*: "The initial search team included his brother Ron and a computer school classmate, Alan Russell. Three unsuccessful attempts followed between March 10, and April 20, 1985. Much of the failure stemmed from the inability to latch onto the wreck using a Danforth anchor instead of the boat's grappling hook; it had been lost earlier on another wreck.

"On June 29, 1985, a new grappling hook caught and held. Lovas and Russell landed on the lower gun deck behind the conning tower. Despite the low visibility of two to three feet, their excitement and enthusiasm knew no bounds. Lovas had fulfilled his ambition; he had found his U-boat. All hatches were still closed and artifacts lay scattered about the wreck site – proof positive that none had been there before.

"On a subsequent dive Lovas opened the conning tower hatch and found to his surprise that the U-boat's interior was as well preserved as the exterior. White paint still covered interior walls and most metal surfaces were in excellent shape, except those that were aluminum: they were severely corroded. The Navy had done a thorough job of stripping the inside of the conning tower. Major items, such as repeaters and telegraphs had been removed. Even the seat and optics for the attack periscope were gone, leaving only the stainless steel shaft."

After six years of secrecy, the publication of Keatts' article brought the *U-1105* into the limelight. Quick to take advantage of Lovas' discovery were the Maryland Historical Trust and the Naval Historical Center. They begrudgingly acknowledged Lovas's discovery with comments (which I heard through the grapevine) to the effect that he had blabbed his secret to a journalist who had then let the cat out of the bag. This was poor sportsmanship on the part of officialdom. Lovas did not "blab" anything. He recounted his efforts to Keatts for the specific purpose of bringing his discovery to public attention.

Subsequently, the Maryland Historical Trust and the Naval Historical Center sponsored surveys that were conducted on the site in 1992 and 1993. In November 1994, the *U-1105* was officially designated as "Maryland's first historic shipwreck preserve." According to a press release from the Maryland Department of Housing and Community Development, Division of Historical and Cultural Programs, "On May 8, 1995, the State of Maryland, in partnership with the U.S. Navy, formally opened its first underwater dive preserve off Piney Point in the Potomac River. The subject of the preserve is the rubber-sheathed German submarine *U-1105*."

To facilitate diver access, and to obviate the need to grapple into the wreck, the State established marker buoys at the site. According to Maryland's "Diving Safety and Emergency Management Guidelines," published in April 1995, "The site is marked by 2 buoys, a large blue and white can buoy identifies the site and acts as a mooring for vessels waiting to access the site and a smaller orange buy which is connected directly to the bridge on the submarine."

The buoys are in place from April through November. Buoys are removed during the winter. Divers should note that the buoy system may not always exist as described in the State's formal announcement.

In 2000, the *U-1105* was nominated for inclusion on the National Register of Historic Places. The nomination was accepted on January 11, 2001. To substantiate the reason for its inclusion on the register, the registration form noted that each Type VII-C U-boat "was armed with 14 torpedoes, an 8.8 cm deck gun and one 2 cm gun on the conning tower and was manned by a crew of 44. The deck gun was removed and variations in bridge configurations included heavier anti-aircraft weapons and a larger number of these. The design of the *U-1105* reflects many of the late war modifications making it a technologically unique specimen. In addition to a schnorkel for ventilation and recharging batteries while still submerged, it also carried other technical innovations including a GHG Balkon (Group Listening Apparatus Balcony); an advanced passive sonar system. This pod housed an array of 24 crystal receivers and allowed the sonar operator to determine the direction and location of other vessels as far away as 12-15 km. Very few Type VIIC vessels received this and only late in the war. The Black Panther also sported a Hohentweil U radar unit in the conning tower used to detect low-flying aircraft up to 20 km away with an accuracy of 1-2°. This unit is still in place on the vessel. Of course, the most unusual attribute is the rubber sheathing on the hull to deflect sonar. Of the 660 Type VIIC vessels constructed during the war, only 10 received this treatment and the *U-1105* is the only known remaining example. . . .

"Not only does this vessel represent the only known example of this early stealth technology but its study directly provided the data that led to subsequent treatment of American and Soviet submarines. Today all submarines are covered with anechoic coating to reduce their sonar signature; a direct outgrowth of the Alberich process."

The nomination form also included disinformation as well as misinformation: "The vessel was located by a team of sport divers in 1985. It sits upright on the bottom with an 8-12 inch wide crack in the pressure hull from the deck to the keel just forward of the conning tower. The rubberized hull is otherwise intact although the interior is filled with silt from the opening of the hatches by the discovering divers. The Maryland Historical Trust has since had the U.S. Navy seal all hatches to prevent accidental entrapment."

This paragraph declines to credit Uwe Lovas for making the intellectual breakthrough that the folks at the Naval Historical Center and the Maryland Historical Trust failed to make. Nor does it credit Ron Lovas and Alan Russell for their assistance and persistence in locating and diving on the wreck. In the same breath, it blames these unnamed recreational divers for being responsible for the interior being filled with silt (because they removed hatches) – despite the observation in the immediately preceding sentence that the pressure hull was already breached by a crack that measured eight to twelve inches across, and that this crack extended from the deck all the way to the keel. It does not take much imagination to perceive that the pressure hull was already filled with silt that filtered through this foot-wide crack over a period of forty-two years.

Perhaps worse is the laughable irony that the nomination form gave in the wreck's location incorrectly. It did not repeat the original error of transposing two numbers; it created an error of its own. The loran numbers were given as 27476.5 and 42085.5, which are okay for what they are worth. The latitude is given as "30°08"10'N;" the longitude is given as "76°33"10'W." The *numbers* in the latitude and longitude are the same as the numbers in the *Windlass's* log. This time the transposition is between the symbols for minutes (') and seconds ("). The proper order for latitude and longitude is degrees (°) followed by minutes (') followed by seconds (").

Most of the hull is covered by sediment. The only parts that are exposed are the conning tower, and two short segments of the deck atop the pressure hull both forward and aft of the conning tower. The maximum depth is 80 feet, with the conning tower rising some 12 feet above the muddy bottom. Divers are warned to exercise caution when kicking their fins around the wreck because the silt is easily stirred.

According to the St. Mary's County Department of Recreation and Parks, "Points of interest include the command center, the upper and lower gun decks, the deck gun support pedestals and ammunition containers, and the starboard saddle tank with the rupture line caused by the 1949 demolition tests."

Astute divers may also notice a section of the original standpipe that was used as a guide marker, guardrail posts, and a large letter N that is painted on the side of the conning tower. Thanks to Tom Edwards for bringing this capital N to my attention.

The *U-1105* is known as the Black Panther. The origination of the nickname is curious. In 1991, Larry Hewitt wrote to Schwarz in Germany and asked how the U-boat got its colorized moniker. Schwarz replied:

"The name and the heraldic figure were the result of a competition in the crew. A black panther is a beast of prey in the open country. In wartime, a U-boat is also a beast of prey, which attacks ships on the surface. Because the boat was covered with a black rubber coat, we thought that the name was very suitable for *U-1105*."

Artifacts from the *U-1105* are on display at the Piney Point Lighthouse Museum.

The conning tower emblem of the *U-1105*. (From *Embleme Wappen Malings deutscher U-Boote 1939-1945*, by Georg Hogel.)

WAWASET

Built: 1863
Previous names: None
Gross tonnage: 328
Type of vessel: Wooden-hulled side-wheel steamer
Builder: Pusey & Jones, Wilmington, Delaware
Owner: Potomac (or Washington) Ferry Company
Port of registry: Washington, DC
Cause of sinking: Fire
Location: Potomac River, 150 yards off Chatterton's Landing, Virginia

Sunk: August 8, 1873
Depth: 6 to 12 feet
Dimensions: 125' x 28' x 6'
Power: Coal-fired steam

When the *Wawaset* was first constructed, America was in the middle of its Civil War. The Union sorely needed vessels of all descriptions for a multitude of purposes. The U.S. Quartermaster Corps chartered the *Wawaset* as a troop transport at the cost of $85 per day, from November 17, 1863 to May 8, 1865.

After the cessation of hostilities, the *Wawaset* was sold to private interests, in which capacity she ferried freight and passengers along the Potomac River, between Washington, DC and the Coan River, Virginia, near the confluence with the Chesapeake Bay. She was only one of a number of such vessels the plied Potomac waters. She caromed along the river like a slow-moving billiard ball, making whistle stops on both sides to embark and discharge people and cargo in accordance with their needs.

The *Wawaset's* shallow draft enabled her to approach close to landings that did not have docks extending from shore to deep water in the river. In these situations, passengers were rowed on small boats between ship and shore. She performed this valuable service for eight years.

According to the records of the Steamboat Inspection Service for 1869, the *Wawaset* was proceeding in thick fog when she collided with the tug *Rescue*. Neither vessel was materially damaged. Otherwise, she led a career that was free of contention – that is, until August 8, 1873. On that date the *Wawaset* caught fire, ran aground near the Virginia shore, and burned to the waterline with the loss of more than eighty lives.

Newspapers had a heyday with this terrible catastrophe. Personal accounts trickled in day after day, much of it guesswork and speculation which, while sometimes grossly inaccurate, served the purpose of selling newspapers to a gullible public that thirsted for information about the event. The story as it was told in the tabloids was rife with misinformation, and was written with such purple prose that it incited official investigation not only into the cause of the fire, but about what could have been done to save lives after the fire started; and ultimately, what could be done in the future to prevent such a situation from recurring.

To get the facts straight, I will skip over the yellow journalism and go straight to the report of the Steamboat Inspection Service, which was compiled after the true facts were obtained from surviving witnesses. This report may not read as glamorously as the daily accounts, but it has the advantage of being balanced and accurate in hindsight. It was published on August 25, 1873.

No pictures or illustrations of the *Wawaset* have come to light. The *Harvest Moon* and the *Governor Safford* were built at around the same time, and are similar in appearance. (The top image is from *Early American Steamers*, by Erik Heyl. The two other images are from the author's collection.) Note the minor differences in the *Governor Safford* photos, which were taken at different times.

"The investigation was commenced on Friday morning, August 15th, 1873, in the office of the supervising inspector, at the United States Treasury Department, in the city of Washington, and was continued from day to day and closed on Friday, August 22, 1873, having held seven sessions, embracing in all seven days. Forty-five witnesses were examined, including the inspectors by whom the steamer was last inspected, the officers of the vessel, and several of the surviving passengers. The facts developed by the testimony are briefly as follows:

"The *Wawaset* was one of those steamers plying between Washington and Cone [sic] River, a distance of about one hundred miles, touching at intermediate points, and owned by the Washington Ferry Company. She was built at Wilmington, in the state of Delaware in the year 1863, and was of 328 90/100 tons burden, was constructed of wood in a substantial manner, and was considered in all respects seaworthy; her boiler was built at Chester, Pa., by Rearney Sons & Co., year not known. She was provided with one condensing engine, and all appearance in accordance with law. By her certificate of inspection she was authorized to carry thirty cabin and twenty deck passengers, with fifteen men as her complement of officers and crew; persons legally permitted to be carried on board; her equipment consisted of two good and efficient fire extinguishers (Gardner's), one good steam fire pump worked by steam (Woodward's patent) with suitable pipes leading therefrom and fitted and supplied as required by law, and one good double acting fire pump worked by hand, furnished with 175 feet of good hose with nozzles and couplings complete, all being fitted to suit both steam and hand pumps; 75 life preservers, adjustable to the body, each containing six pounds of good cork and having a buoyancy of at least 25 pounds; sufficient and reliable steering apparatus, suitable arrangements for signaling the engineer from the pilot house with steam whistle and signal lights complete; all of which the inspectors confirmed on the stand. The steamer *Wawaset* left Washington for Cone [sic] River on one of her regular trips at or about six o'clock on the morning of the 8th of August, 1873; upon approaching Chatterton's landing about sixty-five miles below Washington, between the hours of 11:30 and 12 o'clock a.m. the whistle was sounded and the boat lowered for the conveyance of passengers to the shore, as was usual at this landing, when smoke was discovered issuing from the fireman's room, under the main deck forward, and the alarm was given that the boat was on fire. It is alleged that the flames burst forth with such fury as to leave but little time for anyone to obtain life preservers or utilize the life boats. From the same cause the officers of the boat claim to have been unable to render assistance to the one hundred and twenty-five odd passengers on board, hence the deplorable loss of life which ensued, while all the officers, as also the crew, with but one exception, were saved.

"We are constrained to believe that the fire raged with fearful rapidity, and that from the position of the passengers they were exposed to imminent peril; but we do not believe the statement of the officers that they did all that could possibly have been done under the circumstances to save the lives of the passengers, which opinion is fully and clearly borne out by the evidence in the case. It would appear from the testimony that the fire originated in the fireman's room, forward of the boiler; that it had been burning some time, and was first discovered by one of the firemen when attempting to enter the room, the opening of the door of which admitted the air to the fire, and thereby caused the vessel to be enveloped in flames and smoke, and driving the engineer from his post; that there were no means of getting to the after-part of the boat to assist the passengers, and that there was not one of the officers aft at the time the fire was raging; that a lady, supposed to be Miss Reed, ran over the wheel-house, and was caught in the master's arms, who passed her below to the clerk, but she was subsequently lost.

"John R. Woods, master of the *Wawaset* at the time of the disaster, testified that he was in the pilot house at the time of the alarm of fire was given; that he did not know where or how the fire originated; that thinking the fire was in the hold, he would go down quietly and put it out, but that in a very short time the flames were at the hurricane deck coming up by the walking beam of the engine, and he 'knew that she was gone and that it was impossible to save her,' and the only chance was to 'beach her as soon as possible.' This is his own unprompted statement of what he saw and of what he thought. The saving of the boat seemed to be uppermost in his mind to the exclusion at that time of the preservation of the lives of the passengers, most of whom were helpless women and children. Accordingly, he says, he ordered the pilot to head the vessel for the shore, then very near. Instead, however, of assuming command, and directing passengers to a position on the boat where they might provide themselves with life preservers, or of ordering the crew to prepare the life-boats for use, he took some of the fire buckets with which to throw water on the tiller rope, leaving the passengers to crowd together so as to cut off all chance of escape. He told them to keep cool, and they would all be saved. Just at that time the engine ceased to work, the boat stopped, the supreme moment passed, and with it all possibility of saving life through the appliances on board.

"Robert Nash, the engineer, testifies that he was at his post, and herein he is supported by the other officers. Indeed, the evidence of the officers and crew of the steamer *Wawaset* coincide in all particulars; they assert there was no time to do more than was done; no opportunity to save life; that every man was employed in the best manner, wherever he happened to be on board; that boxes, planks, etc., were thrown to those overboard. The hose was laid, but water could not be applied; that all appreciated their own and the danger of the passengers, all that they only barely succeeded in escaping from the burning vessel, while the passengers were unaided in making their escape.

"Robert W. Gravatt, the mate; John W.L. Boswell, the pilot; J.W. Wheeler, clerk, and several of the deck hands confirm the testimony of the other officers, and the evidence of some of the passengers was also of a confirmatory nature, while that of other passengers of more intelligence, perhaps, and cooler observation seriously contradict the statements of the officers; these passengers assert that the officers permitted time to be lost; that they made no effort to save the lives of their passengers, especially the women and children; that the hose was not in its proper place; that the metallic life-boat had no davits or falls attached to it and that the other boat was seized by a number of colored men, in the absence of any officer to prevent it, and thrown overboard in such a manner as to cause the loss of all its occupants.

"After a careful review of the whole testimony produced before us, we regret to have to acknowledge that the cause of the fire on the steamer *Wawaset* still remains a mystery; but we are of the opinion that it originated in the fireman's room, under the forward deck, adjoining the forecastle, and near the back connection of the boiler, and we recommend that inspectors require all bulkheads, boilers, hatches or other woodwork near or around the boilers of all steam vessels to be covered with metal, leaving sufficient space for the air to circulate between such metal coverings and the woodwork as a preventative against future disasters to steamers by fire.

"Further we find from his own evidence that John R. Wood was acting in the capacity of master of the steamer *Wawaset* without having a United States certificate of license as such and the evidence also clearly shows that he had not made himself acquainted with the provisions of the act of Congress and the rules and regulations relating to steam vessels, and the duties of the officers navigating them; that he had no organization or discipline whatever in the fire department on board his vessel, expecting, as he said, each officer and crew to assist and do the best they could in case of fire or other emergency; none of the officers were specially designated to take charge of the boats, life preservers, or pumps, and no printed instructions were posted up concerning the manner of using the life preservers or other life saving appliances. As soon as the alarm of fire was sounded confusion reigned on board, no officer to give directions, and no one to distribute the life preservers to the passengers, particularly to the helpless women and children, who were deserted in the hour of their direct extremity.

"Captain Wood further confesses that he never examined or tested the fire extinguishers, one of which was illegally removed from the steamer since her last inspection; never called the officers and crew to quarters for exercise in the fire department, as required by law to be done, at least once in each month and in many other respects failed to meet the requirements of the law in his capacity as master or acting master of a passenger steamer.

"Robert W. Gravatt, who was acting in the capacity of mate on the *Wawaset* at the time of the disaster, was, like her captain, without a United States certificate or license, and equally as ignorant of the requirement of the laws, rules and regulations governing the steamboat inspection service.

"In his own testimony, the chief engineer of the steamer *Wawaset*, Robert Nash, admitted the fact of his trading in truck produce, etc., at different landings when the steamer was running on her regular trips, and particularly on the day of the disaster; the evidence adduced also proved that he was at different times in attendance at the bar of the steamer, during his watch, and when the law positively demanded his presence at his post of duty in the engine room. It was also shown that the hose was not connected with the fire pumps, and that when the alarm of fire was given, Mr. Nash became perfectly paralyzed, and made little or no effort to extinguish the fire and none to save the lives of the passengers. If the hose had been attached to either of the pumps, and one or both of these pumps used in connection with the fire extinguisher, and the steam smothering pipe – the latter of which was under the entire charge of the engineer – we firmly believe the fire on the *Wawaset* could have been put out and the dreadful calamity avoided.

"The negligence and misconduct of the chief engineer of the steamer *Wawaset* prior to the burning of the steamer, as well as his unofficer-like conduct after the fire occurred, are, in our opinion, deserving of the severest condemnation and the highest penalty prescribed by law.

"We have therefore no alternative than to revoke the license of Robert Nash as an engineer on steam vessels navigating waters within the jurisdiction of the United States, and it is so ordered.

"The fire on the steamer *Wawaset* occurred, as will be seen by the evidence, at midday, when all the officers and crew were supposed to be on duty, and at a time when the chances for extinguishing the fire and saving the passengers were far better than if the fire had occurred at night, and yet it is our painful duty to record the sacrifice of some eighty odd souls by that appalling calamity.

"As a further safeguard against the recurrence of similar disasters to steam vessels, we respectfully recommend the necessity for inspectors in the various districts, making it a special duty to visit steamers from time to time, and without previous notification sound alarm of fire and call all hands to quarters and in this way ascertain and correct defects in the organization and equipment of such steamers.

"We are of the opinion that if the fire department on the steamer *Wawaset* had been organized in accordance with the steamboat act, and the officers and crew instructed in their respective duties, that the life-preservers could have been distributed among the passengers, the boats safely lowered, and the greater portion, if not all the passengers saved.

"So far as the general equipment of the steamer *Wawaset* at the time of her last inspection (March 24th, 1873), is concerned, it is in evidence that she was fully up to standard required by the laws and relating to steam vessels, and therefore can discover no dereliction of duty on the part of the inspectors under whose jurisdiction the steamer belonged; we believe they performed their duty impartially and efficiently.

"James I. Lowry, inspector of hulls, testified positively to preparing the original certificate of the steamer so as to admit of the carriage of but fifty passengers and fifteen officers and crew, making a total of sixty-five in all, and this evidence was fully confirmed by the subsequent production of the original certificate itself from the files of the Georgetown custom-house. He therefore has no hesitation in declaring that the Potomac Ferry Company was running the steamer *Wawaset*, on the eighth day of August, 1873, in open violation of the law, not only as regards the carriage of an excessive number of passengers, but also in employing unlicensed officers, and we earnestly recommend that steps be promptly taken by the proper officers of the government to impose upon said company the extreme penalties of the law for such violations; as also upon John R. Woods, the master, and Robert W. Gravatt, mate of the *Wawaset*, for plying their respective vocations without United States licenses, in defiance of the law.

"In submitting this report, sir, we can truthfully say that we have endeavored to discharge the responsible duty imposed upon us with entire impartiality, always keeping in mind the principal object of the law under which the investigation was conducted, viz: the preservation of human life on steamer vessels; and we are led to believe that hereafter steamboat owners will make themselves fully and thoroughly acquainted with the act of Congress relating to steam vessels, and then yield a full and ready compliance thereto, equipping them with all life-saving appliances required by law, and in command of men who know and possess the courage to perform their whole duty in any emergency that may arise."

The document was signed by William Rose and John E. Edgar of the Bureau of Investigation.

As is too often the case, official documents tend to concentrate on bland facts and points of law, and lack all semblance of human interest. The *Wawaset* investigation was no exception. The full story is greater than the one that is told above, which, while largely accurate, lacks many salient features and nitty-gritty details of equal if not greater importance to modern readers and armchair historians. What was left out of the report is just as important as what was put in the report.

It should be noted at the outset that the *Wawaset* had previously been authorized to carry one hundred fifty passengers (one hundred thirty cabin and twenty steerage passengers), not fifty (thirty cabin and twenty deck passengers). Captain Samuel Gedney, Superintendent of the Potomac Ferry Company, appeared before the investigating committee and produced his copy of the license, which clearly specified one hundred fifty passengers.

Assistant engineer Samuel Nash testified that the certificate "was hung up on the boat in a walnut frame covered with glass." The posted certificate specified that the *Wawaset* was authorized to carry one hundred fifty passengers.

No explanation was given for the reason why the passenger capacity was reduced by one hundred passengers on the copy of the license held by the Steamboat Inspection Service. Company officials claimed that an error was made on the duplicate certificate, on which the number 1 was accidentally deleted from the number 150. They also claimed that fifty paying passengers were not enough to pay for the coal that was consumed on the passage.

Gedney went one better and produced for the investigating committee a permit that had been issued to the *Wawaset* by James Lowry and W.O. Saville, U.S. Local Inspectors. The permit was dated June 3, 1872; it read: "Application having been made to the undersigned local inspectors of steam vessels for the district of Baltimore for permission to steamer *Wawaset* to run on excursions said steamer having complied with the necessary requirements of law in regard to life-saving appliance, permission is hereby given to said steamer to carry 500 additional passengers, the route and distance of said excursion not to exceed 80 miles on the Potomac River."

Adding credence to the company's claim was that, only a few months previous to the accident, the *Wawaset* "was completely overhauled on the ways at Baltimore, a saloon cabin was put on her upper deck aft, newly furnished and newly upholstered and painted throughout." This expensive upkeep and modernization does not sound like a vessel that was let run down.

The number of life preservers given in the inquiry (75) was contradicted in the Proceedings of the Board of Supervising Inspectors of Steam Vessels, in which it was noted that the *Wawaset* was equipped with "between three and four hundred good cork jackets," and that the jackets were "accessible to passengers, but two of which were used, by a Mr. Emmerson, for himself and child, both of whom were saved thereby."

Some outspoken critics claimed in writing that the cork jackets were inaccessible. But these self-proclaimed critics had no way of ascertaining accessibility, never having been onboard the *Wawaset*.

With respect to Captain Wood, while it may be true that he did not have a current license, he was known as an "experienced seaman and the full corps of officers and men are old and careful hands at steamboating." The fact that his license had expired did not make him less capable of operating a steamboat, any more than a modern day motorist who loses his driver's license would become less capable of driving a car. The same can be said for the unlicensed mate.

One editorial noted frankly that engineer Nash was unjustly vilified; that he was "made the scapegoat for the sins of his employers and superiors."

I do not mean to sound like an apologist for the steamboat company or its officers and crew, but I cannot help but point out that all too often, inquiries are conducted in order to cast blame so as to mollify an irate public and their representatives, not necessarily to ascertain the full truth of a situation. More than one inquiry has been little more than a whitewash for political expedience.

The same editorial that defended Nash also stated, "The American forgets that in all such cases public opinion in this country demands that somebody be 'made an example of.' Without arguing the question of the culpability of the officers of the *Wawaset*, one or all of them . . . it is safe to say that hundreds of steamers on American waters are daily navigated by men no wiser, no braver, no better qualified for their duties and no better fitted to meet a great emergency. This last mentioned test – fitness to meet a great emergency – is one which steamboat inspectors cannot apply at will, and it is the most important." This seems to me to be a rational and unprejudiced viewpoint.

In my opinion, the official investigation ignored the fact that sometimes people are overcome by events that are beyond their ability to control; that perhaps are beyond *anyone's* ability to control. The fact that neither the captain nor his officers nor the crew failed to handle the emergency better than they did in nowise infers their lack of ability, especially in light of the extraordinary circumstances with which they were faced, and in the incredibly short time that they had to face those circumstances.

As far as punishing the company and the unlicensed officers to the full extent of the law, that extent was not very extensive. By not giving credence to the company's copy of the certificate of inspection, which allowed for one hundred fifty passengers, "the owners are liable to a fine of $100 for engaging the Captain and mate, respectively, without licenses, and are also liable to a fine of $10 for every passenger carried in excess of fifty."

In addition, the official investigative report did not dwell on – indeed, did not even mention – the human factor: how individuals dealt with the terrible circumstances that were facing them. This was where the newspapers performed an invaluable service: by interviewing survivors and publishing their remarks for posterity.

Passenger John Reed exonerated the captain and his officers and crew: "After the excitement became general I advised the passengers to keep cool, as the boat I knew would ground in low water. Many jumped overboard before she struck, and I threw planks to them. I don't think a single person was drowned off the forward deck after the boat struck. Capt. Wood was the last man that left the boat. I don't think there was a live passenger afloat when Capt. Wood left the boat. I don't think anything was left undone by the officers to save lives and the boat. I told many of the passengers, 'For God's sake, don't jump overboard; we will be aground in low water soon, and you can wade ashore.' They would not heed me, but jumped excitedly into the water. I had a cousin who jumped overboard before the boat stopped, who was lost. If we could have got all the planks overboard many would have been saved. The shrieks of the women and children were enough to appall the stoutest heart." Reed was badly burned on the face and head.

Elsewhere Reed's observation was confirmed: "The captain was the last person who left the boat. He was on the bow, and did all in his power to render assistance to the panic-stricken women. Finally the flames drove him overboard, considerably burned about the head and face, and he swam ashore."

Captain Woods provided correspondents with a succinct version of events: "The fire broke out at twenty-five minutes past 12 o'clock, between Thorn's Gut and Chatterton. I was in the pilot house at the time. A fireman came and told me that the boat was on fire below. I immediately came out, and found the flames reached quite to the hurricane deck along the walking beam. I then saw that it was impossible to get to the life-boats, which were on after-quarters on each, to lower them, although they were full of passengers. I threw water on the wheel ropes so as to keep her steerage all right, and passed buckets of water from below to the hurricane deck for the purpose, as I became satisfied there was no hope of saving the vessel, and that the only chance to save the passengers was to keep her going, she heading to the beach. The boat reached the beach in about twelve or thirteen minutes after the alarm was given – in less than five minutes after the alarm was given the fire was in the rear of the pilot-house – the engine refused to work about a half a minute before she struck the shore, and the boat ran a length before she came to a dead stop and grounded in less than five feet of water from the bow. I remained on the hurricane deck until the flames had burnt the window curtain in my room and the saloon windows, below, were shooting forth fiery darts. I then came down on the forward deck and did what I could to save the passengers. A great many were afraid to jump overboard. I assured them they were safe in jumping, as the water off the bow was not over their heads, and upon this assurance one or two made a leap, and many others seeing that the water was shallow followed their example, and

The headline for this woodcut from *The Daily Graphic* reads: "The *Wawasset* [sic] Disaster on the Potomac." The caption reads: "Dredging for the dead, with a general view of the wreck, from a sketch made on Sunday by Mr. Lautrup, our special art correspondent in Washington."

were saved. It was with difficulty I checked them jumping over in large bodies, and drowning each other during the excitement. I am satisfied as nearly all was lost were lost in the stern of the boat, the flames driving that way, and forcing the passengers to jump or be burnt. Just before I left the boat I heard a lady (Mrs. Taylor, of Alexandria) crying for help from the rear of the vessel. I saw her clinging to the middle chains, and sent a boat to her rescue and saved her. I am satisfied the excitement caused undue loss of life and that every passenger was saved who jumped overboard forward. A great many lives were lost on the life-boats by being overcrowded. Before the boat stopped one of them was crowded with colored passengers and when she was cut loose the stern bulged out and swamped the craft. About a dozen small children were aboard, and I think five or six were lost."

It is interesting to note that at an inquest that was held near the scene of the disaster on the day after the catastrophe, "The jury entirely exonerated Capt. Woods from all blame in the matter, and gave him a certificate to that effect. When the captain saw there was no hope of extinguishing the flames, he took his station at the wheel, and heading for the shore prevented the rudder ropes from burning by pouring water on them, until finally they were consumed – a short time before she touched the shore." These actions do not sound like those of a person who was derelict in his duty.

The pilot was John Boswell. He was standing at the helm when the fire alarm was given. "I says, 'Captain, the best thing we can do is to run her ashore the nearest place – Chatterton's landing.' I headed her for the shore, and she struck in five feet of water. I staid [sic] in the pilot house until the wheel ropes broke in two and the fire was coming into the pilot-house. I then jumped overboard and swam ashore with two ladies, whom I saved. I then brought out [the lifeboat] and landed six or eight passengers. I made a second trip with the boat, and took in three colored women, with a child, who were hanging to the rudder, and landed them safely. I then swam out again and made two unsuccessful attempts to rescue Officer Reed's wife, but she twisted away from me in each instance, I presume not knowing what she was doing through excitement. When I came back to the stern of the boat for the last time, three children – two white and one colored – were there. I tried to get at them, but the flames prevented me, and they were all burnt. I think two of them were Mr. Reed's children. I then went astern, and bailed out the life-boat, and took nine dead bodies to Stewart's wharf, four white and five colored. . . . I kept the deck hands pouring water on the wheel ropes until the fire drove them off deck. . . . I don't think any but Mr. Reed's cousin, Miss Bettie Reed, were lost in jumping off the bow of the boat. She jumped before the boat struck, and was lost."

Samuel Nash, assistant engineer, "swam ashore with an old man before he returned and saved his father. He does not know the name of the old gentleman, but describes him as short and stout." Samuel Nash's father was chief engineer Robert Nash, who was so vilified in the investigative report. The fact that father Nash remained onboard long enough for his son to swim ashore with an old man, then return for his father, implies that father Nash did not abandon his post until the very last minute.

Robert Nash: "I tried to get in the hold to discover the place of burning, but the smoke was so thick I could not. I then turned in a fire-extinguisher; I went on the forward deck and used buckets of water. After I saw I was of no further service I jumped overboard, and clung to a peach box until rescued by my son. Many were saved by clinging to the peach boxes which were thrown overboard. . . . When in the water I saw a man and small child struggling. I tried to save the child by placing it on the peach box, but by some means both got away from me, and it was the last I saw of them. I presume both were drowned. The boats could not be used because the fire broke out amidships, and the flames prevented reaching them. One of the boats was so crowded before being cut away that she broke upon striking the water and swamped. I think many lives could have been saved if the life-boat could have been reached by the passengers after she was finally thrown overboard."

The sad story about George Cook, a grocer, was recounted by one reporter: "He had two little children with him, and while he was struggling in the water making a fight for life, he was seen holding his youngest child to the surface crying 'Oh my God, save my baby!' It was supposed that the older child had already perished. . . . It is probable that he and his two children all perished."

In this case the prediction was partially premature. Leslie Cook survived, and made this statement to the press: "I got frightened and ran back towards the saloon, and the place was full of smoke, and saw father when he came down the steps, and we went on that place round by the stern and climbed over. I believe they call the place we came on the waist. We got to the rudder chains and held to them, and we could see the smoke and flames above us. All this time the people were screaming and hallooing, and we were both frightened. The people kept jumping over the stern and getting on the rudder chains, and I was crowded off; but I got hold of father and clasped him round the waist, but we were both shoved off and sank. I let go my hold and went to the bottom, but I rose in about the same place, and got hold of the chain again. I looked around for father, but did not see him again. I was not on the chains very long – but it seemed a long time – before a boat took me off."

Kate McPherson was onboard the *Wawaset* with a Miss Marbury. They were together "during the first part of the excitement, until the smoke drove them down the gangway; that she [McPherson] missed her [Marbury] on the main deck, and the rush of colored people was so great towards the life-boat that she could not turn to find her; that she was hustled overboard after the life-boat was stove in, with many others, by the rush of the colored people toward the gangway; that she immediately sunk and rose twice, and knew nothing more until she found herself in a boat and being carried ashore." McPherson suffered a slight burn on her shoulder. "The flames burst out all around and swept aft, driving women and children over into the water. She saw four little children hanging by their hands on the waist of the steamer, and one after the other drop into the water, the flames driving them off. The colored people were perfectly wild, and no remonstrance on the part of the officers was heeded, they jumped into the boat, piling it full, and declared that it was the colored people's boat; refusing all whites admission; when it went down all were dumped into the water together and many others followed, being pushed overboard. . . . The screams of the women and children were deafening."

An unnamed woman whom the newspaper described as "an old colored women" gave this account: "I tell you what, chile, I got 'cited when I saw de flames an' de smoke; I got frightened shure, and run back as far as I could. I was too skeered fur anything, and de people was hollering, and de women and chillen screamin' and some jumpin' over. De fire got closer and closer, and when it commenced to lick right roun' me, I tink dis old woman might as well drown as bunup in de fire. Den, honey, I jup, and helt my bref while I went down. When I come up I cotch holt of a white man, and he turn roun' and raise h's fist and say, 'You d——d black wench, if you don't let go I'll drown you.' Den I let go again, and I hole my bref and down I go to the bottom agin, and when I come up dis old head strike agin a peach box, and I tells you I held on to it tight. I didn't 'no whether it would hold me or not, but I clutched it and floundered roun' a little, kicking in the water, and in a little time my feet tech something. I keep holst of de box, and I didn't now but at de water would be deeper, and I kep puttin' one foot afore de other and gets on de shore, but I held on to de box 'til I got way up on de shore, and I was might glad, I tell you, when I got there."

For several days bodies were collected from the river and interred temporarily in the sandy beach until they could be transported to Washington for identification and proper burial. Newspapers provided descriptions such as, "unknown colored woman, 25 or 30 years of age; black skirt, with three flounces, and overskirt; bodice of stripped calico; black lasting gaiters, foxed with morocco;" and "unknown white boy, about 7 years of age; gray cassimere pants, checked calico bodice, lace boots;" and "unknown colored woman, 60 years of age; black dress, black lasting gaiters;" and "unknown colored woman, 4 feet 6 inches high; hair short nap; green dress, black overshirt, white apron, black gaiter shoes;" and so on . . .

"The body of Mrs. Reed was brought in just above Chatterton. It was so much disfigured that it could only be recognized by the clothing and jewelry. . . .

"The body of Mr. George Cook, of South Washington, was brought in between Chatterton and Boyd's Hole, about 12 o'clock, by Mr. Robert Adams, and was at once recognized. On his person were found $54 and a silver watch. By the papers in the pockets he was at once known. . . .

"The body of a colored man rose about the same spot shortly after, and was towed in. It had on a striped colored shirt, striped pants, and black frock coat. No one could have recognized him except by his clothing; every particle of the flesh being eaten from his face, his eyes and ears gone, and large spots eaten to the skull-bone. He was buried at once. . . .

"Another colored woman suddenly appeared further up. When she rose her white apron appeared to cover her face, and all on shore supposed it to be a white women until she was floated in. On the body was a white and black striped dress and black leather boots."

And so it went. Decomposing and fish-eaten bodies drifted with the current and tide, some not rising to the surface until several days after the fire. Some bodies were recovered by dragging grapples in the vicinity of the wreck. Two bodies were found inside the burned out hulk, where they were visible through knee-deep water.

For miles around the landing, the river was dotted with "hats and bonnets, fans and small articles." This is to say nothing of planks, peach boxes, and miscellaneous debris.

Then there was the seedy side of the calamity. There were allegations that local citizens brought bodies ashore only to strip them of their valuables.

A woman who called herself Margaret Lewis told how she had walked from Laurel to Washington "in search of her four children, who were passengers on the ill-fated *Wawaset*." She stopped at police headquarters with a story of how she had been robbed

The caption for this woodcut from *The Daily Graphic* reads: "Peace hath her slaughters as well as war - a cartoon on the Potomac disaster."

on a street car of her only $2, and "a gold cross belonging to one of her lost children." The policemen gave her breakfast and took up a collection for her, aggregating $8.50. Then it was ascertained that stories that she told to different persons did not agree. Finally, Lieutenant Kelly "came in and recognized her as a professional 'dead-beat.' She had imposed upon him two years ago by telling him about her husband being crushed to death on a railroad, and he raised $25 by subscription and gave it to her. Other officers came in and at once recognized her as a confidence woman." Her real name was Bridget McGarvey. She "had her mug taken and will be sent to Police Court under charges."

There is no doubt that the loss of the *Wawaset* was a terrible tragedy. There *is* doubt about whether the extent of the tragedy could have been avoided or at the very least ameliorated if the officers and crew had acted more heroically than they did. I suspect, however, that the greatest factor that contributed to the large loss of life was due to the way panic-stricken passengers conducted, or misconducted, themselves. A little rationality on the part of individuals would have gone a long way to saving lives.

The charred hull of the *Wawaset* lay in water that was as deep as twelve feet at high tide, some one hundred fifty yards from shore. There was little if anything that could be salvaged from the wreck. It was abandoned on the muddy bottom. The *Wawaset* was insured for $25,000.

Skip 137 years, to 2010. Among worldwide vessel catastrophes the *Wawaset* was nothing more than a footnote. But in King County, Virginia, the *Wawaset* reigned supreme as a big frog in a little pond. Her memory was kept alive by the King County Historical Society. Through perseverance, society members managed to get the U.S. Navy involved in searching for the long-lost steamer. The Navy justified its involvement by calling the operation a training mission for the Explosive Ordnance Division.

First they located the wreck by means of side-scan sonar. Then they placed marker buoys around the area. Finally they sent a pair of divers into the water to examine the site. Jim Ryan and John Mavis swam in circles on the bottom – not aimless circles, but planned, ever-widening circles from a central point. For a long time they swam within twenty feet of the wreck, but couldn't see it. In fact, they couldn't see anything: not even their hands in front of their face masks. Underwater visibility was zero.

According to Gary Furr, the master diver who was in charge of the operation, "It was all touch and feel. . . . but it's just hard to locate anything in those conditions. Toward the end of the day, we found it, structure that felt like it extended 3 to 4 feet up from the bottom. From the sonar, it seems to extend about 75 feet."

Oddly, the diving unit claimed that the wreck lay in 20 feet of water some 250 yards from shore. The depth and distance make it appear that they found the stern of the wreck. The bow must be buried under thick Potomac mud.

This artist's conception of the *Wilson Small* was drawn by Edwin Forbes (1839-1895).

WILSON SMALL

Built: 1851
Previous names: None
Gross tonnage: 258
Type of vessel: Wooden-hulled side-wheel steamer
Builder: Isaac C. Smith, Hoboken, New Jersey
Owner: W.D. Wallach, Washington, DC
Port of registry: Baltimore, Maryland
Cause of sinking: Collision with *Mary Augusta*
Location: Off Poplar Island

Sunk: August 9, 1867
Depth: 20 feet
Dimensions: 150' x 23' x 7'
Power: Coal-fired steam

The *Wilson Small* was built for Joseph Coffee and Wilson Small. The hull was constructed by Isaac Smith at Hoboken, New Jersey. The engine was built at Coffee's West Point Foundry. The vessel was launched on May 29, 1851. During her sea trials on August 13, she was found to be "quite fast." Her first home port was New York City.

She was originally scheduled to run between New York City and Keyport, New Jersey, which lay opposite each other across the Lower Bay and the Raritan Bay. Almost immediately after her initial service, Wilson Small sold his interests to Edward Elsworth and D.R. Martin. Ownership changed hands several more times until 1857, when the *Wilson Small* commenced operating out of Baltimore. Ownership continued to change hands until "Moses C. Smith & others" sold the vessel to Anthony Reybold, George Needham, and Asa Needham, shortly after the onset of hostilities that came to be known as the War of the Rebellion or the War of Secession, depending upon the allegiance of the writer.

In September 1861, the United States Quartermaster Corps started chartering the *Wilson Small* for use as a tender and supply boat. These charters continued throughout the war at rates that varied from a high of $210 per day to a low of $85 per day. During this time of government occupation, she also served with the Hospital Transport Service; this was a division of the United States Sanitary Commission. In this capacity she soon became the headquarters of the Commission. At times she was used to evacuate wounded soldiers from the battlefield to the District of Columbia.

After the war she returned to merchant service in the Chesapeake Bay, under the ownership of W.D. Wallach. The summer of 1867 found her working in consort with the *Mary Augusta*, transporting peaches from the Choptank River on the Eastern Shore of Maryland, to Baltimore. Her end came ignominiously on August 9:

"The steamer *Wilson Small*, Captain Leonard, which left this port [Baltimore] on Thursday evening at 8 o'clock for various landings on the Choptank River, was sunk by collision with the steamer *Mary Augusta*, about one o'clock yesterday morning, off Poplar Island. Some of the passengers and crew reached the city [Baltimore] at an early hour yesterday morning in the steamer *Louisiana*, from Norfolk, which was in the vicinity at the time of the collision. The *Wilson Small* was the property of W.D. Wallach, Esq., of Washington, and was engaged in the regular trade to the Choptank. The *Mary Augusta*, a powerful double ender, commanded by Captain Lewis, had been chartered by Mr. Wallach to run in connection with the *Wilson Small* during the peach season, and was on her return from the Choptank, fully loaded with peaches, when the accident occurred. Mr. Wallach was on board the *Wilson Small*.

"It is alleged that when off Poplar Island the *Wilson Small* ran into the *Mary Augusta*, striking her on the port side, and cutting away her upper works, injuring her to the amount of several hundred dollars. The *Wilson Small* sunk almost immediately in twenty feet of water, but fortunately all on board were saved by the steamer *Louisiana* and the *Mary Augusta* except for two female colored passengers, who were asleep at the time of the collision and who were drowned. The *Mary Augusta* was compelled to throw overboard 700 boxes of peaches, but by canting her on the side opposite to which she was struck she was enabled, by the efforts of Captain Lewis, to reach her wharf shortly after 11 o'clock yesterday morning. The *Wilson Small* was valued at $30,000, and is supposed to be fully insured. The accident will, doubtless, cause some disappointment to the peach growers of the Eastern Shore, as they are just now in the midst of gathering their abundant crops of fruit, and it will necessarily be some days before the places of the *Wilson Small* and *Mary Augusta* can be supplied."

Other sources stated that three people perished, and that the *Wilson Small* was valued at $25,000. All sources agreed that the vessel was fully insured.

Each skipper blamed the other for causing the collision. The Steamboat Inspection Service conducted an investigation, and ascertained facts and arrived at conclusions that differed somewhat from those of newspaper correspondents – who, it must be allowed, might have heard only one side of the story. According to the official report that was published in 1867:

"The steamers *Wilson Small* and *Mary Augusta* collided on the night of the 9th of August, near Poplar island [sic]; the former sunk [sic] in a few minutes, carrying down two colored girls, who were passengers, and one fireman; an investigation disclosed the fact that the *Mary Augusta* was in charge of an inexperienced man as pilot, and who had no license. The *Mary Augusta* was also without signal lights, which doubtless deceived the *Wilson Small* as to her course; loss, $15,000."

According to Bob Burgess, the wreck of the *Wilson Small* was "raised and brought to Baltimore where her engine was removed and salvaged. The hull was later abandoned on mud flats now occupied by the American Sugar Refinery in that city."

MISCELLANEOUS SHIPWRECKS

Curtis Bay

The arms of this bay have long been convenient seafaring disposal areas: places where unwanted watercraft were taken for burial. It is much like an elephant's graveyard filled with skeletal remains but without the tusks. It seems that vessels go there to die; or rather, they are towed there when they have outlived their usefulness and other forms of disposal are not economically feasible: much like a vehicle which, having been totaled in a crash, was left forever by the side of the road instead of being towed to a junkyard and either dismantled for parts or melted down for its scrap metal.

The wrecks that inhabit Curtis Bay are undignified reminders of the past importance of waterborne trade. It might be said that yesterday's majesty is today's eyesore. This particular eyesore is located in a watery municipal wasteland; or rather, in several wastelands.

Yet to people like me – who find artistry in crumbling buildings and collapsing shipwrecks – Curtis Bay is more like a photographic opportunity to examine and explore some partially sunken hulls without having to worry about remaining air supply and decompression penalty. Whereas many people stroll along paths in parks to smell the flowers in springtime, I like to photograph the vestiges of mankind's architectural and maritime past.

I first learned about the wrecks in Curtis Bay from the books of Robert H. Burgess. Five of his titles are listed in the Suggested Reading section. He wrote about various vessels that ended their careers in ignominy in coves or off points within the bay. Some

This is but a part of the shipwreck graveyard in Curtis Bay.

Top: Close-up of the remains of the ancient wooden-hulled sailing vessel that is pictured on the previous page.

Bottom: Close-up of a concrete-hulled vessel of more recent vintage. Although the sides of the hull look like wooden slats, the horizontal lines are likely impressions that were made by grooves between the timbers that were used to create the mold into which concrete was poured. Note the iron reinforcing bars, and how the concrete is crumbling around the portholes and grooves.

hulks were quite peripatetic, having been moved from one location to another to another before finally disintegrating, at which point they were no longer moveable.

Burgess's stories and photographs prompted me to visit these sites in Baltimore's industrial district, in order to photograph the remains that remained, and to document their state of decay and deterioration at this singular point in time, as well as to provide a record of the current state of collapse for future generations.

One concentration of shipwrecks is located northwest of the intersection of Chemical Road and the parallel highways of Route 173 and Interstate 695, near where the latter roads' bridges pass east and west over the water. The GPS coordinates for the center mass of this gaggle of wrecks are 38° 12' 30.85" and 76° 34' 28.07".

Another concentration is located around the bend: that is, west from the concentration that is noted above, then south under the bridges to the southwest shore just north of the railroad swing bridge. The GPS coordinates for the center mass of this gaggle are 39° 12' 05.75" and 76° 34' 42.54".

In between these two gaggles lies a half-sunken tug, at 39° 12' 22.11" and 76° 34' 56.33". The tug lies close to the west bank slightly south of the bridges. There is no telling how long it will be there, or will be exposed.

Other hulks appear and disappear irregularly, as they are either abandoned in place or fall apart until their metal structures settle beneath the surface of the muddy water. So, for the record . . .

In the foreground are the crumbled ruins of at least two wooden-hull vessels. Over the decades, mounds of dirt and debris have accumulated around the collapsing timbers, so that the hulls are hardly recognizable. Against the shore are two metal hulls, and more wooden hulls are located off-camera to the right, with only bare stubs of wood protruding above the surface of the water. Additional hulls may be completely submerged.

Mallows Bay

Whereas Curtis Bay lies in a busy metropolitan area where forlorn shipwrecks are always visible to ever-present commuters, truckers, and tourists who can see them from the highways, Mallows Bay can be found only with great difficulty, in an uninhabited expanse along the eastern shore of the Potomac River.

Here the river is so wide that even George Washington couldn't throw a dollar across it. (Actually, no one nowadays can throw a dollar across the Potomac River

These shipwrecks are "around the bend" on the other side of the bridges from Curtis Bay. Above is an old tugboat that has seen better days, partially submerged among piles that must have once supported docks. Below is a pair of aged wooden-hulled sailing vessels that are resting on the muddy bottom: rotting away with no one to care for them. The bays and coves in Baltimore Harbor are littered with the remnants of yesteryear's shipping discards. Equivalent to automobile junk yards, this is where unwanted vessels are towed to die.

where Washington is purported to have thrown it, because today a dollar doesn't go as far.) The river at this point is more than three miles wide.

The major portion of Mallows Bay's shipwreck history commenced with America's entry in the first war of German aggression. At the onset of the Great War, the United States Shipping Board created the Emergency Fleet Corporation, which was charged with the responsibility of buying, borrowing, or building "bottoms" (as merchant vessels were called), in order to deliver much needed supplies and war materiel to the fighting fronts, and to replace those bottoms that were being sunk at a prodigious rate by enemy mines and U-boats.

The EFC initiated a massive shipbuilding program that concentrated its efforts on constructing types of steamships in which the amount of iron that was used in construction could be minimized – this because most of the available iron was needed to manufacture guns and to build tanks and warships.

One experimental – some might say radical – design called for molding hulls from ferro-concrete. The raw materials that were necessary to make concrete were readily available, and their use would not significantly reduce the production of concrete that was needed for military applications: either domestic or overseas. Reinforcing rods (called "rebars") helped to stiffen and support the shaped concrete in the way screen mesh or chicken wire is used as a substrate for plaster walls.

A dozen concrete ships were built before inherent flaws made themselves obvious: the thick concrete hull and bulkheads made the ships 30% heavier than their iron or steel counterparts, thus reducing their speed in open water and making them less maneuverable, plus increasing their fuel consumption; and their cargo carrying capacity was 5% less than a ferrous metal vessel of similar size.

For the same ironic reason, the EFC determined that wooden-hulled steamships might satisfy the demand for oceanic transport. After all, the American hinterlands were filled with unending forests of timber that were just aching to be felled and converted to lumber. And wooden-hulled vessel designs were nearly as old as mankind: proven through millennia of ancient sailing history.

Even though the thick-beamed and -planked hulls possessed a smaller carrying capacity than concrete hulls – by about 8% - the country's shipbuilding efforts moved effortlessly in this direction. Across the nation trees fell by the thousands, and dozens of shipyards sprang up like weeds: on the east coast, on the west coast, and in the Great Lakes. These new shipyards were operated by people who knew a great deal about how to make money from government contracts, but practically nothing about the how to build ships. They were slow in getting started, and by the time the ship construction project was in full swing, the war was over.

Of nearly five hundred wooden bottoms for which the U.S. government issued contracts, fewer than one hundred were completed by the time the Armistice was signed. Fewer than another hundred were completed afterward and saw postwar service. The rest were laid up before completion when their contracts were canceled; many of these they were mothballed. What began as a hopeful idea for an enormous and perpetual transatlantic conveyor system became a three billion dollar white elephant.

The government then tried to sell off its newly constructed wood-framed argosy in order to help pay off some of the debt that had been incurred by the American war machine, only to discover that the "bottoms" had dropped out of the market. Wooden-

The gross burning commences. (Courtesy of the National Archives.)

hulled vessels could not compete in the open market with steel-hulled vessels because they were slower, less maneuverable, and contained less cargo space than their metallic brethren.

Worse yet, due to the rush to produce bottoms in accordance with wartime deadlines, most hulls were fabricated from freshly cut wood that was still green. Hulls constructed from unseasoned lumber leaked enormously, and soon rotted and fell apart. And those were only a few of a legion of structural deficiencies.

Hardly any buyers could be found to purchase these undesirable steamships. A few were sold for merchant service, largely to foreign countries. One in particular – the *Corvallis* – was sold to First National Pictures for use in the silent film *The Half-Way Girl*. In 1925, the vessel was dynamited on camera for the movie's spectacular finale. A freighter that cost the government $800,000 to build, was sold to the picture company for $45,000 – an awful lot of depreciation even in pre-depression days. (For full details, see *Shipwrecks of New Jersey: Central*, by this author.)

More than two hundred wooden bottoms were sold to a single company for less than one million dollars – total, not per vessel. After their machinery was removed, most of these vessels were towed to Mallows Bay in the 1920's, and burned for the iron fastenings that constituted the only value that the bottoms retained: scrap metal.

Whereas Curtis Bay can be viewed as an elephant's graveyard, Mallows Bay can be viewed as a white elephant's graveyard.

Enough metal was left in the wooden hulls to serve as a magnet that attracted additional discarded hulks throughout subsequent decades. This snowball effect mirrored a common attitude: who would notice another scuttled hulk among those that already littered the bay? Thus Mallows Bay became a common dumping ground for abandoned derelicts (the watery kind, not the alcoholic kind). The bay can best be described as a waterborne junkyard.

According to the Maryland Department of Natural Resources, "In the 1960's during the Congressional hearings regarding possible removal of the ships, several groups provided testimony suggesting that the ship hulls, having been there for almost 40 years, had become an integral part of the Mallows Bay ecosystem and the local fishery. For various reasons they were never removed, and the ships remain today. Many of the sunken ships have trapped sediments and collected plant life to become artificial islands. In addition to the wooden ships, other ship remains have been found, including 12 barges, several 19th Century log canoes and schooners, various workboats, a car ferry called the *Accomac*, and possibly a Revolutionary War longboat."

The Maryland DNR did not provide evidence to substantiate the suggestion that a "possible" longboat of Revolutionary War vintage actually inhabits the bay, but the suggestion makes good press. Hyperbole notwithstanding, Mallows Bay continues to serve as a reminder of the folly of rushing into shipbuilding where "anglers" fear to tread.

Today, the most visible member of the Mallows Bay shipwreck museum is the car ferry *Accomac*. According to Robert H. Burgess (in *Chesapeake Circle*), this centerpiece vessel began her career in 1928 as the *Virginia Lee*, when she conducted ferry service between Cape Charles and Norfolk, Virginia:

"Many miles of strange seas had flowed under her keel since she gave up her original ferry route in 1942. The Government had acquired her for service overseas in the

The burning in full swing. (Courtesy of the National Archives.)

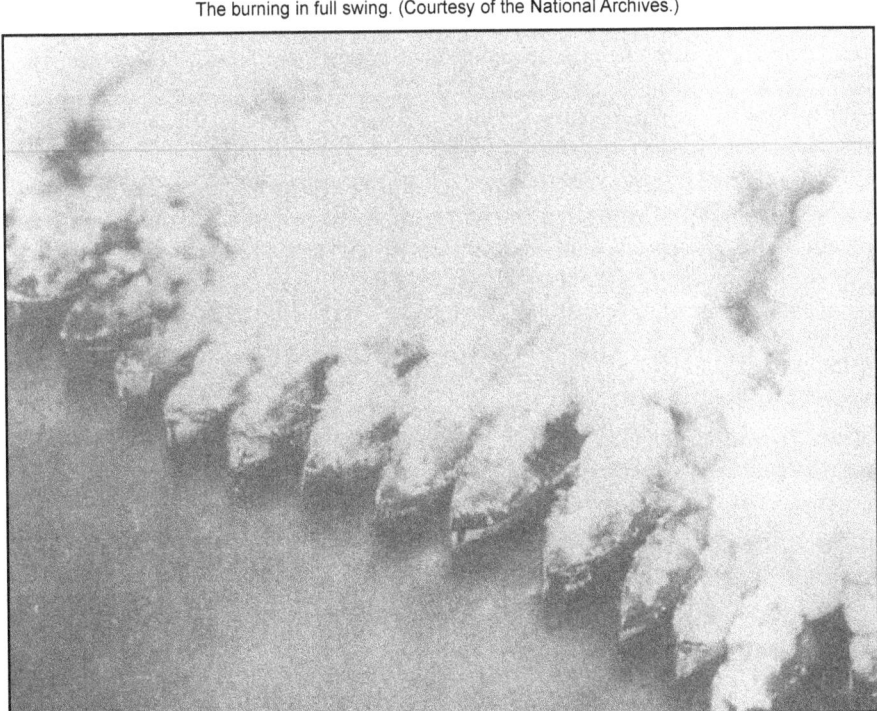

A picture postcard of the *Accomac* in better days.

European theatre, but for some reason her destination was changed and she was sent to the Amazon River to transport rubber. She returned to the States in 1948 and was tied up at Baltimore. She was later purchased by B.B. Willis and in 1949-50 operated between Boston and Provincetown as the excursion vessel *Holiday*. February 1951 found her back in Baltimore on her way to Miami to again enter the excursion business. Off Diamond Shoals she encountered heavy weather which broke her steering cable and caused other damage and had to be towed to Morehead City, North Carolina. In May 1951 she was purchased by the Virginia Ferry Corporation [a subsidiary of the Pennsylvania Railroad], renovated for their use and renamed *Accomac*."

Ghosts on the *Accomac* must have experienced déjà vu when they learned that she was returning to her first operational route, and ferried vehicles and people across the mouth of the Chesapeake Bay. She remained in this service until the opening of the Chesapeake Bay Bridge-Tunnel, on April 15, 1964. Six weeks later, while undergoing renovations, a fire of undetermined origin broke out onboard the *Accomac* in the early morning hours of May 28.

She was tied to a wharf in Portsmouth, Virginia when the conflagration erupted. The Portsmouth fire department responded to the alarm, but was unable to contain the blaze. High winds fanned the flames, which then leaped from ship to shore, torching adjacent piers and spreading fire to other vessels.

The Coast Guard was called to assist the local firefighters. Five cutters and five patrol vessels poured water onto the blaze. Three of the cutters were equipped with high-pressure nozzles. Nearby vessels were pulled from the wharf and were towed to the middle of the Elizabeth River.

Up in flames went a small excursion boat, a Navy utility craft, an LST (Landing Ship, Tank), and a tanker barge loaded with diesel fuel. According to a contemporary newspaper account, "The flames were reported so fierce they had driven firemen back from the only point along the shore from which water could be pumped." Three piers and a warehouse were also destroyed before the fire was brought under control by the concentrated efforts of Portsmouth and Coast Guard firefighters.

The *Accomac* was almost completely razed and not worth the cost of repairs. Subsequently, the burned-out hull ended up at Mallows Bay, to languish in league with the burned out wooden hulls from four decades earlier.

Recently the *Accomac* became a geocache site. For those of you who are not in the know, geocaching is a quasi-treasure hunting game in which people stash a "treasure" in a waterproof container, then advertise the coordinates to prospective treasure seekers, who then search for the site by means of a hand-held GPS receiver. It's essentially a grown-up version of hide and seek utilizing modern technological toys.

The so-called treasure in the cache consists of toys or trinkets and usually a logbook. Finders sign the logbook to prove that they have located the site. Sometimes they exchange gifts by taking a trinket from the container and leaving one of their own.

Geocachers and other boaters should beware of water hazards that are barely awash. More than one hundred hulks have been scuttled in Mallows Bay. Many of them are not exposed but lurk maliciously beneath the surface. Sharp wood or metal objects that are barely submerged can easily puncture inflatable hulls.

Canoes and kayaks are the best forms of transportation for tooling among the wrecks. Canoeists have the advantage of a stable platform, but kayakers should proceed slowly and be careful of striking parts of wrecks that might capsize the boat; the water might not be deep enough to execute an Eskimo roll, even if you have a spray skirt. Motorboaters are especially warned not to cruise among the wrecks with their motors

The *Accomac* today.

Above: The stern of the *Accomac*, with a view of the scuttled fleet in the background. Although the hull appears intact when viewed from shore, from this angle you can see that the after port hull is broken down.

Below: Most of the scuttled fleet is totally submerged. This close-up view shows iron fasteners that were not salvaged from the wooden hulls.

engaged; row row row your boat gently down the stream, or you might leave your propeller or a least a couple of blades among the wreckage.

A powerboat launching ramp is located at GPS coordinates 38° 28' 07.49" and 77° 15' 47.10". For small boats (canoes and kayaks), it is easier and more convenient to put in the water alongside the small floating pier some fifty feet northward.

The distance from the launching ramp to the *Accomac* is nearly half a mile. The other wrecks stretch for three-quarters of a mile to the north. Don't overlook the wrecks in the back bay, adjacent to and northeast of the launching ramp.

Above: The flooded interior of the *Accomac*, showing some of the rusted machinery.

Below: This scuttled wooden hull is one of the few that is largely exposed. The view is looking westward, beyond Mallows Bay to the opposite shore of the Potomac River.

Above: The highest standing wreckage of the incinerated fleet.

Below: This wreck lies in the back bay with some other wreckage, most of which is completely submerged.

185

Above: Trees and other vegetation have taken root on exposed wreckage, siphoning water from the bay and drawing nourishment from windborne dirt that has accumulated on horizontal surfaces, and from soil that was generated from rotting wood. Note the firmly embedded iron fastenings that were never salvaged. The boat launch lies in the open space between trees in the upper right corner. Partially submerged shipwrecks appear in the middle distance.

Below: Another view of back bay wreckage, looking outward from the back bay, across Mallows Bay, and showing the opposite shore of the Potomac River on the horizon.

AWOIS

Wreck Site Locations

The method for relocating wreck sites has changed in recent years. Early in the history of wreck-diving, the only way to return to a wreck was by the alignment of land ranges. In this system, one would look for two pairs of alignments, such as a telephone pole behind the northwest corner of a beach house with blue shingles, and the leg of a water tower a finger's width southwest of a red brick building. If only one pair was aligned and not the other, the boat was either too close or too far from shore, and not directly over the wreck. Only when both pairs of alignments coincided would triangulation place the boat in the exact position over the site. A grapnel was then deployed in order to hook into wreckage. As cumbersome and as difficult as this system sounds, some skippers were quite expert at locating relatively small targets in a short period of time. The process could be frustrating, however, if the skipper was inexperienced or untalented. And the system did not work in fog or rain, when the landmarks were obscured, or too far from shore from where the landmarks were difficult to see. And of course, it did not work at all from over the horizon.

Then the depth recorder made its appearance. This device enabled a skipper to read the depth and the contours of the bottom. This additional piece of information helped skippers to fine-tune the process.

Loran was the next distinct improvement. LORAN is the acronym for Long Range Navigation. This radio navigation system was developed during World War Two for military purposes, but did not become commercially available until the 1960's, when the cost of receiving units was reduced to the point at which they became affordable to charter boat skippers. In loran, a transmitting station, designated as the master station, emits synchronized pulses to several secondary stations. Signals are then transmitted from the secondary stations. The receiving unit on the boat (or in a plane) measures the time difference (called a TD) between the pulses from the secondary stations to the receiver. A position can be triangulated by plotting TD's from two or more stations.

At first there was loran A. In a comparison between the history of radio navigation and that of written language, loran A is equivalent to chiseling hieroglyphics on rock. The receiving units were difficult to read. The screen displayed a pair of jagged, close-cropped vertical lines that looked like compressed electrocardiogram waves on a hospital monitor. To obtain a readout in numerical form, it was necessary to coordinate the dual displays until they were identical. Then one had to switch channels and repeat the process in order to obtain the correct triangulation. To pinpoint a set of coordinates, one had to switch back and forth until both correct numbers were obtained. To make matters worse, all too often one of the secondary stations ceased transmission due to mechanical malfunction, and left boaters without a means of locating offshore sites. More than once over the years I have returned to the dock without ever having gotten into the water.

Loran C was a more distinct improvement. (I don't know what happened to loran B – or if there ever *was* a loran B.) The transmitting stations were more reliable, and the receiving units were digital and therefore easy to read. Referring to my written language comparison, loran C was equivalent to writing on paper with a ballpoint pen.

Still, there were problems with precise repeatability. The propagation rates of the signals varied in accordance with surface features of the Earth (particularly land masses) and atmospheric conditions, thereby introducing non-uniform inaccuracy in the transmission rates: specific coordinates could change from day to day. Also, the receiving units contained inherent differences in their electronic configurations, antenna location, electrical grounding, and so on, so that one unit displayed a readout that might be slightly different from the readout of another unit. The accumulation of these inaccuracies meant that a set of "numbers" (the pair of digital readouts expressed in microseconds) could change from unit to unit (or boat to boat). Coordinates that coincided with a wreck on one day on one boat, might not coincide with the wreck on another day or on another boat. The difference in accuracy of these various components could be a hundred feet or more on a good day, three to four hundred feet when conditions were less than optimal. You could still find the wreck, but you might have to run a few circles around a marker buoy before seeing a spike on the depth recorder.

Then the Global Positioning System (GPS) was developed. This system was like word processing with spell-check. GPS was made possible by America's vigorous pursuit to achieve dominance in the space race against the Soviet Union. GPS is only one of thousands of spinoffs that people take for granted when they complain about the money that is spent on shooting rockets into outer space.

GPS was created and is currently maintained by the U.S. Department of Defense primarily for military applications. The signals are transmitted from satellites with such incredible pinpoint accuracy that the DOD inserted filters to make the "numbers" less precise (on the theory that enemy nations or terrorists might make harmful use of the accuracy). This Selective Availability (SA) purposely introduced errors into the transmitting system so that accuracy was reduced to about fifty feet. (In the military mind, this is beyond of the effective blast radius of a nuclear device.)

GPS receiving units are pathetically reliable as long as the integral antenna can obtain a clear view of the sky – pretty much of a given on a boat. The unit locks on to any number of satellites (as many as half a dozen) in order to triangulate its position. The unit determines not only its horizontal position with respect to the surface of the Earth, but its vertical position – which is great for flyers and mountain climbers. The unit can also track its movements like a plotter. And units may be as small as a pack of cigarettes.

Selective Availability has been disabled, but it can be switched on again at a moment's notice and without warning. In fact, GPS can be switched off entirely in the event of hostile activity.

In the next stage of the progression, standard GPS was replaced by differential GPS. In DGPS, the satellite signals are referenced to a coastal transmitting station, which broadcasts correction signals that increase the accuracy range to about five feet with near perfect repeatability. One can not only locate a wreck promptly and with precision, but can locate discrete *places* on a wreck.

The latest evolution in GPS is the Wide Area Augmentation System (WAAS). This system utilizes ground reference stations that are uplinked to a geosynchronous satellite (a satellite in a geostationary orbit; that is, one that hovers over the same spot on the planet all the time). What comes next is anybody's guess.

As a result of this procession of changes, "numbers" are available in several different formats. If you have loran A numbers, throw them away. Loran C has been shut down but the numbers may still prove useful – and may become invaluable if the DOD decides for military expedience to switch off the GPS, and renovate the closed-down loran transmitting stations. Although the loran C system has been discontinued, many GPS receivers can convert loran numbers to GPS – *but* not without some inherent inaccuracy, perhaps even gross inaccuracy.

There are computer programs that can convert loran C numbers to GPS numbers. For reasons that I cannot understand, I am told that none of them work with any degree of reliability. It seems to me that an algorithmic formula *has* to work – but in this regard I must accept the professional opinion of experienced boat captains and other interested users. Due to algorithmic problems associated with loran C coordinates (dissimilar signal propagation rates over land and sea, atmospheric disturbances (weather), receiving unit differences, local anomalies, and so on), the inherent imprecision and unpredictable variability obtains products that cannot be reproduced with any degree of accuracy, and therefore cannot be converted to precise GPS coordinates. When loran C was being phased out, the only reliable method for converting loran C numbers to GPS numbers was to locate the site by means of loran, then take a GPS reading.

Another but less reliable conversion method is to insert a correction factor into the computer program. This is done by first finding a wreck for which you have GPS numbers: a wreck that lies in the vicinity of the wreck you want to find but for which you have only loran C number. Next, correlate that wreck's loran number with the GPS number. This correlation provides a correction factor that becomes less precise with increasing distance.

For all these reasons, the list of locations in the back of the book includes loran numbers.

AWOIS Background

As I wrote in the first sentence of the previous section, the process of conversion is in a state of change. I have obtained numbers from a variety of sources. For various reasons, there are wrecks for which I have obtained loran C numbers but not GPS numbers. In addition, one of my sources for GPS numbers was the Automated Wreck and Information System (AWOIS) that is maintained by the National Oceanic and Atmospheric Administration (NOAA). Sometimes, instead of providing GPS numbers in the usual format (degrees, minutes, and decimals) AWOIS provides the numbers in latitude/longitude format (degrees, minutes, seconds, and decimals). Fortunately, all but the cheapest handheld GPS receiving units possess functions and capabilities that can read the lat/lon format.

Furthermore, GPS coordinates on the AWOIS list are printed in formats that sometimes differ from that of most GPS lists and receiving unit readouts. Then again, an entry in today's AWOIS list may differ from an entry for the same wreck or obstruction from several years earlier, as individual entries are updated and revised.

The AWOIS list is more useful for inland waters than it is for the ocean, because more surveys have been conducted where shipping and boating traffic is concentrated. The primary purpose of these hydrographic surveys is not to search for historic shipwrecks. The primary purpose is to locate shoals and obstructions in navigable waterways as an aid to mariners so that they can operate their vessels without fear of running aground or striking a submerged object: in other words, to achieve safe navigation along the country's waterways. Finding shipwrecks is only a spinoff.

The AWOIS list is particularly useful for the Chesapeake Bay and its major tributaries not only because of the requirements of the sheer volume of commercial traffic, but because of the volume of naval traffic, and because of the increasing draft of modern day supertankers, all of which necessitate continual surveying and dredging in order to prevent vessels from grounding on shifting shoals and from striking submerged wrecks and obstructions. Region 6 is the region that focuses on the Chesapeake Bay.

However, to utilize the list effectively, users must have an in-depth understanding of its origin, evolution, and deficiencies.

The list was initially cobbled together from various official sources such as the 1945 Wreck Information List, its revised form as the 1957 Navy Wreck List, Hydrographic Office surveys, Life-Saving Service reports, and Coast Guard records. The position accuracy for many offshore shipwrecks was often given as 3 to 5 miles; or, under better circumstances, as 1 to 3 miles. This information may be helpful for historical purposes, but it hardly enables one to locate the wreck in question. This kind of location is often called PA, for "position approximate."

Later, commercial publications were added to the AWOIS. A glance at the bibliography of source materials will show that early titles of my Popular Dive Guide Series were included. In recent years, the practice of citing sources has pretty much ceased, I suspect because some of the new sources are classified (such as the 1968 Non-Submarine Contacts list and the more accurate subsequent editions that were published by the Defense Mapping Agency only for eyes that held the proper security clearances).

AWOIS is revised and updated on a continuing basis. That is, the *system* is revised and updated, but not necessarily the individual records. Some records still show wartime positional accuracies – or *in*accuracies, as the case may be. AWOIS notes four levels of accuracy: high, medium, low, and poor. A high level of accuracy is assigned only when the position was ascertained by one of two methods: from anchoring into a wreck which a diver actually explored; or, less often, confirmed by side-scan sonar or other electronic detection means, in which the towfish was integrated with an onboard GPS unit so as to interpolate the correct position of the wreck or obstruction.

A medium level of accuracy means that a wreck or obstruction was reported in a general area, but was never investigated and confirmed. Low level and poor level are meaningless.

One should never put faith in an AWOIS location – even if that number is given in GPS – without first obtaining its level of accuracy. AWOIS often provides a precise GPS number for a location that is inaccurate. Keep in mind the difference between precision and accuracy.

In order to demonstrate the progression of accuracy, and the variety of ways in which AWOIS prints numbers, I will use Record 2561: the Union sloop-of-war *Cumberland*, which was rammed and sunk by the Confederate ironclad *Virginia* (ex-*Merrimac*). So-called GPS numbers were provided in two formats that represented conversions from latitude and longitude: (1) Lat 36/58/13.53 and Lon 076/26/02.81, and (2) Lat 36.970425 and Lon 76.434113888889. These extremely precise numbers (especially the last, which is taken to twelve decimals), were scaled off an old sketch of the Battle of Hampton Roads. The position quality was given as poor, and the wreck was not even charted. So the number is precise but the location is inaccurate.

Over the last decade, the Homeland Security Project has been responsible for re-evaluating old (or ancient) locations, so that the position quality of many wrecks and obstructions has now been raised to "high" as wreck sites were actually located and marked. GPS numbers have been refined as divers have been put down on the wrecks, or modern electronic detection equipment was used to upgrade positional data.

The AWOIS location of the *Cumberland* is now given as (1) Lat 36-58-07.61 and Lon 76-26-07.73, and (2) Lat 36.968781 and Lon 76.435481. Note that the strokes in the previous lat/lon format have been replaced with dashes. Unfortunately, this change is not uniform throughout the system. For reasons of conformity, in my list I have used dashes wherever AWOIS numbers were given with strokes.

Keep in mind that AWOIS is largely a list of obstructions: concrete blocks, disused piles, submerged dolphins (a cluster of piles for the purpose of mooring), sunken buoys, rocks and other geological formations, lost anchors, small craft such a rowboats and cabin cruisers, dredge pipes, sewer lines, containers that fell overboard, fish havens, derelict nets, fish pounds, tree trunks and stumps, broken down piers, natural oyster bars, shoals, sand bars, old rip rap, dumping grounds, automobiles, railroad cars, and miscellaneous debris. Occasionally there is a wreck, and usually it is unidentified.

New surveys have recommended that old obstructions and their symbols be deleted from the chart because the obstruction was not found. But if the recommendation was heeded, often the wreck or obstruction was not deleted from the list. Thus a lot of chaff is listed with the wheat. For example, a 1980 survey lists *Capt Nick's Dreamboat* as a 235-foot vessel that was beached and employed as a "floating" restaurant; the "wreck" no longer exists, but AWOIS continues to list it.

My wreck list incorporates AWOIS shipwrecks that have a high level of accuracy. I did not list a lot of small craft because most of them were put on the AWOIS list several decades ago, and by now likely are completely broken down and buried in the mud. I listed no sites whose level of accuracy was given as medium, low, or poor.

Wrecks that AWOIS listed by name, *I* listed by name; they can be distinguished from standard GPS numbers that I obtained by actually locating the wreck by means of the format in which the numbers are given: eight digits instead of seven, two dashes instead of one, two decimal digits instead of three.

If an AWOIS wreck was listed as unknown, I listed it by its Record number. This way the user can look it up on the AWOIS website or on a download. In most cases, I have taken the liberty of extracting a descriptive cognomen from the text in the descriptive entry, in order to enable the reader to perceive at first glance what kind of wreck was observed by NOAA evaluators – say, a wooden barge or pile driver – so the user will know whether he wishes to learn more about what the evaluators wrote about the wreck.

The AWOIS database is searchable. I have downloaded the eastern seaboard sections onto my computer. Whether users access the database online or on their personal computer, they can search for specific wrecks either by name or Record number. The keyboard command is "control f". Type the name or number or any other search criterion into the rectangular search window, tap Enter, and follow the yellow brick road.

For listings in which the footage is given in parentheses, the footage refers to the length of the vessel, not the depth. For example, Oyster Barge (180') is an unidentified wreck whose hull measures 180 feet in length. This information might prove useful to the ultimate user of this book.

As a result of all the foregoing, the GPS/Loran list at the back of the book is a hodgepodge of number variations. Take your pick and shovel out the numbers that work best for you.

More on AWOIS

AWOIS is not only a source of wreck locations but, in some cases, of useful wreck descriptions. By way of example, I would like to reprint some descriptions that NOAA divers made in the 1970's and 1980's. These descriptions are not always published in the AWOIS list, but may be found in the Field Examinations that were used as a basis for the list. The following may be somewhat confusing, but it will also be somewhat edifying.

* * * * *

1

"NOAA ship *Heck* located and positioned the remains of a deteriorated vessel approximately 100 feet in length. The wreck is currently uncharted and lies at position LAT. 038° 37' 35.0" N. LONG. 076° 25' 13.8" N [sic: should be W] (on chart 12266) with a least depth, corrected for predicted tides, of 65.5 ft (MLLW) taken on the vessel's shoalest point."

There is now a symbol on the chart at this location: the number "67" inside a dotted circle. The wreck lies about three-quarters of a mile northwest of the *New Jersey* (which see). In the GPS and loran list at the back of this book, I call this wreck "AWOIS Unidentified" because AWOIS did not assign a Record Number to it at that time.

* * * * *

2

Perhaps that site is not very interesting, but take a gander at this description that is published on the AWOIS list as Record Number 3683:

"WHILE SEARCHING FOR ITEM 6, 150FT BARGE *ECKIE*, A DIFFERENT WK WAS HUNG. DIVERS REP. A 40FT X 12FT STEEL HULL TUG (PUSH BOAT TYPE) LYING UPSIDE DOWN AND RESTING ON SMALL PILOT HOUSE. TRANSOM PARTLY BURIED WITH HULL INCLINED UPWARD FROM BOTTOM TO APPROX. 50FT. WRECK CLEARED BY 46.5FT (PREDICTED TIDES) IN LAT.38-36-27N, LONG.76-25-51W. HYDRO. RECOMMENDS CHARTING WK. CLEARED BY 46.5FT AT POS. LISTED ABOVE."

Now look at the different and expanded version that was published in the Field Examination: "A forty foot pusher type tug boat resting starboard side down and leaning over on the pilothouse was found by ship's divers. The highest point on the wreck was the bow, and the wreck was buried lower on the stern. The wreck was in the early stages of decomposition. A plaque on the portside of the pilothouse read:

SEATENDER
SERVICE
SEARIGHT
NJ

"No readily apparent reason was seen to explain the sinking of the vessel. A least depth was taken on the high point using a pneumofathometer (0-140 FSW GAUGE). All deck gear, including the remnants of towing lines, were in good condition. See attached sketch."

The report doesn't state whether the divers read the plaque on the bottom in limited visibility, or recovered it and read it on the survey boat. Record Number 3683 was assigned to this wreck. On the list of GPS and loran numbers, I call this wreck "AWOIS 3683 (40' steel push tug)."

* * * * *

3

Record number 2366 also looks interesting. According to the initial 1952 Notice to Mariners: "WK OF LOADED BARGE, 150FT LONG, REP. SUNK IN 70FT DEPTHS, ABOUT 3M NORTH OF SHARPS ISLAND LT BY 18A IN APPROX. POS. LAT.38-33-18N, LONG.76-25-41."

The wreck was surveyed and a description was added: "BUILT 1920, 3/11/52, SUNK OWNER S.C. LOVELAND CO., INC., 151 SOUTH FRONT ST., PHILADELPHIA, PA., CARGO 55T NITRATE OF SODA, STEEL CONSTRUCTION, LOA 149FT, BEAM 20FT, AND DEPTH 11FT. WK PARTIALLY BURIED NEAR BOW, RESTING ON STBD PLATE, IN AN UPRIGHT POS. STBD LIST OF 25 DEG."

According to the 1978 survey: "DIVERS IDENTIFIED WRECK AS THE BARGE "EKIE". EVALUATOR RECOMMENDS CHARTING A DANGEROUS SUBM. WRECK, COVERED 42FT. AT SURVEYED POSITION." Note that the correct spelling of the name of the barge is *Eckie*, which is noted in the section above.

Gale force winds struck the eastern seaboard on March 11, 1952. Offshore, the hull of the *E.H. Blum* cracked. The Coast Guard cutter *Agassiz* towed the stricken tanker to safe harbor. The tanker *Saxon Star* sent an SOS because she was in critical condition with her cargo overflowing their tanks. The Coast Guard cutter *Mendota* went to her assistance.

Conditions in the Chesapeake Bay were not much better. Unusually large waves whipped the water to froth. During the worst of the storm, the tug *Gertrude Loveland* was proceeding northbound with two barges in tow. As tug and tows approached the Sharps Island Light, off the mouth of the Choptank River, the barge *Eckie* sank with one man aboard.

And according to the 1987 survey: "BARGE FOUND TO BE 17FT WIDE AT A DISTANCE OF 48FT FROM THE END. IT IS PARTIALLY BURIED IN BOTTOM SEDIMENTS, SHOWS MODERATE DECOMPOSITION AND HEAVY ENCRUSTATION. IT IS COMPLETELY FILLED WITH BOTTOM SEDIMENTS. THE BARGE WAS LOCATED IN LAT. 38-35-43.9N; LONG 76-24-43.71W WITH A LEAST DEPTH OF 46FT BY DIVER PNEUMATIC DEPTH GAUGE IT IS RECOMMENDED THAT WK BE CHARTED AS A 46FT DEPTH, LABELED WK WITH SURROUNDING DANGER CURVE. LORAN-C RATES: 9960-CHAIN; 16121.1W, 27519.8X, 42428.5Y, 58856.8Z."

Here's where it gets both confusing and interesting.

Confusing: notice the startling difference between the coordinates given in the 1952 report and those given in the 1987 report. Both descriptions are published on the AWOIS list. So which location is correct: either, neither, or both? If both, each location could refer to a different wreck. To make matters worse, although the first cited location is given as three miles *north* of Sharps Island Light, the plotted coordinates fall three miles *south* of the light.

Furthermore, the two locations are a couple of miles apart. How could the skipper of the survey vessel *Heck* not have noticed that he was nowhere near the location that he was supposed to scan? And why didn't the report evaluator in the office pick up the error?

Interesting: the Field Examination reveals information that was deleted from the version that was published on the AWOIS list: "The contact was found to be the remains of a standard type square barge. The barge was 17 feet wide. At a distance of 48 feet from the end, the barge is buried in the bottom sediment; consequently, no overall length measurement was possible. The barge shows moderate decomposition and heavy encrustation. Several openings leading into the barge were found. The barge is completely filled with bottom sediment."

Unless one assumes that a hundred feet of the barge was completely buried beneath the mud, this wreck is far too short to be the *Eckie*. On the GPS and loran list, I give both coordinates and call the wrecks "AWOIS barge 1" and "AWOIS barge 2."

* * * * *

4

One last sample is record number 3684. I am providing the record number so you can find the text within the AWOIS list. Initially in 1966: "NM25/66—145 FT. STEEL BARGE LOCATED IN APPROX. POS. LAT. 38-37-41.0N, LONG. 76-26-02.0W IN 54-55 FT. 38-39 FT. REP. OVER WRECK." NM stands for Notice to Mariners.

The *Rude* and *Heck* conducted a wire-drag survey in 1978, at which time the wire cleared at 43 feet. According to the 1987 survey: "LOCATED REMAINS OF LARGE METAL STRUCTURE CONSISTING OF LARGE PLATES AND I-BEAMS IN LAT 38-37-40.91N, LONG 76-26-00.90W."

Not much published information, but the description in the 1987 Field Examination is far more extensive: "The contact appeared to be the remains of a large wooden hulled vessel carrying a large amount of coal. A bow and a stern were identified with an approximate length of 100+ feet. Remains of the hull ribbing ran down both sides with a large bulkhead running down a portion of the centerline of the vessel. Heaped in the remaining hull of the vessel was a large amount of coal. Near the bow the divers found a large windlass with portions of chain still wound around the wildcat. The bow of the vessel appeared to be severely damaged on the starboard side with the pieces found mostly intact with a large metal closed chock on the undamaged port side. The vessel was lying in a north-south line, keel down. The approximate beam between the remaining ribs was estimated at 40 feet. The highest point of the vessel was at the stern where a long wooden pole like object protruded 12-15 feet above the rest of the wreck. A least depth was taken on the last dive."

I don't have to tell you that the 1987 description of a *wooden* barge bears no resemblance to the 1966 description of a *steel* barge.

Nonetheless, this kind of structure might provide a haven for fish that feel the need to hide from pelagic predators. It also might prove fascinating to a wreck-diver with an exploratory sense of adventure. My point is that the AWOIS list contains much *mis*information, but even so the information that it does contain might be of value to a number of people. Furthermore, the Field Examinations contain even more information, although the accuracy might be in doubt.

* * * * *

The Field Examinations have been digitized and can be found on NOAA's website – although admittedly, my search for FE307 – the one that described the wrecks above as well as the *New Jersey* and *Levin J. Marvel* – proved fruitless. The place to look on the website is not intuitive, and when I followed links to where I thought the FE's should be located and typed criteria into the search engine, I kept getting an error message that read "subject not found." I had to contact the website help desk, whose respondent located the FE for me. He agreed with me that the search mechanism was less than efficient.

For what it's worth, the original hard copies of the Field Examinations have been turned over to the National Archives. (As historic information, in the 1980's, I used to obtain these Field Examinations by visiting the office of the National Ocean Survey in Rockville, Maryland.)

My other point is that the serious Chesapeake Bay wreck hunter should pay a great deal of attention to the AWOIS list. This list is not static, but is growing all the time. As I noted above, the Homeland Security Project has intensified the search for wrecks and obstructions in the Chesapeake Bay. Why, I have no idea.

The U.S. Navy searched for offshore shipwrecks during World War Two in the belief that German U-boats might be able to hide from then-nascent sonar detection systems by lying next to a wreck: using the wreck as a shield to disguise the U-boat's sonar signature and presence on the bottom. In reality, it was virtually impossible for a U-boat to locate a shipwreck. U-boats were not equipped with sonar, and they did not have windows.

Salvage of the *Cuyahoga*. Note the gash in the hull. (Courtesy of the U.S. Coast Guard.)

To be fair, the Navy didn't know what level of technology the Nazi's had developed. As a result of this ignorance and belief, the Navy dropped an uncounted number of depth charges and hedgehogs on East Coast shipwrecks, doing tremendous damage to those sunken hulls in the process. Better to be safe than sorry, I suppose.

The Navy plotted the locations of a number of shipwrecks and created the Wreck Information List. In 1957, this list was modified and enlarged to the Navy Wreck List. Approximate positions were given in latitude and longitude with accuracy at best of one to three miles, at worst three to five.

In 1968, the Navy compiled a list called Non-Submarine Contacts. This list was highly classified. It was *not* included in the AWOIS database. The location information on the Non-Sub Contacts is now long out of date.

So why is Homeland Security interested in shipwrecks in the Chesapeake Bay? As I noted above, I have no idea. I hope they don't entertain the thought that a terrorist submarine could hide next to a pile of debris that couldn't conceal anything larger than a rowboat. But who knows? Such beliefs have been entertained before and, all too often, have had a habit of repeating themselves. As the saying goes, those who do not study history are bound to repeat it.

Notwithstanding all of the above, these hydrographic surveys are a boon to Chesapeake Bay anglers and wreck-divers. A light perusal of the list reveals some interesting wreck data. An in-depth study of the Field Examinations reveals a whole lot more. And while some of the descriptive information may be incorrect, the locations should be valid if they were based upon an integrated side-scan sonar survey, or if divers were put into the water.

To reiterate my point, AWOIS is a valuable tool that contains a wealth of information that is growing wealthier all the time.

Salvage of the *Cuyahoga*. Note the gash in the hull. (Courtesy of the U.S. Coast Guard.)

SUGGESTED READING

Anonymous (1884-1922) *Official Records of the Union and Confederate Navies in the War of the Rebellion*, 31 volumes, Government Printing Office, Washington, DC.

Berman, Bruce D. (1972) *Encyclopedia of American Shipwrecks*, The Mariners Press, Boston, Massachusetts.

Brown, Alexander Crosby (1961) *Steam Packets on the Chesapeake*, Tidewater Publishers, Centreville, MD. (Note: this is a revised edition of (1940) *The Old Bay Line: 1840-1940*, The Dietz Press, Richmond, VA.

Bunker, John Gorley (1972) *Liberty Ships: the Ugly Ducklings of World War II*, Naval Institute Press, Annapolis, Maryland.

Burgess, Robert H. (1965) *Chesapeake Circle*, Cornell Maritime Press, Cambridge, MD.

Burgess, Robert H. (1975) *Chesapeake Sailing Craft*, Tidewater Publishers, Cambridge, MD.

Burgess, Robert H. (1970) *Sea, Sails and Shipwreck: Career of the four-masted schooner Purnell T. White*, Tidewater Publishers, Cambridge, Maryland.

Burgess, Robert H. (1963) *This Was Chesapeake Bay*, Cornell Maritime Press, Cambridge, Maryland.

Burgess, Robert H. and Wood, H. Graham (1968) *Steamboats out of Baltimore*, Tidewater Publishers, Cambridge, Maryland.

Earle, Swepson (1923) *The Chesapeake Bay Country*, Thomsen-Ellis Company, Baltimore, Maryland.

Gaines, W. Craig (2008) *Encyclopedia of Civil War Shipwrecks*, Louisiana State University Press, Baton Rouge, Louisiana.

Gentile, Gary *The Nautical Cyclopedia*, GGP, 3 Lehigh Gorge Drive, Jim Thorpe, PA 18229 ($20).

Gentile, Gary (2002) *Shipwrecks of Delaware and Maryland*, GGP, 3 Lehigh Gorge Drive, Jim Thorpe, PA 18229 ($20).

Gentile, Gary (1992) *Shipwrecks of Virginia*, GGP, 3 Lehigh Gorge Drive, Jim Thorpe, PA 18229 ($20).

Hahn, Herbert Paul (1990) *American Mariner: a Documentary Biography*, American Merchant Marine Museum Foundation, Kings Point, New York.

Hildebrand, Samuel F and Schroeder, William C. (1928) *Fishes of Chesapeake Bay*, United States Bureau of Fisheries.

Holly, David C. (1994) *Chesapeake Steamboats: Vanished Fleet*, Tidewater Publishers, Centreville, Maryland.

Holly, David C. (1987) *Steamboat on the Chesapeake: Emma Giles and the Tolchester Line*, Tidewater Publishers, Centreville, Maryland.

Holly, David C. (1991) *Tidewater by Steamboat: a Saga of the Chesapeake*, The Johns Hopkins University Press, Baltimore, Maryland.

Keith, Robert C. (1982) *Baltimore Harbor: A Picture History*, Ocean World Publishing, 401 South High St., Baltimore, Maryland 21202.

Oickle, Alvin F. (2009) *Disaster on the Potomac: the Last Run of the Steamboat Wawaset*, The History Press, Charleston, South Carolina.

Sawyer, L.A. and Mitchell, W.H. (1970) *The Liberty Ships: the History of the 'Emergency' Type Cargo Ships Constructed in the United States During World War II*, David & Charles, Newton Abbot, Devon, England.

GPS and LORAN NUMBERS
ALPHABETICAL

American Mariner	38-02.403	76-09.314		
Amphibious Craft (35')	36-55-46.56	76-03-11.61		
Anglo African	37-03-25.12	75-53-57.53	27163.2	41372.6
Anglo African	37-03-23.4	75-55-09		
Armed Sailing Vessel (with cannons)	36-54-49.53	76-05-22.76		
AWOIS 10006 (wreck)	38-48-33.71	76-48-33.71		
AWOIS 10675 (dangerous wreck)	38-00-18.36	76-19-58.13		
AWOIS 10792 (wood ship remains)	37-00-47.40	76-03-09.2		
AWOIS 10794 (30' large metal box)	37-01-03.22	76-02-45.21		
AWOIS 10804 (dangerous wreck)	39-04-06.54	76-16-14.33		
AWOIS 11877 (menhaden trawler)	38-23-02.70	76-20-20.20		
AWOIS 11903 (container)	39-02-16.97	76-19-53.41		
AWOIS 11904 (wreck)	39-02-38.75	76-20-31.45		
AWOIS 12490 (dangerous wreck)	37-09-19.52	76-38-09.83		
AWOIS 12491 (dangerous wreck)	37-07-38.88	76-38-14.00		
AWOIS 13714 (barge)	38.067069	76.446386		
AWOIS 14174	37-14-14.77	76-27-09.39		
AWOIS 3190 (barge)	37-08-53.95	76-09-07.91		
AWOIS 3191 (60' vessel)	37-13-29.73	76-11-30.36	27255.4	41459.9
AWOIS 3420 (barge on side)	36-55-04.58	75-43-42.50		
AWOIS 3424 (wreck largely buried)	38-05-08.25	76-14-33.50		
AWOIS 3425 (wreck)	38-05-24.48	76-15-05.18		
AWOIS 3673 (197' LSM barge)	37-55-12.48	76-11-11.74		
AWOIS 3683 (40' steel push tug)	38-36-27.03	76-25-50.88		
AWOIS 3684 (145' steel barge)	38-37-40.91	76-26-00.90		
AWOIS 3875 (195' barge)	37-56-52.22	76-11-46.49		
AWOIS 4007 (359-ton barge Columbia ?)	38-18-44.91	76-25-00.60		
AWOIS 433 (steel barge)	37-19-47.14	76-08-31.41	27256.2	41538.7
AWOIS 4436 (60' steel pile driver)	38-55-57.72	76-23-37.73		
AWOIS 4692 (172' wreck-like contact)	38-42-11.26	76-25-28.22		
AWOIS 4696 (41' yacht)	38-46-05.97	76-29-36.26		
AWOIS 6878 (2 wrecks awash)	38-20-20.51	76-27-51.55		
AWOIS 7238 (100' wood vessel w/coal)	38-37-34.98	76-25-13.77	27527.8	42450.4
AWOIS 7239 (52' bargelike wood fiberg	38-37-40.13	76-26-08.51	27532.2	42450.6
AWOIS 7240 (120' wood vessel)	37-57-44.88	76-11-42.11	27356.3	41984.7
AWOIS 7260 (100' wood barge)	39-00-56.55	76-22-31.46		
AWOIS 7438 (large wood vessel)	38-53-54.31	76-24-04.65		
AWOIS 8673 (low-lying timbers)	39.131444	76.239889		
AWOIS 8875 (60' barge)	37-08-54.01	76-09-08.12		
AWOIS 8875 (60' barge)	37-08-53.88	76-09-08.05		
AWOIS 8897 (armed sailing vessel)	36-54-48.70	76-05-23.90		
AWOIS 908 (30' crane barge)	37-00-50.37	76-09-56.77		
AWOIS 912 (wreck)	37-01-13.47	76-30-24.91		
AWOIS 9544 (steel vessel wood beams)	36-55-56.87	76-03-17.06	27187.7	41269.4
AWOIS 9545 (steel vessel wood mast)	36-56-02.70	76-03-19.60	27108.4	41270.4
AWOIS 9555 (barge or pontoon float)	36-56-48.23	76-02-55.68	27188.1	41279.9
AWOIS barge 1	38-33-18	76-25-41		

Name	Lat	Lon		
AWOIS barge 2	38-35-43.9	76-24-43.71		
AWOIS Unidentified	38-35.0	76-25.8		
Barge	39-12-33.99	76-26-48.05		
Barge	36-55-05.11	75-43-41.20		
Bean Boat	38-18.591	76-27.898		
Big D (pile driver)	36-59-47.37	76-06-03.87	27206.5	41308.7
Big D (pile driver)	36-59-46.85	76-06-05.11		
Bigger Steel Barge	38-30.692	76-23.510		
Blair (tug)	38-47-40.09	76-26-54.34		
Brazil	37-51.793	76-09.465	27332.1	41916.3
Bright (114' wood barge)	38-33-32.57	76-25-41.67		
C.G. Willis (190' barge)	37-53.434	76-07-969		
Cabin Cruiser (30')	38-30-26.85	76-23-35.75		
Carmina (pilot boat)	36-57-35.01	76-01-16.90	27182.9	41292.0
Charlotte (barge)	38-01-49.66	76-22-22.81		
Chase (124' schooner)	39-08-25.07	76-15-46.02		
Chilore	36-57-38.02	76-00-38.31	27180.4	41293.1
City of Annapolis	37-51.312	76-10.191	27334.0	41909.5
Coal Barge	38-25-26.33	76-23-27.23		
Cockroach Wreck	38-18.816	76-25.504		
Columbia	38-18-45.35	76-24-59.42		
Columbus	37-57-49.56	76-11-54.61		
Crab Boat	38-44-44.99	76-27-27.55		
Crane Barge	37-00-50.89	76-09-55.54		
Cumberland	36-58-07.61	76-26-07.73		
Diamond Shoals (lightship)	36-56-58-76	76-01-20.20		
Dispersed Wreck	36-54-14.31	75-53-28.90		
Dorothy	37-51.605	76-09.683	27332.5	41913.8
Dottie (40' work boat)	38-42-24.53	76-24-57.68	16141.9	27541.7
Dragonet	38-20.521	76-18.213	27446.0	42250.6
Eckie (150' barge)	38-36-27.03	76-25-50.88		
Ekie (barge 149')	38-35-43.9	76-24-43.71	27519.8	42428.5
Ekie (barge)	38-35-44.33	76-24-42.53		
Favorite	38-06.927	76-30.625		
Florida	36-58-17.66	76-26-17.45		
General J.A. Dumont	39-00.20	76-29.30		
Herbert D. Maxwell	38-55.593	76-23.610		
Julia Luckenbach	37-40.476	76-10.364		
Kent	37-55-00.45	76-12-58.79		
Large Wooden Vessel (machinery)	38-53-54.00	76-24-05.11		
Levin J. Marvel (schooner)	38-45-23.30	76-31-26.27		
Mary A. DeKnight	38-56-27.57	76-23-11.89		
Mary L. McAllister	37-46-47.19	76-11-03.97	27023.7	41854.9
New Jersey	38-37-03.20	76-24-35.90	27523.2	42444.4
Purse Seiner (20 feet relief)	38-23.028	76-20.339		
Railroad Car	36-54-53.81	76-10-41.55		
Railroad Cars (3)	36-54-53.12	76-10-41.94		
S-49	38-19.898	76-29.269		
Sailboat (22')	38-45-02.32	76-26-56.00		
Sailboat (32')	38-34-30.65	76-22-24.21		
San Marcos	37-43.153	76-04.670	27290.8	41820.8

199

Santore	36-53-53.18	75-46-51.07	27117.0	41276.9
Schooner	38-18-15.20	76-10-54.55		
Skidbladnir (58' vessel)	38-41-15	76-31-40		
Small Steel Barge	38-18.826	76-26.429		
Steel Steamer (180')	37-51-48.16	76-09-27.39		
Tautog Barge	37-47.940	76-03.841		
Ted's Wreck	37-53.434	76-07.969		
Texaco (tanker)	37-14-57.82	76-05-05.73	27232.1	41487.8
Texas	37-43.153	76-04.670	27290.8	41820.4
Thomas F. Pollard (possibly)	36-54-22	75-57-47		
Three Hulks	36-57-43.35	76-24-53.77		
Tulip (northwest end)	38-10.048	76-35.992		
Tulip (southeast end)	38-10.038	76-35.981	27493.9	42105.0
U-1105 (conning tower)	38-08-173	76-33-106	27476.5	42085.5
Westmoreland (barge)	36-56-45.35	75-57-29.96	27165.9	41289.6
William D. Sanner	36-57-35.01	76-01-16.90	27182.9	41292.0
Wood Wreck (frame, 2 rails; 100')	36-58-52.40	76-59-37.70		
Wooden Vessel (deteriorated)	38-52-23.33	76-25-15.99		
Wreck	38-48-33.71	76-22-44.88		
Wreck	38-05-08.69	76-14-32.29		
Wreck	37-52-54.54	76-08-25.69		
Wreck (42')	38-43-56.99	76-24-25.63		
Wreck (broken up)	38-05-20.72	76-15-00.80		
Wreck (keel and ribs)	37-03-53.31	76-03-24.70		

GPS and LORAN NUMBERS NORTH to SOUTH

Barge	39-12-33.99	76-26-48.05
Chase (124' schooner)	39-08-25.07	76-15-46.02
AWOIS 10804 (dangerous wreck)	39-04-06.54	76-16-14.33
AWOIS 11904 (wreck)	39-02-38.75	76-20-31.45
AWOIS 11903 (container)	39-02-16.97	76-19-53.41
AWOIS 7260 (100' wood barge)	39-00-56.55	76-22-31.46
General J.A. Dumont	39-00.20	76-29.30
Mary A. DeKnight	38-56-27.57	76-23-11.89
AWOIS 4436 (60' steel pile driver)	38-55-57.72	76-23-37.73
Herbert D. Maxwell	38-55.593	76-23.610
AWOIS 7438 (large wood vessel)	38-53-54.31	76-24-04.65
Large Wooden Vessel (machinery)	38-53-54.00	76-24-05.11
Wooden Vessel (deteriorated)	38-52-23.33	76-25-15.99
AWOIS 10006 (wreck)	38-48-33.71	76-48-33.71
Wreck	38-48-33.71	76-22-44.88
Blair (tug)	38-47-40.09	76-26-54.34
AWOIS 4696 (41' yacht)	38-46-05.97	76-29-36.26
Levin J. Marvel (schooner)	38-45-23.30	76-31-26.27
Sailboat (22')	38-45-02.32	76-26-56.00
Crab Boat	38-44-44.99	76-27-27.55

Name	Lat	Lon		
Wreck (42')	38-43-56.99	76-24-25.63		
Dottie (40' work boat)	38-42-24.53	76-24-57.68	16141.9	27541.7
AWOIS 4692 (172' wreck-like contact)	38-42-11.26	76-25-28.22		
Skidbladnir (58' vessel)	38-41-15	76-31-40		
AWOIS 3684 (145' steel barge)	38-37-40.91	76-26-00.90		
AWOIS 7239 (52' bargelike wood fiber)	38-37-40.13	76-26-08.51	27532.2	42450.6
AWOIS 7238 (100' wood vessel w/coal)	38-37-34.98	76-25-13.77	27527.8	42450.4
New Jersey	38-37-03.20	76-24-35.90	27523.2	42444.4
AWOIS 3683 (40' steel push tug)	38-36-27.03	76-25-50.88		
Eckie (150' barge)	38-36-27.03	76-25-50.88		
Ekie (barge)	38-35-44.33	76-24-42.53		
AWOIS barge 2	38-35-43.9	76-24-43.71		
Ekie (barge 149')	38-35-43.9	76-24-43.71	27519.8	42428.5
AWOIS Unidentified	38-35.0	76-25.8		
Sailboat (32')	38-34-30.65	76-22-24.21		
Bright (114' wood barge)	38-33-32.57	76-25-41.67		
AWOIS barge 1	38-33-18	76-25-41		
Cabin Cruiser (30')	38-30-26.85	76-23-35.75		
Bigger Steel Barge	38-30.692	76-23.510		
Coal Barge	38-25-26.33	76-23-27.23		
AWOIS 11877 (menhaden trawler)	38-23-02.70	76-20-20.20		
Purse Seiner (20 feet relief)	38-23.028	76-20.339		
AWOIS 6878 (2 wrecks awash)	38-20-20.51	76-27-51.55		
Dragonet	38-20.521	76-18.213	27446.0	42250.6
S-49	38-19.898	76-29.269		
Columbia	38-18-45.35	76-24-59.42		
AWOIS 4007 (359-ton barge Columbia ?)	38-18-44.91	76-25-00.60		
Schooner	38-18-15.20	76-10-54.55		
Small Steel Barge	38-18.826	76-26.429		
Cockroach Wreck	38-18.816	76-25.504		
Bean Boat	38-18.591	76-27.898		
Tulip (northwest end)	38-10.048	76-35.992		
Tulip (southeast end)	38-10.038	76-35.981	27493.9	42105.0
U-1105 (conning tower)	38-08-173	76-33-106	27476.5	42085.5
Favorite	38-06.927	76-30.625		
AWOIS 3425 (wreck)	38-05-24.48	76-15-05.18		
Wreck (broken up)	38-05-20.72	76-15-00.80		
Wreck	38-05-08.69	76-14-32.29		
AWOIS 3424 (wreck largely buried)	38-05-08.25	76-14-33.50		
American Mariner	38-02.403	76-09.314		
Charlotte (barge)	38-01-49.66	76-22-22.81		
AWOIS 10675 (dangerous wreck)	38-00-18.36	76-19-58.13		
Columbus	37-57-49.56	76-11-54.61		
AWOIS 7240 (120' wood vessel)	37-57-44.88	76-11-42.11	27356.3	41984.7
AWOIS 3875 (195' barge)	37-56-52.22	76-11-46.49		
AWOIS 3673 (197' LSM barge)	37-55-12.48	76-11-11.74		
Kent	37-55-00.45	76-12-58.79		
C.G. Willis (190' barge)	37-53.434	76-07-969		
Ted's Wreck	37-53.434	76-07.969		
Wreck	37-52-54.54	76-08-25.69		
Steel Steamer (180')	37-51-48.16	76-09-27.39		

Name				
Brazil	37-51.793	76-09.465	27332.1	41916.3
Dorothy	37-51.605	76-09.683	27332.5	41913.8
City of Annapolis	37-51.312	76-10.191	27334.0	41909.5
Tautog Barge	37-47.940	76-03.841		
Mary L. McAllister	37-46-47.19	76-11-03.97	27023.7	41854.9
San Marcos	37-43.153	76-04.670	27290.8	41820.8
Texas	37-43.153	76-04.670	27290.8	41820.4
Julia Luckenbach	37-40.476	76-10.364		
AWOIS 433 (steel barge)	37-19-47.14	76-08-31.41	27256.2	41538.7
Texaco (tanker)	37-14-57.82	76-05-05.73	27232.1	41487.8
AWOIS 14174	37-14-14.77	76-27-09.39		
AWOIS 3191 (60' vessel)	37-13-29.73	76-11-30.36	27255.4	41459.9
AWOIS 12490 (dangerous wreck)	37-09-19.52	76-38-09.83		
AWOIS 8875 (60' barge)	37-08-54.01	76-09-08.12		
AWOIS 3190 (barge)	37-08-53.95	76-09-07.91		
AWOIS 8875 (60' barge)	37-08-53.88	76-09-08.05		
AWOIS 12491 (dangerous wreck)	37-07-38.88	76-38-14.00		
Wreck (keel and ribs)	37-03-53.31	76-03-24.70		
Anglo African	37-03-25.12	75-53-57.53	27163.2	41372.6
Anglo African	37-03-23.4	75-55-09		
AWOIS 912 (wreck)	37-01-13.47	76-30-24.91		
AWOIS 10794 (30' large metal box)	37-01-03.22	76-02-45.21		
Crane Barge	37-00-50.89	76-09-55.54		
AWOIS 908 (30' crane barge)	37-00-50.37	76-09-56.77		
AWOIS 10792 (wood ship remains)	37-00-47.40	76-03-09.2		
Big D (pile driver)	36-59-47.37	76-06-03.87	27206.5	41308.7
Big D (pile driver)	36-59-46.85	76-06-05.11		
Wood Wreck (frame, 2 rails; 100')	36-58-52.40	76-59-37.70		
Florida	36-58-17.66	76-26-17.45		
Cumberland	36-58-07.61	76-26-07.73		
Three Hulks	36-57-43.35	76-24-53.77		
Chilore	36-57-38.02	76-00-38.31	27180.4	41293.1
Carmina (pilot boat)	36-57-35.01	76-01-16.90	27182.9	41292.0
William D. Sanner	36-57-35.01	76-01-16.90	27182.9	41292.0
Diamond Shoals (lightship)	36-56-58-76	76-01-20.20		
AWOIS 9555 (barge or pontoon float)	36-56-48.23	76-02-55.68	27188.1	41279.9
Westmoreland (barge)	36-56-45.35	75-57-29.96	27165.9	41289.6
AWOIS 9545 (steel vessel wood mast)	36-56-02.70	76-03-19.60	27108.4	41270.4
AWOIS 9544 (steel vessel wood beams)	36-55-56.87	76-03-17.06	27187.7	41269.4
Amphibious Craft (35')	36-55-46.56	76-03-11.61		
Barge	36-55-05.11	75-43-41.20		
AWOIS 3420 (barge on side)	36-55-04.58	75-43-42.50		
Railroad Car	36-54-53.81	76-10-41.55		
Railroad Cars (3)	36-54-53.12	76-10-41.94		
Armed Sailing Vessel (with cannons)	36-54-49.53	76-05-22.76		
AWOIS 8897 (armed sailing vessel)	36-54-48.70	76-05-23.90		
Thomas F. Pollard (possibly)	36-54-22	75-57-47		
Dispersed Wreck	36-54-14.31	75-53-28.90		
Santore	36-53-53.18	75-46-51.07	27117.0	41276.9
AWOIS 8673 (low-lying timbers)	39.131444	76.239889		
AWOIS 13714 (barge)	38.067069	76.446386		

Books by the Author

The Popular Dive Guide Series
Shipwrecks of Massachusetts: North
Shipwrecks of Massachusetts: South
Shipwrecks of Rhode Island and Connecticut
Shipwrecks of New York
Shipwrecks of New Jersey (1988)
Shipwrecks of New Jersey: North
Shipwrecks of New Jersey: Central
Shipwrecks of New Jersey: South
Shipwrecks of Delaware and Maryland (1990 Edition)
Shipwrecks of Delaware and Maryland (2002 Edition)
Shipwrecks of the Chesapeake Bay in Maryland Waters
Shipwrecks of the Chesapeake Bay in Virginia Waters
Shipwrecks of Virginia
Shipwrecks of North Carolina: from the Diamond Shoals North
Shipwrecks of North Carolina: from Hatteras Inlet South
Shipwrecks of South Carolina and Georgia

Shipwreck and Nautical History
Andrea Doria: Dive to an Era
Deep, Dark, and Dangerous: Adventures and Reflections on the Andrea Doria
Great Lakes Shipwrecks: a Photographic Odyssey
The Fuhrer's U-boats in American Waters
Ironclad Legacy: Battles of the USS Monitor
The Kaiser's U-boats in American Waters
The Lusitania Controversies: Atrocity of War and a Wreck-Diving History (Book One)
The Lusitania Controversies: Dangerous Descents into Shipwrecks and Law (Book Two)
The Nautical Cyclopedia
NOAA's Ark: the Rise of the Fourth Reich
Shadow Divers Exposed: the Real Saga of the U-869
Shipwreck Heresies
The Shipwreck Research Handbook
Shipwreck Sagas
Stolen Heritage: the Grand Theft of the Hamilton and Scourge
Track of the Gray Wolf
Underwater Reflections
USS San Diego: the Last Armored Cruiser
Wreck Diving Adventures

Dive Training
Primary Wreck Diving Guide
Advanced Wreck Diving Guide
The Advanced Wreck Diving Handbook
Ultimate Wreck Diving Guide
The Technical Diving Handbook

Nonfiction
The Absurdity Principle
Wilderness Canoeing

Science Fiction
A Different Universe
A Different Dimension
A Different Continuum
Entropy (a novel of conceptual breakthrough)
A Journey to the Center of the Earth
The Mold
Return to Mars
Second Coming
Silent Autumn
Subaqueous
The Time Dragons Trilogy
- *A Time for Dragons*
- *Dragons Past*
- *No Future for Dragons*

Sci-Fi Action/Adventure Novels
Memory Lane
Mind Set
The Peking Papers

Supernatural Horror Novel
The Lurking: Curse of the Jersey Devil

Vietnam Novel
Lonely Conflict

Videotape or DVD
The Battle for the USS Monitor

Visit the GGP website for availability of titles:
http://www.ggentile.com

www.ingramcontent.com/pod-product-compliance
Lightning Source LLC
Chambersburg PA
CBHW051054160426
43193CB00010B/1176